blue
rider
press

BOSS LIFE

BOSS LIFE

SURVIVING MY OWN SMALL BUSINESS

Paul Downs

BLUE RIDER PRESS
New York

blue
rider
press

An imprint of Penguin Random House LLC
375 Hudson Street
New York, New York 10014

Copyright © 2015 by Paul Downs

Blue Rider Press is a registered trademark and its colophon
is a trademark of Penguin Random House LLC

Library of Congress Cataloging-in-Publication Data

Downs, Paul.
Boss life : surviving my own small business / Paul Downs.
p.   cm.
ISBN 978-0-399-17233-5
1. Cabinetmakers—United States.   2. Small business—United States—Management.
3. New business enterprises—United States—Management.   I. Title.
HD8039.C152U63   2015   2015016068
338.7'684104092—dc23
[B]

Printed in the United States of America
1   3   5   7   9   10   8   6   4   2

Book design by Michelle McMillian

For my mother,
who never got to see how it all turned out

Contents

Preface

I've been living the boss life since 1986. I own a small company that builds custom furniture. I started fresh out of college, with no experience. Ever since, my business has been my life, my education, and my struggle.

When I began, I had no training as a businessman and no mentors to help me. I just wanted to make stuff and have fun. I found that I was good at designing products and making sales, and the business started to grow. In 1987, I hired my first employee, and soon found myself struggling with management, cash flow, taxes, and all the other details required to keep a business running. After globalization and the Internet brought new competition and new opportunity, my company experienced unsustainable growth and, in 2008, a devastating crash. But we've endured—and even had one very profitable year. I am a survivor, but not a financial success.

In 2010, by sheer luck, I was given the chance to write about my experiences in *The New York Times* for their "You're the Boss" blog.

I became a regular contributor. I've used that forum to describe the shabby treatment that business owners suffer at the hands of large and powerful institutions, in particular the health insurance and credit card industries. The main focus of my writing, though, has been my own company.

I decided to tell the difficult parts of my story, concentrating on my deficiencies as a businessman. I have written about fighting with my former partner, struggling with cash flow and unhappy customers, firing employees, and dealing with a rapidly changing economic landscape.

Many readers have written to tell me of their own struggles, and thanked me for publicly airing my many failures. Apparently a humble and honest look at small business life is rare. But I've found myself struggling with the limits of the blog format. Complex and sensitive situations must be oversimplified or omitted.

This book will be an opportunity to dig deeper into my experiences. It is an accurate portrait of a real business, the boss who leads it, the people who work in it, and the challenges we face. I hope that I can promote a better understanding of the factors that drive the behavior of small business owners and, by extension, show how a significant part of our economy functions. There's a lot of chatter about "job creators" from people who have never created a job. Politicians make rules, but aren't required to follow them. Employees complain without understanding why bosses act the way they do. And prospective entrepreneurs gamble their future without a clear picture of the challenges they will face. All these people need to know the other side of the story. This book is for them.

Some disclaimers: the world of woodshops is almost entirely a male domain. I don't know why this is, other than tradition. I have hired women whenever I found one who was qualified, but they are a very small percentage of the total workforce. In order to simplify the language of this book, I use the male form of certain common nouns, "craftsmen" and "salesmen" in particular. Please do not take this as a denigration of women who perform those roles.

The names of some people and customers have been changed, and the quoted dialogue is my best recollection of what was said at the time. That said, all the events in the book happened. If this account offends anyone, my apologies in advance.

BOSS LIFE

Introduction

If this were a standard business book, I would tell you all the smart things I did to achieve financial success, and maybe trot out a few mistakes to show some humility. Unfortunately, I'm no business genius and I'm not rich. My story has neither tidy conclusions nor a triumphant ending. So this book will be different.

I'd like to tell you what happened to my company in 2012, as we struggled to replicate profits earned in the previous year. We started strong, but then sales took a puzzling turn for the worse. The vast majority of our clients were delighted with our work, but a couple of them weren't satisfied with reasonable efforts and cost us huge amounts of money. I presided over a very good crew, except for a couple of workers who gave me serious trouble. We made some money, then lost a whole lot more, then clawed most of it back. Meanwhile, my complicated family life couldn't be ignored. This is real life. The triumph and tragedy of small business. The uncertainty and challenges of being the boss.

What do I mean by "boss"? It's commonly understood to mean someone who's in charge of others, but that could be a middle manager in a big corporation. Instead, I'm talking about bosses who both own and run their businesses—small companies with fewer than twenty employees. More than seven million American businesses, employing nearly thirty million people, are in this category. These bosses answer to nobody and are responsible for everybody. Their own money is at risk. Every problem goes straight to them, and they have to come up with the solution, figure out how to pay for it, and then implement it. The position guarantees long hours, hard work, and overwhelming stress.

Every day, these bosses wear multiple hats: managing employees, keeping track of the money, dealing with bureaucrats, negotiating with the landlord—the list goes on and on. Larger companies, with more resources, can hire individuals or create whole departments to do these jobs, but a small company can't generate enough cash to cover that expense. So these tasks land in the boss's lap. No matter that the boss may have little or no training, and no desire to spend time on them. Done wrong, the company fails, either slowly or quickly. Done right, the boss gets to do them again. A sudden crisis— a cash shortage, or an equipment breakdown, or a personnel crisis— requires even greater effort. Even if the business survives, there is never a guarantee of easy sailing ahead. The situation goes back only to the routine level of toil and stress.

That's not to say that being the boss is relentlessly terrible. Inventing the processes that enable successful operations is like solving an intricate puzzle. It's highly satisfying to see your business running well, delivering the product or service that inspired its creation. There is no thrill like receiving payment from a satisfied client. Most workers try hard to do a good job, and most people are good to work with. Consistently meeting a payroll is a real accomplishment. A business can provide for the security and growth of both boss and employees. It might be able to expand and enter markets all over the world. It might even make a healthy profit. The boss can take delight in each small victory and, over the course of a career, be proud of all that has been accomplished, whether it added up to fabulous wealth or not.

Every business has a dual nature: the real-life version with its countless imperfections, and the ideal theoretical business the boss imagined when he started, where everything works as it should and money is made. Good money. Steady money. Maybe even outrageous money.

Money is the unavoidable scorecard. Any business can be great at making a product, great with its employees, great with the customers, but if it doesn't make profits, it isn't considered a success.

While recounting the events of 2012, I'll concentrate on four subjects: *Sales* focuses on how my very small company interacts with a wide variety of clients, from enormous institutions to individuals. *Operations* is about how my company makes its products, how I manage the people I employ, and my attempts to move our workshop from a nineteenth-century model to the twenty-first-century version. This transition is an incredibly complex problem and the solutions we find (or fail to find) have implications for the whole economy. The third theme, *Money*, describes how cash flow, or lack thereof, affects my decision making. And finally, I'll describe how I exercise my *Powers as boss*, balancing those demands with my duties as a father and husband. The details of this story are particular to my company and my life. The lessons, I hope, are useful to everyone.

The shop floor from the southeast corner.

The Company S table on the shop floor for final inspection.

Top right: The table that started it all, built in 1999.

Top left: The Downs family: Hugh, Paul, Henry, Peter, and Nancy.

Bottom left: Paul Downs with a set of chairs he made in 2013.

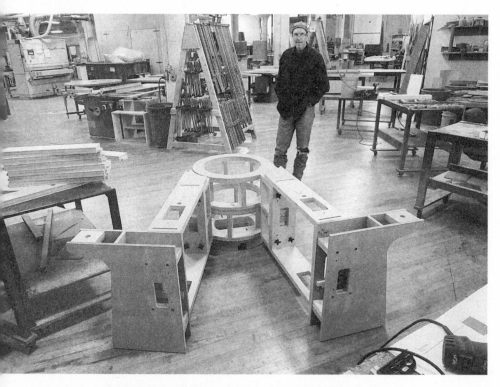

Paul on a shop walk, inspecting the base of a scissoring table.

JANUARY

DATE: MONDAY, JANUARY 2, 2012

STARTING BANK BALANCE: $137,154.32

CASH RELATIVE TO START OF YEAR ("NET CASH"): $0

NEW-CONTRACT VALUE, YEAR-TO-DATE: $0

Nine a.m., January 2. Paul Downs Cabinetmakers, custom board-room table maker, starts its twenty-sixth year with a meeting. We are on the fourth floor of an old factory in Bridgeport, Pennsylvania. I stand at a battered table, returned to us for storage when our client, a New York bank, downsized in 2008. Thirteen sleepy workers, sitting, wait for me to speak.

We meet every week at this time. The usual agenda is a review of our progress toward meeting monthly and yearly sales goals, a review of projects in progress, and a report on our cash reserves. I'll get to all that, but start with a surprise: good news—2011 has ended on a high note. We have a record amount of cash on hand and a full order book to take us through the next two months. I confidently state that we have achieved success at last. The business has finally done more than build tables. It has also made good money.

Two years ago, as 2010 began, I was not so confident. A decade of my incompetent stewardship, capped by two brutal years of recession, had left the company at death's door. We had shrunk from twenty-three employees to six, and I had just $16,239 in the bank— enough to operate for three days. A small business lives or dies on cash. It is the fuel that pays the rent, buys the materials, funds the ads, and makes the payroll. If I ran out, the shop, the tools, the Web site, the trained employees, the catalogue of designs: all would sit idle. The business would be dead.

I desperately needed clients with cash in hand. This is the perennial cry of the incompetent boss—if we just had more sales, everything would be great! But for me it was true. Before 2008, I had been very bad at cash management. Then, as the world slid into recession, buyers disappeared. My partner and I fought about the money we had left, and one night he took our cash reserves and paid down our line of credit. Eighty-eight thousand dollars of the $105,000 I had on hand was gone. I immediately laid off half my people. With a shrinking order book, a demoralized workforce, and a hundred thousand dollars in past-due bills, I had one question: how soon would I have to shut the doors? QuickBooks couldn't tell me, so I wrote a spreadsheet that gave me a running bank balance, taking into account all income and expenses, for as far forward as I cared to look. I could move transactions from one day to another to see how delaying or accelerating payments affected my bank balance. As long as it never went below zero, I was in business. My sheet was a new way to see my cash situation. Unfortunately, it showed that I'd go broke in three weeks.

I barely survived the terrible year 2009. Customers purchase our product, custom conference tables, when a business moves or expands. As 2008 ended, we still got a few orders from projects initiated before the crash, but sales volume soon took a huge drop. I took any job I could find, but I had to lay off five of my eleven remaining employees. I cut all my workers' pay by 15 percent and set my own salary at just $36,000 a year. I rarely had more than a week's worth of cash on hand. The stress of wondering whether I would have to close the doors was relentless. I experienced shooting chest pains and sleepless nights. But I never quite failed. By juggling incoming and outgoing payments, I managed to pay off my vendors and survive to see another year. The year 2010 started with no relief—in January, I came within a day of running out of money. But in February, buyers started calling. By March 2010, with orders appearing at a sustainable rate, I was able to restore everyone's pay to previous levels and rehire some laid-off workers. By year's end, I had ten employees and a bank balance of $106,777.

The favorable trend continued in 2011. I added more people and completed more jobs. At the end of the year, we got a large order that generated a huge payment. Our bank balance topped out at $303,834, and I was able to distribute big bonuses to my workers and to myself, totaling $166,680. I was a happy man. I had survived the worst of the recession and learned how to manage cash flow. In three years, I had gone from nearly bankrupt to reasonably secure, paid off a pile of vendor debt, and was looking forward to further growth in 2012.

Does compressing three years of disaster and regeneration into dollars communicate what it was like? Do those numbers really depict my own stress, my workers' fear for their jobs, and my debtors' doubts that I would pay them back? Definitely not. But those balances are an objective measure of the success or failure of a business. In the end it has to be about the money. Numbers don't lie.

Back to my meeting. On this day I have $137,154 on hand, but my other numbers get reset. Inquiries, sales, profits: all zero. Every year I start from scratch, worrying that this time the phone won't ring, orders will stop, and my cash will dry up. I don't believe that the things we do to generate sales will suddenly stop working, but I've been through bad times and it's hard to have faith in the future.

THE NUMBERS THAT TRACK our expenses also start at zero, but increase with every passing minute. Rent, electricity, and equipment leases never stop. Payroll and material costs start the instant someone shows up to work. It all adds up. Operating the shop, including pay for fifteen workers and a decent salary for myself, costs about $9,000 a day.

We generate cash to cover those costs in two ways: write new orders, or ship product. Our usual terms are to get half of the money on order placement, 35 percent before we ship, and 15 percent within ten days of delivery. If we sell and produce at a steady pace, we receive many payments each week. Our goal is to take in more than we spend, but every table we make generates significant costs. So even when things go smoothly on the shop floor, most of our cash is paid out to cover the rent, materials, payroll, and other expenses. Our plan is to have a little bit left over and to steadily accumulate that surplus over the course of the year. This is known as "positive cash flow."

You might assume that that is the same thing as profits. Not so. You can have positive cash flow without profits, and profits without positive cash flow. How? Profit, for a manufacturer, is a technical term that describes a particular situation: when the value of product shipped exceeds the costs incurred during a given time period. "Sales" does not mean what you think it does, either. Again, the accounting definition, as it applies to a factory like mine, is that a sale occurs when finished product is delivered to the client. That thing where the client signed our quote and gave us a big deposit? Not a sale. As far as our accountant is concerned, the client just loaned us some cash, which we can repay by delivering a finished table. When it arrives, the deposit and preship payments become ours to keep, the value of the table is added to our income statement as a sale, and any amounts outstanding are added to our list of assets, even though we don't have them in hand and can't use them to cover expenses.

You can have profits without positive cash flow: we might make and ship tables and pay for the costs of production, but not get paid by the client. If our costs are lower than the value of delivered product for a given period, we are making a profit, even though we don't have the money in hand. Without cash on hand to buy materials and pay the workers, operations will eventually stop. Moral of story: get paid. Profits don't mean much otherwise.

And positive cash flow without profit? If we ink a bunch of deals, we might suddenly get a lot of deposit payments. During that same time, our factory may not be operating efficiently, and the costs of making goods might exceed the value of the products we deliver. We have cash, but we aren't making profits. This can easily happen if a company has effective marketing but poorly managed production. This is how I operated for many years. We were growing a little faster than we were failing. Money from new clients compensated for the losses incurred as we produced furniture for the old clients. Everyone got the product they ordered, but hiccups in sales resulted in cash shortfalls, and I had to dip into my own pocket to cover expenses.

There's a third way to bring in cash: borrow it. Income, raised by whatever means, counts in cash-flow calculations. The problem with borrowed money is that eventually it needs to be paid back. Or not, if you can find a fool to lend to you. In my own company, that fool would be me. When I covered cash shortfalls from my own savings, as I often did, I was loaning money to the company. I always intended to pay myself back right away, but the bad management that got me into trouble in the first place prevented me from making sufficient profits for a payback. Over the course of twenty-six years, I have loaned Paul Downs Cabinetmakers $508,774 and managed to pay back $121,676. I am still owed $387,098. Am I a rich man who has half a million lying around to keep my company going? No. The money came out of the company to me as salary and went back in as loans, over and over. Not very smart, as every dollar that took this trip was subject to payroll taxes as it went out of the company.

I AIM TO HAVE positive cash flow at all times. Unfortunately, it doesn't happen that way. We have a regular rhythm to our expenses: rent at the beginning of the month, payroll every other Tuesday, two credit card due dates, and the ongoing purchases of materials and other items. Income is much more erratic. Some days we get lots of cash; some days we get nothing. This is why I want to have a healthy bank balance: to cover the days or weeks when cash flow is negative. The $137,154 that I start the year with is fifteen days of working capital. I can use it to pay bills and make payroll. If I want to, I can spend some of it on projects that might enhance the business, like more advertising or a new machine. But if we spend $9,000 a day, a conservative estimate, I have three weeks to figure out what to do if the money stops coming in.

I already know what to do: sign new contracts, ship finished product. The magic number for 2012 is $200,000. That's my monthly target for both incoming orders and outgoing shipments. This will produce a steady cash flow of $200,000 a month. If expenses are at $9,000 per day, and the work year consists of 250 workdays, we will have positive cash flow of $150,000 over the course of the year.

Sell $200,000, ship $200,000. We will have to build a lot of tables. Not a trivial task—far beyond the capabilities of any one person. In small woodshops, a ratio of employees to sales of $120,000 per worker is good, $150,000 per worker is excellent. I have fourteen people to meet a goal of $2,400,000, which means output of $171,428 per worker in the next year. We will need to be very efficient.

WHAT WILL WE DO to meet that goal? You might picture everyone at a workbench, cutting wood. But building the tables is only one step in our process. A manufacturing business must perform six major functions to stay alive: Design, Marketing, Production, Logistics, Warranty Service, and Administration. *Design* operates at both the conceptual level, which in my case is the decision to make furniture, and at the individual level, which is the specific design of each table we make. *Marketing* attracts paying customers to your door by describing to the world the goods that you have available. It includes sales. *Production* is the actual making of the product, including setup of the factory, acquisition of materials, hiring and management of labor, and design of the work processes that lead to finished goods. *Logistics* is the process of moving your finished goods to the customer: packaging, shipping, and installation. *Warranty Service*, which might be considered a form of Marketing or Production, is in my mind a separate function. It consists of responding to customer issues and communicating them back up the function chain to improve the overall performance of the organization. *Administration* keeps track of all the other functions, and includes bookkeeping, accounting, dealing with government regulations, and human resource duties.

Note that the six functions are all connected, not just in a linear progression but also through feedback loops from one function to each of the others. For instance, Design must respond to the expectations of potential customers (Marketing), to the capabilities of the factory (Production), to the problem of shipping and delivery (Logistics), and to issues encountered in the real world (Warranty). Changing the nature and capacity of one function has implications for the entire operation.

It is entirely possible to break out any of these functions and have them performed by others. This is called "outsourcing," and it often makes perfect sense. If you are not competent at one of the functions, hire someone who is. Managing that vendor takes money and time and drastically interferes with effective feedback loops. But it allows access to expertise that can be very difficult to develop in-house. Note, also, that in an extremely small company, one person can perform all these functions, and probably will when the company is starting up. In that case, the feedback loops are instant and so continual that their existence might not even be noticed. This can be good or bad, depending on whether the feedback loops lead to changes in behavior.

It is worth mentioning the difference between a hobby and a real business. It is commonly believed that it's easy to step from one to the other, but that underestimates the difficulty of establishing all six functions. A hobbyist needs to perform only two: Design and Production. Marketing is not required, as the client is the hobbyist. Logistics might be an issue, but usually a trivial one, as the item is produced very close to where it will be used. Warranty issues are easily handled—there is no paying customer, and the hobbyist's response will depend on how he feels at the moment. Administration is insignificant. Being a hobbyist is much, much simpler than being a business. There are far fewer problems to solve, and almost all the time and effort can be spent on the fun stuff.

My constant challenge has been to perform all six functions competently using the limited resources of a small company. In 1986, I had a desire to make furniture but no experience. Of necessity, I first mastered Design and Production, working alone as I taught myself my trade. Eventually I learned to perform all six functions, some just well enough to stay in business. Production has been the pipeline through which new people enter the company. I hire people to work at the bench, and move some into other jobs.

At the beginning of 2012, we have thirteen full-time employees, a part-time bookkeeper, and one temporary worker. Six of us work in the office: myself; Emma Watson, the admin; Dan Smolen and Nick Rothman, who, along with me, are the sales force; Andy Stahl, the engineer; and Pam Potter, the bookkeeper. Nine work on the shop floor building tables: Steve Maturin, shop foreman, accompanied by Ron Dedrick; Sean Slovinski, Tyler Powell, Will Krieger, and Eduardo Lopez, cabinetmakers; Dave Violi, who does the finishing; Bob Foote, our shipping manager; and Jésus Moreno, the temporary worker.

With the exception of Emma and Jésus, all my workers are craftsmen who have worked in shops for years. Woodworkers have a calm and quietly confident demeanor, grounded in their ability to build things well and quickly. The best ones have what I call "good hands": they can make things without undue fuss, at high speed, without sacrificing quality. They can visualize how to break a complex project into discrete steps, recover when things go wrong, and always keep moving toward the final goal. In my experience, this talent is very rare. At the same time, it is present in every culture. In any group of humans, some have a special ability to manipulate materials to produce useful things. A few craftsmen have done spectacular work that ends up in museums. But most make ordinary items that serve their purpose and then are discarded. That is the kind of work we produce, the kind of workers we are: not in it for fame and fortune. The opportunity to make good things is a satisfaction in itself.

Building things out of wood is a cumulative process. You need each step to go well before you can move on to the next. Lots of things can go wrong: difficult wood, malfunctioning machines, and mistakes in design or construction. Error, in the form of small deviations from specifications, accumulates as a piece passes through production. At the same time, clients expect us to deliver what the salesman sold them. Bench workers can't change the design.

Given the need to manage small errors and the occasional disaster, my workers place great value in predictability. They are masters of execution. Their special skill is understanding the nature of the material they work with, the exact behavior of the tools they use, and the precise execution of production processes. They want each step to succeed. They understand that we get paid only once for a table, even if things go wrong on the shop floor and we end up remaking it. So they are suspicious of innovation, whether it is a new design, material, machine, or process. "New" often means "unreliable," so they are inherently conservative.

Unfortunately, new marketing methods, technologies, and competition arrive every day. Buyers will order from the company that offers the coolest products at the lowest price. We need to be creative, to be on constant lookout for better ways to do things, or we will be out of business. So one of my biggest challenges is how to be innovative when my company is composed of non-innovators.

BEFORE THE MONDAY MEETING became a weekly event, in 2010, I'd never established any formal, regular communication with my employees. For more than twenty-three years, my preferred method of finding out what was happening was to walk around the shop a couple of times a day. Our shop is very large—the main room is more than twenty thousand square feet. It's noisy, filled with machinery, workbenches, wood, and partially finished projects. The six people out there are often far away from one another, so instructions given to one person don't necessarily make their way to everyone else. Problems that I thought had been solved kept popping up in another corner of the shop. I finally figured out that it would be a good idea to gather in a quiet place once a week. Hence the Monday meeting.

I always open with new orders we've received. Then I review our cash position—how much money came in and out last week, how much we expect this week—and predict the week's closing cash position relative to our balance at the beginning of the year, a number that I call "Net Cash." I ask whether anyone has any production issues: broken machines, experimental techniques that either failed or succeeded, and anything else. I've made it clear that the point of these discussions is to solve problems, not to punish anyone. If we discuss something, it tends to be very dispassionate and technical. They aren't a chatty bunch. This fifteen- to twenty-minute meeting is the one fixed point in my week. So what keeps me busy? Making sales.

SALES IS A SUBSET of Marketing, but it's critical to the success of the company. It's the step that connects us to customers, who are a part of all six functions of the business. Design determines what we make for the customer; Marketing tells the customer that we have something for them to buy; Production makes what the customer ordered; Logistics moves the finished goods to the customer; Administration makes sure that the customer's order is defined and completed correctly; and Warranty Service takes care of any customer complaints. Customer, customer, customer. The people at the other end of every deal we make, their desires and needs, direct every part of the operation.

When I opened my doors, I had never sold anything in my life. It was a struggle just to meet a potential customer, let alone close a deal. Since opportunities were scarce, I formed a strategy that we still use today: listen to the client, identify their needs, and design a product to suit. In this way, I avoided a mismatch between what I was offering and what the client was looking for. Unfortunately, my early customers wanted a very wide range of items, many requiring specialized manufacturing capabilities that I didn't have. So I modified my strategy: I would design products that I could produce in my own humble shop and customize them to suit buyers' needs. The subsequent modified design could form the basis for new offerings. I would steadily expand my catalogue, guided by customer requests and financed by them as well.

As it turned out, I had the personality and design skills required to make this work. (Not a given: many fine craftsmen can't design or sell.) Nowadays we have wonderful tools—digital photography, Web sites, cheap modeling software, and e-mail—that empower small companies like mine to communicate our ideas at very low cost. We can inspire the confidence that is required for customers to write us a large check. Back when I started, though, none of that existed. I'm still amazed that anyone bought from me. But they did, and here I am.

In the early years, I built all the work myself, but after my first hires I concentrated on Design, Marketing, and Sales. In 1992, I abandoned the bench for good. My company was small then, but growing steadily. Fortunately, tools to increase my productivity were appearing. I stopped drawing with pencils and started using a computer in 1997. I discovered e-mail and digital photography in 1999. I put up my first Web site in 2000. In 2003, we started getting clients who found us using Google, and in 2004, started our Google AdWords campaign, which greatly expanded our marketing reach.

In 2006, we started using SketchUp, a 3-D modeling program that allowed us to show potential clients exactly what we would build for them. All this made our sales process more efficient and effective, leading to significant sales growth. Until 2007, I was the sole salesperson. In 2007 and 2008, I hired an outside salesman, who concentrated on the New York market. He had a nice run until that business dried up in the fall of 2008. Then he left, and I was alone with the job for the next two years.

SELLING OUR WORK takes a lot of time: fielding inquiries; writing proposals; closing deals; and managing jobs through the factory to make sure that they are built as promised. Each transaction is highly customized and of significant dollar value. Our average order in 2011 was more than thirteen thousand dollars.

To increase efficiency, I developed a standard work flow. This involves analyzing a client's situation and then sending a detailed proposal, including plans and elevations of the table, a virtual model of the design, and pricing. This method has worked well and has a satisfying rhythm to it. It's just like building furniture: a defined process that can be executed as a series of discrete, repeatable steps.

I can turn a simple proposal around in three hours. A complex job might take a couple of days. I believe that a complete proposal, delivered very quickly, is an impressive example of our custom design and engineering capabilities. This seems to work. If what we offer is the client's best choice, they place the order. If not, then they don't. I've always been too busy with incoming inquiries to spend time following up on sent proposals.

In early 2010, after two slow years, the number of incoming calls picked up considerably. I was desperate to close deals, so every caller, no matter how unpromising, got an absolutely fabulous proposal within twenty-four hours. I worked some very, very long days and ended up with a wicked case of carpal tunnel syndrome. Our order book started to fill up, but the pain in my wrists was so bad that I could no longer respond to every call. In May 2010, I decided that it was time to make a risky move: transfer one of my people from the workbench into the office to help me with sales. I didn't think that I could find someone outside the company who understood our production methods. I had to promote from within.

This had the potential to go badly wrong. Removing an efficient worker from the shop floor would mean losing some of our production capacity. Our cash flow and profits would take a big hit. I would need to train the new person, so there would be a period when we'd send out fewer proposals and close fewer deals. In the end, the effort might fail. Perfectly good clients might be lost to bad sales technique, and I would have to send a discouraged worker back to the bench. But I could not continue as the lone salesman—it was ruining my health.

I had someone in mind. Nick Rothman had been working for me for eleven years. He has great bench skills and regularly found ways to improve our process. He has a spark to him and is very easy to talk to. This is unusual for a talented woodworker; most are quiet, reflective types. Nick had worked with some of our software, so I knew that he could handle a computer. He had also told me that he would do whatever it took to help the organization succeed and had expressed a desire to move ahead in the company. In May 2010, I announced to Nick: "You are now a salesman." I didn't think about how this might change his view of his work and himself. Being a craftsman is one thing; being a salesman is quite a different job. I now know that he had hoped for an engineering job, and his view of sales was stereotypically negative: salesmen are oily manipulators who trick people into parting with their hard-earned money. He didn't consider that the sales I made were the source of all the company's money, and, by extension, every dollar that he had ever earned. Despite his qualms, Nick agreed to make the switch. Next I had to consider how I would teach him our process. At the time, there were just two people in our office—my engineer, Andy Stahl, and me.

The office is quite large: six thousand square feet, with one central space and nine smaller offices up against the windows. It has fourteen-foot ceilings and exposed pipes. But it's not a sexy, TV-style industrial space. It's decrepit, messy, blazing hot in the summer and freezing in the winter. The walls are unpainted drywall; the bare concrete floor is still stained with glue left behind when we stripped off the hideous carpet in 2007.

Andy and I had chosen windowed offices at opposite ends of the room. The privacy was nice, but it made for very poor communication between both of us and the rest of the company. The office is at one end of our building. The workbenches on the shop floor are almost three hundred feet away. I had long known that this arrangement was inefficient and led to misunderstandings, but had done nothing about it. Now I rethought the problem. Should I let Nick choose his own office? Much of what he needed to learn was very subtle, like how to talk to a customer and provide instant design feedback. So I decided that the best way for him to learn was to put him right next to me, in my office.

Having had my own space for more than twenty years, I was keenly aware of the freedom I was giving up. No more loud music. On hot days, I'd been in the habit of working with no shirt on and a wet handkerchief on my head. On cold days, I'd sit swathed in blankets. Sometimes I would yell and scream in frustration, or sit staring out the window. I keep a BB gun to shoot the starlings that get into the shop, and when everyone else went home, I liked to take target practice in the main space. When I was tired, I took a nap on the floor.

Now Nick was sitting three feet from me. And I found that I enjoyed the company. My daily struggle to make sales had been out of sight of the rest of the company. I often felt that I was killing myself for an indifferent audience. I had the impression that the workers saw their paychecks as theirs by right, that the money just magically appeared. Now Nick was getting a firsthand look at my job and all it entailed. For the first time ever, I was explaining to one of my employees all the ways that the company interacted with the outside world. I started teaching him what I knew about design and sales and found that we both enjoyed it.

Nick is a good student—interested, enthusiastic, willing to ask questions, and able to take his new knowledge and come up with further innovations. I was surprised to find that he is dyslexic. This was never an impediment when he worked on the shop floor, but it was an issue in sales.

Written communication is a very important part of our process. We do some of our work on the phone, but most of the follow-up is done with e-mail. I am a competent writer. Nick was not. I started cc'ing him on every e-mail, so he could see my style. He cut and pasted, built a library of answers to common questions, and eventually got much better.

It took three months of shoulder-to-shoulder training before I gave him his own customer, and another month to close his first sale. Once he got comfortable with the idea of selling, he proved to be a steady producer. He was good on the phone with clients. He mastered all the software and learned how to put together an attractive proposal. He realized that there was no trickery involved—that people buy our product only because they want it. And by bringing his shop-floor experience into his own work, he proved to be an imaginative designer, with a lot of good ideas that I hadn't thought of.

By the spring of 2011, Nick and I were selling at about the same rate and I began thinking of hiring another salesman. There's a pleasure in closing a deal and getting the money, but after twenty-five years of sales, I was tired. I wanted to ease myself out of that job in order to concentrate on improving the company in other ways.

But I would not find my next salesman on the shop floor. None of my other employees were good candidates. Out of the blue I got a call from someone who might be a solution to my problem. Dan Smolen had worked in shops in Colorado for years, eventually moving from the bench to management. He was relocating to Philadelphia to be closer to his wife's family. He was calling around, looking for a project manager position. Common in the construction industry, this job involves shepherding a project through production, delivery, and punch-list completion. Dan was used to dealing with clients, although not as a salesman. He has a typical shop-guy demeanor—calm, careful, and competent.

Dan's references checked out and I interviewed him a couple of weeks later. I told him that I needed a salesman who could design projects as well. He told me that it sounded like an interesting challenge and that he'd give it a try.

The offer I made Dan conforms to a pattern I have followed over the years—hire the first person I can find who might possibly be able to do the job. I'm particularly inclined to favor people who show up unbidden and announce that they want to work for me. A number of my best workers, including Nick; my engineer, Andy Stahl; and my shipping manager, Bob Foote, came to me this way. I have found placing want ads to be discouraging. I have to conduct the entire process myself: write the ads and place them, field phone calls, read résumés, do follow-ups, interview, and make the final decision. Technology has eased some of that, particularly writing and placing ads, but the rest can't be automated, and it takes a lot of time.

Furthermore, in the trades, the whole résumé/interview thing is not a very useful predictor of skills. Good craftsmen are generally not big talkers. Interviews don't tell me much about how well a worker might perform. Putting a candidate out on the shop floor for a tryout also presents difficulties. The guys out there are very busy. Who will spend a couple of days with a new person? And what would he work on? I don't want untested workers making anything that customers have paid for. And I can't run the risk of someone getting hurt, or one of our machines being damaged because of an inexperienced operator. My solution was to pick one of the candidates, make the hire, and hope for the best. And, predictably, it did not work out well. Not only was the initial choice a crapshoot, but what happened next was worse.

We don't really have a training program to bring new people up to speed. Steve Maturin, the shop foreman, is in charge of integrating new hires. He's a superb craftsman but not a people person. His method is simple: put the new guy at a bench, give him some work, show him how to do it, just once. If that lesson does not sink in, the guy sucks and is not worth further effort. Steve will do his best to find work for him to do, but he does not run a school. If the newbie is smart, he will observe work being done, ask the other workers, and get the information he needs. If talented, he'll be able to build at a high level. If he is not so talented, or not such a fast learner, he'll flounder until I notice the problem and fire him. As you might imagine, with such a bad process, we have trouble finding new workers.

Before I hired Dan Smolen, all new employees started on the shop floor. I believed that the foundation of success at Paul Downs Cabinetmakers was the ability to build furniture. I considered starting Dan in the shop for a few weeks to give him a sense of how we made our product, but decided against it. I needed him to learn my methods as soon as possible. Whether he was great with a sander or could splice veneer was not relevant. I decided to put him through the same process as Nick: set his desk next to mine and let him see what I did all day.

I had also hired an administrative assistant, Emma Watson, who also needed training. It was time to put everyone together. We replaced a wall between two empty offices with a sliding patio door and moved five desks into that space. Nick and Andy are on one side of the door; Emma, Dan, and I are on the other. If the door is open, we can easily speak to one another. If the door is closed, we can carry on two phone conversations simultaneously. Nobody has any privacy, but we have other offices if we want that. Andy, like me, found that sharing space is energizing and makes communications much easier. He is the link between the sales operation and the shop floor, and being in constant touch with the salespeople facilitated that part of his workload.

Dan started in May 2011. He quickly learned to use our software but had a tougher time when on the phone with clients. It is difficult to think and speak on the fly, to provide instant answers to highly technical questions, even when one is very familiar with the subject. And Dan was still learning about conference tables: what sizes work in which rooms, which configurations work best for which situations, which woods look good together, how to integrate wiring. If he could survive the initial conversation, though, he did OK. His written communications and design ideas were good. He made his first sale in July 2011. By the end of the year, he had closed sixteen deals, worth $270,870. As a comparison, Nick wrote fifty-one orders for $972,601; I did forty-eight, totaling $887,356.

The record for booking orders is held by me, as you might expect. In 2006, I closed 101 deals, worth $1,570,954. I accomplished this along with all my other duties running the company. At the end of 2011, it looked like my record would not be threatened any time soon. Both Nick and Dan could sell, but they were streaky. There would be a week or two when one or the other would be crowing about his successes, and then weeks when nothing came in. I could not tell whether the pattern was something they were doing or whether it was baked into our business model.

We get calls from all kinds of potential clients, and the resulting orders vary in size by a factor of ten, from a couple thousand to hundreds of thousands of dollars. Some callers need fast shipment, and some can wait months or years. So it is not surprising that the timing of orders varies. I had experienced sales streaks myself, but Dan's and Nick's dry patches were more frequent and longer than any of mine. Was it due to some failure on their part? Or was it just chance? And yet, I pay those guys every two weeks whether they sell or not. When I moved Nick from the bench to sales, his biggest fear was that his income would go down. So I offered him a salary that was equivalent to what he had earned as an hourly worker: $62,000 a year. He would also get an additional 2 percent commission on any orders he booked. I gave Dan the same deal. A lot of bosses put their salesmen on 100 percent commission and let them sink or swim. I am not so hard-hearted. Selling is tough. I have been subject to its roller-coaster ride for twenty-five years, and I want to do what I can to shield my people from it. So I wimped out and gave both of them most of their pay as salary, with the opportunity to make another twenty thousand dollars if they got to a million in sales.

———————

THE FIRST MONDAY of 2012 was just like every other Monday. After the meeting, everyone scattered to their work stations. Six on the shop floor, cutting wood and making furniture. One in the finishing room, putting a smooth and gleaming coating on raw wood. Two packing finished work for shipment, with pauses to clean the shop. For the shop guys, each day is much like the others. The projects change, but they are always in the same shop, with the same machines, cutting up the same material, and working alongside the same people.

In the office, it's entirely different. The six of us live the triumphs and tragedies of sales. My mood closely tracks the frequency of inquiries and the arrival of orders. In the first week of January, we get fourteen calls and e-mails, an improvement on 2011's average of twelve per week, but no orders come in. The second week, inquiries remain strong: seventeen strangers reach out to us, each a potential buyer. Still no sales. Now I am starting to worry. Two weeks without a deal isn't unheard of, but as the dry patch lengthens, my discomfort rises. I relive the agonies of days without work, without money. Thankfully, on the morning of Friday the 13th, Nick closes the first deal of the year: an order worth $16,940 to a housing developer in Baltimore. That same afternoon, he chalks up $8,038 for a table inlaid with the purchaser's initials. In the next week, Nick books four more orders, worth $123,986. In the last week of January, he sells three more, worth $25,041. His total for the month is $174,005, a fantastic start to his year.

We will not make our goal of $200,000 in sales, though, because Dan has not sold anything. In fact, he hasn't made a sale since before Christmas. I could also blame myself for not closing any deals, but I hired a second salesman so I could get out of that game. I still pick up the phone when it rings, and if it is a sales call, I talk to the client, do the initial consultation, then pass the job to Dan or Nick. I want to take the lead on certain kinds of jobs, especially when there is the potential for a very large order. I don't trust either Nick or Dan that much, yet. But I send them the bread-and-butter jobs, the ones that might yield from five to twenty thousand dollars.

On the last day of January, a Tuesday, just as I am seriously considering whether hiring Dan has been a mistake, one of his clients pulls the trigger. He closes a deal with a telecommunications firm in Maryland for $18,694. We finish the month with new orders worth $193,602. Not quite my $200,000 goal, but pretty close. And Nick's hot streak continues into the new month, with a $23,327 sale on the third. Our total for new orders as of Monday, February 6, is $216,929. Nick has sold $197,332. Dan has sold $18,694. I took a $903 order for some replacement parts. I'm happy, and I'm unhappy. One of my salesmen is killing, the other is dying. I know that I can step into Dan's shoes on any day, do a better job, and put his salary into my own pocket. Should I pull the plug? It's a tempting thought, but I know better than to act rashly. I've put a lot of effort into training Dan. Better to wait for a while and see what happens.

FEBRUARY

DATE: MONDAY, FEBRUARY 6, 2012

BANK BALANCE: $125,891.42

CASH RELATIVE TO START OF YEAR ("NET CASH"): -$11,262.90

NEW-CONTRACT VALUE, YEAR-TO-DATE: $216,929

I deliver a mixed message in the first February meeting. Along with all the new orders, the value of jobs constructed last month was $216,614, and we're poised for strong shipments in February. It's a great performance by the shop. So why do I have $11,262 less than I had at the beginning of the year?

Because money goes out the door as fast as it comes in, often faster. We've received deposit payments for most of the new orders, and preship and final payments for the jobs we delivered in January. That's a nice pile of cash: $215,034. But we spent even more: $226,297. We've had twenty-six working days so far this year, and it's cost $7,803 a day to run my factory. At that burn rate, I have sixteen days of working capital on hand.

I use QuickBooks to make sure that my accounting conforms to standard methods, but its cash management tools are very poor. I rely on the spreadsheet I designed in 2008 to look into the future. Directly after the meeting, I bring it up to date. I add all the incoming and outgoing payments I know about. The sheet is divided into weeks. I can see my cash balance each day, and, of course, each week's ending balance is the next week's starting balance. If I see a negative balance on any day, I'll move payments around. There's always a day in the future when I've used up all the income I know about. The trick is to keep bringing in cash so that this day never arrives.

After completing my update, I can see that working capital will hold steady throughout February, but only if we can book new orders as fast as we did in January. We'll need those deposits to keep up with the current rate of spending.

I don't want to give you the impression that I worry about money all the time. It's probably only several hundred times a day. If I feel like thinking about something else, I make a visit to the shop floor.

It's a big space, 252 feet long, 122 feet across. It has a fourteen-foot ceiling and big windows on the outer walls. Concrete columns, set on a twenty-four-foot grid, break up the expanse. I can see carts loaded with completed table parts waiting to go into the finishing room. Beyond that are stacks of lumber, long rolling racks with shelves of veneer, and then the machines.

There are so many machines that it's hard to spot the workers. The smallest are hand held, the largest as big as a minivan. They fall into three categories: cutting wood parts, sanding them, and clamping them together. When I began my career, woodworking machines were relatively crude and relied on the skill of their operator to prepare them for use. Workers are not consistent about how they do this. Every person who uses a tool ends up with a slightly different result, and it is impossible to duplicate an earlier setup. A project with many steps will start to accumulate errors. A good craftsman makes adjustments as the job progresses, but it takes great skill to produce complex work successfully. The best way to ensure high quality in that environment is to have one person take a job from start to finish, so that he can compensate for these inconsistencies. Another approach is to break the construction into small parts that are built repetitively: mass production. In my shop, we've never sold enough of any one item to need an assembly line, so we stick with the single-maker model.

In recent years I've bought a newer generation of machines. These are called CNC (computer numerical controlled) machines, but they're better called robots. Instead of shop floor setups, they follow instructions in the form of computer code, written by Andy Stahl. We have two machines that operate this way: a laser and a CNC milling machine. The laser cuts very intricate, delicate shapes, like the logos we cut from veneer. The CNC is for big parts. It has a working area five feet wide and ten feet long and can make heavier cuts in bigger pieces of wood. Both these machines can cut to within a thousandth of an inch of the planned dimensions. This means that we don't have to worry so much about accumulated errors. We can design complex work knowing that the pieces will fit together without a lot of adjustments, and we can have multiple guys working on a single project.

Another newer type of machine uses digital sensors to adjust to varying workpieces, but still requires an operator. We have two very expensive German veneer sanders. One can sand the pencil marks off a sheet of paper. A very skilled person with a hand sander can also do this, but not nearly as fast, and with a higher rate of failure.

A surprising truth about machines is that they have varying capabilities, just like human workers. Our second veneer sander is supposed to perform to the same high level as the first, but it cannot. It simply isn't as good: every now and then a part put through it comes out ruined. We bought it first, but now we rarely use it.

There are very strict limits on the size of the material that our machines can process. This has changed the way we design our work. The largest piece that our CNC machine can handle is five feet by ten feet, and our veneer sanders max out at 54-inch width. Many of our raw materials come in sheets that are four feet wide and eight feet long. It's hard for one worker to lift pieces bigger than that, so we use four feet by eight feet as a target for the maximum size of any component, even if the finished table is considerably larger. This is a good limit for other reasons as well: bigger pieces are more expensive to ship and won't fit in elevators when we get to a customer's site. Remember the feedback loops between the various functions of the business? Here's a good example: the needs of Manufacturing and Logistics influence Design and Marketing to limit part sizes.

Most of the time, the salesmen can steer a client to decisions about table size and shape that are within our targets. But would I decline a job if it looks like it will be difficult to build, or ship? Or just suck it up and do it anyway? It depends on the amount of money involved. It's always tempting to close a large deal. But what if the client has a lot of money, wants something tricky to build, and we are not sure whether the budget is sufficient to cover the cost?

There's a job like this on our shop floor now: a big U-shaped table. Each arm is thirteen feet long, and the base is twelve feet wide. We're building it for Company S, a food giant with headquarters in the Midwest. The job took a long time to develop. They first called in the spring of 2011, but didn't give the go-ahead to submit a proposal until November. Nick did the initial design, working from a very simple sketch provided by the architect. The only detail on the drawing, other than the size and shape of the table, was that the top was in three pieces, with a top depth (the dimension from the outer edge to the inside of the U) of five feet. Big problem, as the two pieces forming the arms of the table would be thirteen feet long, and the piece forming the base of the table would be twelve feet long and five feet wide. None of these would fit in our sanders, and they would be hard to move around the shop. Company S also wanted a very traditional look, with lots of intricate detailing on the base of the table.

Nick submitted a first design in November 2011. They thought it was promising but wanted some changes. Nick made some changes. It was better, but they wanted a few more tweaks. Nick made a few more tweaks. Now they liked the design but were nervous about hiring us, since we are far away from their headquarters.

I offered to jump on a plane and make our final presentation in person. In early December 2011, I spent several hours working with the chairman and his team. Face time did the trick. I was able to tease out their biggest concerns: that the table would be late and over budget, and that it would be flimsy. I closed the deal by agreeing that the tabletop would be made in three pieces as originally specified and that the mid-March delivery date was inviolable. And we'd absolutely stick to the original budget of forty-five thousand dollars. The timing was difficult, but not impossible. The budget would be a crapshoot.

We price our tables using a very complex Excel spreadsheet that takes into account the size, shape, materials, number of pieces in the top, power/data configuration, and other factors. It spits out two important numbers: the overall price and time estimates for the number of man-hours needed to complete the job, broken down by design, construction, finishing, and shipping. Our spreadsheet is reasonably accurate for most tables, but for very large and/or very complicated jobs, its algorithms become questionable. When we can't predict how some jobs will go, we guess and hope for the best. We've estimated 314 man-hours to do the Company S table.

Steve Maturin, Ron Dedrick, and Sean Slovinski are building it. All three guys have superb hands. This project requires them to dust off old skills and complete some very difficult tasks without help from our new machines. We're using our CNC as much as possible. The U-shaped top is made of subsections, each small enough to fit on the CNC, that will be glued together to make the three large panels. The entire perimeter of the U is composed of a band four inches wide, made of solid cherry. This outlines a six-inch-wide band of mahogany. The mahogany band surrounds the center panels of the table. These are thirty inches wide and veneered with pommelle sapele, a highly figured African wood. Each of these bands, composed of multiple pieces, will be cut by the CNC machine, then glued together so that the top surfaces are perfectly aligned. Those assembled top pieces will then be hand-sanded to perfect flatness, a task we'd normally do with machines.

If you watched Steve and Ron build this top, which took two weeks, you wouldn't see anything spectacular. No shouts of triumph or end-zone dances. They started with the glue-ups. All those pieces, almost three hundred feet of perimeter, are held together with clumsy iron clamps. Each inch of that length needs to be tapped into perfect alignment, while the clamps are being tightened and before the glue dries. Glue-up takes the first week. Then they do nothing but sand, for hours and hours without pause. They have to move a hand-held sander at the perfect speed or it will burn through the paper-thin veneer and the top will be ruined. They repeat a single physical motion: starting with hips tight to the edge of the table, bending at the waist until their backs are nearly horizontal, arms fully extended, then returning the sander to the start position. Every pass has to be perfect, or the sanding will be uneven and the finish will not look right. Bend. Extend. Straighten. Bend. Extend.

Straighten. All day long, holding a hot, noisy sander. This is hard, sweaty work that requires the delicate touch of a concert pianist.

It's a pleasure to watch. Unfortunately, as a businessman, I am not so excited. Highly paid workers using traditional skills to build a complex design is something I never want to see in my shop again. Three of my best workers are bogged down in a single project, and simpler jobs are not getting any attention. We could complete the easier work ahead of their time estimates and meet my monthly build and delivery targets. Instead, the Company S table is sucking up labor hours and leaving my guys too tired to do overtime. We are losing money.

Company S is just one of five orders on the shop floor in February. Their values total $187,639. This is short of my $200,000 build target, but we built $216,614 in January, so I am not too worried. There's other activity out there as well. The tables we built last month are being packed and shipped. And in the office we're processing the usual stream of incoming inquiries, trying to convert them into sales.

Customers contact us in two ways: phone calls and e-mails. The vast majority of these are initiated by someone who visits our Web site. We make a very specialized product that lots of people want to buy but cannot find in local stores. So they head to Google. Within a second, the connection is made: interested shoppers meet Paul Downs Cabinetmakers.

Before the Internet, matching a buyer and a seller was far more complicated and expensive. The more specialized the product, and the greater the distance between client and maker, the harder it was to do a deal. Buying ads in media with national or international reach was extraordinarily expensive. Only a business of substantial size, selling a product that everyone needed, could afford to do this.

A tiny company like mine was forced to serve a local market. Direct-mail campaigns and local print advertising were not cheap, but within the realm of possibility. That is exactly how my business developed in its first fourteen years. I spent my marketing budget on print ads in a local magazine.

My first ads appeared in 1993. These fledgling efforts required the services of a professional photographer, writer, and graphic de-signer, who cost me about ten thousand dollars. (Now it's almost free, using digital photography and cheap software.) Monthly ad charges exceeded two thousand dollars, for an eighth of a page in black and white. I raised the money to start this effort by selling some of my company to my father and brother—a pity investment on their part.

The magazine had a monthly circulation of a hundred thousand. How many of those people were looking for custom dining sets at any moment? Not many. A very small number of potential buyers saw my ad, and a subset of them made a trip to my shop to see the designs I offered. Who has time for that kind of shopping? Wealthy women with large houses to fill.

These face-to-face meetings were nerve-racking experiences. We would go through my portfolio of photographs to see if anything was of interest. There was no guarantee that the client would see anything she liked, nor any guarantee that she could afford it if she did. It is amazing that I sold anything at all. As a feedback loop be-tween Design and Sales, though, these meetings were hard to beat. Clients asked me for all kinds of items: dressers, beds, built-in cabi-nets, closets, porches, you name it. I made anything, but dining room furniture was the best fit for my capabilities. As a product, it had advantages. First, clients will spend good money on it, in par-ticular to get a dining table made to fit their room. Second, making sets of chairs offers the shop floor an opportunity for repetitive work, which is considerably more efficient. Third, there are lots of ways to improve on traditional designs.

I had hundreds of meetings with clients and developed table, chair, and server designs that addressed their needs. The more clients I worked for, the more designs I developed. The more designs I had, the better the chance that the next buyers would see something they liked. Feedback loop in action.

My shop grew throughout the 1990s. By the end of that decade, I had six employees and six hundred thousand dollars in annual sales. My salary would fluctuate between thirty and forty thousand dollars annually. I was getting very tired of face-to-face sales, though. Selling custom furniture to affluent couples was a multi-step endeavor, and at some point the husband got involved. Most of those guys had day jobs, so I ended up doing a lot of evening and weekend meetings. At the same time, I was trying to be a helpful husband and father. My wife, Nancy, and I had been blessed with twins in 1994, and had another boy in 1996. One of the twins was born with severe autism and my wife needed a lot of help. So I would work a long day in the shop, rush home to a house full of little kids, and then go out again in the evenings to clients. I worked most Saturdays as well. Then I heard about this wonderful thing called a "Web site." I could display my entire portfolio along with the prices. Anyone could view it anytime and decide for themselves whether they could afford my work. And I could introduce new designs as fast as I thought of them.

I started work on my first site in 1999. By the end of that year, I posted more than a hundred and fifty pieces, each with pricing. I started showing my Web address in my magazine ads. It worked—easier shopping inspired more calls, and I spent a lot less time on tire kickers.

In 1999, an architect who had bought a dining table from me was renovating the offices of a local company. They wanted a flagship boardroom table with the latest power and data connections, so he asked me if I was interested. The table was twenty-four feet long, and five feet wide at the center, with contrasting panels of cherry, bird's-eye maple, and curly anegre. It was a spectacular design.

The biggest table we had made, to that point, was less than half the size of this monster. But it wasn't beyond our capabilities. I fine-tuned the design a bit and gave it to Steve Maturin to build. This was before we had any CNC machinery. In an astonishing feat of craftsmanship, Steve built the entire table by himself and beat the time estimate. We installed it and I photographed it with my first digital camera. I put the photo and specifications onto our Web site in 2000, labeled "Lippincott Boardroom Table."

Fast-forward three years. My ads are still running in the local magazine and sales continue to grow. And the Lippincott Table is going viral. Google started showing it as a top result when people searched for "boardroom table." Suddenly, people all over the world had found my Web site. And in 2003, we started getting the first calls from people who wanted a conference table, along with those who wanted dining tables. The online channel was far more effective, and cheaper, than the print ads. In 2003, less than 5 percent of our business was initiated by a visit to the Web site. By 2005, that percentage had risen to 95 percent, and I abandoned print forever.

Being the top search result for "boardroom table" gave us the opportunity to make money at no cost to us. Apparently we weren't the only ones getting this free lunch, so Google monetized its traffic with the introduction of AdWords. This program reserved the best positions on a search results page for paid advertisements. Here's how it works: a potential advertiser (such as Paul Downs Cabinetmakers) identifies search terms that potential customers might be using (like "boardroom table") and offers to pay Google a certain amount to show an ad whenever someone searches those terms. If we offer more than anyone else, our ad is shown at the top of the search results. If we offer second highest, then our ad appears below the top bidder, and so on. We started using AdWords in 2004—we were very early adopters. I started buying a range of search strings, concentrating my budget on dining tables. But the boardroom table inquiry stream was growing fast, and those buyers were much easier to deal with than residential buyers. I needed to decide between dining tables and conference tables. Eventually I realized that if we were really going to sell conference tables, I would have to rethink the way we designed the product, our sales methods, how we built them, and how we safely shipped them to the customer. Design, Marketing, Production, Logistics, Warranty Administration Service: every function of the business would need to be reinvented for the new world we had entered. That effort consumed me for the next years, right up to the crash in 2008.

This condensed history makes the opportunity presented by the Internet look obvious. Am I a farsighted business visionary? No. I was lucky. Google, itself growing at chaotic speed, used an algorithm to read the whole Internet, and it chose a page on my little Web site as the best depiction of a particular thing. And Google also provided an efficient channel between a world of strangers and me. I had nothing to do with that. At the turn of the century, my day was taken up with ordinary tasks. I was doing all the selling, which took up most of my day. I was also doing the marketing, engineering, scheduling, project management, material ordering, bookkeeping and payroll, banking, hirings and firings, and also driving the truck and making all our deliveries. That was ten to twelve hours of work each day, and then home to a house full of little kids. There is no broad vantage point in that existence. No retreat from the daily grind, no view of the big picture, no time to figure out what it all means and what to do next. Big decisions get made for picayune reasons. I created a Web site so that I could stop working on the weekends. Watching couples bicker over which chair they liked best drove me to create new designs. I took a partner because I was lonely and wanted a mentor to teach me the business skills I lacked. I started thinking about conference tables because people suddenly started asking for them. I made lots of uninformed choices. The good ones turned out a little bit better than the bad ones turned out badly, so the company survived.

My experience with a partner is a very long, complicated story. The extremely short version is that I sold some of my ownership stake to one of my clients in 2002. I was warned that this was a bad idea, but I felt trapped. The company needed to expand so that I could hire some people to help me with my workload, but I couldn't make it bigger without increasing my hours, and I was already tapped out. The partnership seemed like a solution. The Partner, as I will call him, had a good reputation for honesty and fair dealing. He brought an infusion of capital to the business, which we used to move to larger quarters, upgrade our information infrastructure, and introduce CNC machines to the shop floor. We also hired shop workers, willy-nilly, to keep up with our growing sales. All this was expensive and disruptive. During those years, the company made no profits. In fact, it lost substantial amounts of money.

Everything might have turned out differently except for one piece of extraordinarily bad luck. Prior to teaming up with me, The Partner had owned several manufacturing businesses that had done well. I was looking forward to working with someone who could mentor me and help me learn new business skills. I was very good at design and sales but very bad at running the factory, figuring out our costs, dealing with my employees, and many other things that a boss must do.

After our partnership was formed, The Partner said that we absolutely had to clean up our books and properly keep track of our financials. And he had an experienced CPA to recommend: his wife, Jenny, who had been the money manager for all his previous businesses. I liked Jenny. She was extremely intelligent and diligent, very easy to work with. I was delighted to have her take over what had been a classic receipts-in-the-shoe-box operation. She got right to work and set us up with a chart of accounts with the data from my two previous years of operations. This took four months.

And then she died in her sleep, at age fifty-four. The Partner was devastated. And, although nobody realized it at the time, it was going to be a big problem for the business as well. In all their previous companies, The Partner and Jenny had been an effective team: he was the Great Leader and Chief Visionary, she was the Minute-by-Minute Navigator, keeping operations on track.

Jenny passed in April 2003. The Partner rallied, and over the next five years, he and I did our best to expand production and to respond to the changes in our marketing and customer base. We got along well. But without Jenny's guidance, we lost money every year. We did accomplish a lot. His investment (most of which he lost) helped me to get unstuck and take the business to the next level.

Returning to 2012: we can now build and deliver sophisticated tables anywhere in the United States and Canada. Those two countries are huge markets. Using Google, we cast a wide net to find customers over that large area.

Big nets capture some strange fish. We occasionally get inquiries from around the world. On February 13, an e-mail arrives from a furniture dealer in Kuwait looking for pricing for five tables. He's putting together a bid to furnish a new government facility in Kuwait City. He hasn't given us enough information about the design for us to generate real numbers, but I could send him a ballpark estimate.

If I can be bothered, that is. Does it make sense for me to spend any time on this? Does this job have potential? A couple of years ago, the answer would have been a resounding "No!" The difficulty of vetting a foreign partner, the problems of shipping and installation, and the risk of not getting paid: all would have been too much for me. But this time, by chance, I see the opportunity with new eyes.

A year ago, in the winter of 2011, I realized that my increased sales force was generating a lot of routine work—writing contracts, sending finish samples to clients, keeping track of payments. We had systems in place, but they took a lot of my time. I decided to hire an assistant. I'm always looking for the easiest way to fill a position, so I turned to my wife. She knows everyone. As soon as I described the problem, she had a person in mind: her friend Emma Watson. Emma and her husband had moved to the area a few years before, after he had retired from the diplomatic corps. She was looking for a way to supplement his pension.

I hired her and she was perfect: hard-working, smart, and diligent. I worked with her closely as I trained her, and bounced ideas off her whenever I wanted a fresh opinion. Unlike the rest of us, she had not spent her whole life in woodshops and had an outsider's perspective.

When I hire someone, my first consideration is whether they can perform the specific job. People are complicated, though, and often have personalities, skills, and experiences that aren't relevant to the positions I hire them to fill. In large organizations, nobody cares whether an employee might have the ability to perform more than one job—if a problem needs attention, another person will be hired to solve it. In a very small company like ours, employees' secondary abilities become an inventory of possible new functions for the business. Suddenly a boss can consider a course of action that would otherwise have been out of reach.

I mention to Emma that we got an inquiry from Kuwait and wonder whether we should bother with it. Her reaction surprises me. Why don't we contact the U.S. Trade Representative in Kuwait? I never considered asking the government for help and had no idea where to start. But Emma is familiar with the way things work in our embassies. She volunteers to get in touch with the Department of Commerce people in Kuwait. I tell her to go ahead. If their response is promising, then I'll decide whether to devote any of our limited resources to developing it. Emma goes to it with a will. She is seizing the initiative, something that my other employees have rarely done. She's only a part-time administrative assistant, but she's proving her usefulness by increasing her own responsibilities, maybe with hopes of a full-time job.

I've employed more than a hundred and twenty people over the years. I'm willing to assert that you can divide employees into two groups: the ones who want to perform their job competently then go home; and the ones who are always thinking about ways to get ahead. In my experience, the first group vastly outnumbers the second. One of my biggest problems, as a very small company, is to find ways to advance people. We aren't large enough, or growing fast enough, for a career path to be available to every employee. Instead, the shop is divided into various functions, people are hired to do that work, and they are going to stay in the same position unless a vacancy becomes available. And that's not common, particularly for the top-level jobs. Those are filled with people who have been with me for a long time and show no desire to leave. I know that some lower-level people are unhappy about this, but I don't know what to do about it. The size of the business determines our resources for

trying new ideas and exploring other markets. But restricted resources limit our ability to increase our size. Catch-22, small business
edition. The solution is to be more profitable. Profits become a war
chest that could fund further expansion. But I've been particularly
bad at making profits, barely able to find the cash to survive. Without an extra cushion, I have no way to move in new directions. It's
nice to get good ideas, but I need to think carefully about potential
costs to the company and whether we can afford to pursue the opportunity. I have often found myself in the position of having to
squash an employee's enthusiastic suggestions that we do this or
that because of lack of resources. It is discouraging to the worker,
and discouraging to me. And I'm sure that it is one of the main reasons that I haven't seen tons of initiative from my people—I haven't
been able to respond to their suggestions, so they stopped giving
them.

I end up Skyping with the guy in Kuwait, who seems credible. I
send him a short proposal, with some examples of our work and approximate pricing. And then I sit back to see what else Emma comes
up with. If we start exporting, she will be indispensable, and we'll
have access to a very large new market. Everybody wins! I have
some doubts about servicing Middle Eastern customers—post-sale
care might be a problem—but I'm willing to pursue the idea. The
cost of finding out more is very low, and I have some cash on hand.

The approach from Kuwait is not the only foreign opportunity to
consider. In the spring of 2011, a guy called me from New York, asking if I had any interest in doing custom work for his company, a
large European furniture manufacturer. (I'll call it Eurofurn, not its
real name.) I told him that it depended on what they had in mind.
He told me more: Eurofurn had been around for more than a hundred
years. It had outgrown Europe and expanded to the Far East, Aus-
tralia, South Africa, and the Middle East. Now they were moving

into the United States and had opened a New York showroom. My caller, whom I will call Nigel, was an Australian who had been put in charge of American operations. He needed to respond to Eurofurn's clients' requests for custom items. That work could be done at their German factory, but shipping time was an issue, so he had turned to Google to find a custom table maker in the United States.

Nigel came to see our operation in May 2011. I gave him the standard tour: how we designed our work, how we modeled it with software, and how we tracked orders. We toured the shop floor, concentrating on our CNC and veneering capabilities. He was impressed, or so he said. On a shoestring, we had put together sophisticated capabilities for a small company.

I wanted to get a better sense of the Eurofurn product line, so a couple of weeks later I went to Manhattan. Say these words to yourself: "European furniture showroom in Midtown Manhattan." What pops into your head? You probably got it exactly right. A large room in a historic building, with a stunning view of the city. Super sleek tables and chairs, computers everywhere, a crew of young, stylish workers. English is spoken with attractive foreign accents. A wellfunded, impressive operation.

All their designs were quite modern, mixing metal elements of polished stainless steel and chrome with woodwork. The choice of wood and the design of details were understated—no exotic grains, but very clean, uniform, and very well made. The metal components were beyond our capabilities, but we could produce most of the woodwork. It would be different from what we usually make, but we could do it.

Nigel and I discussed what came next. I walked up to one of the chairs around their conference table and pulled it back—an unconscious gesture on my part. To my surprise, the chair didn't move. No casters. It weighed close to fifty pounds. It had a swivel seat, but the chair wasn't designed to be repositioned. I said, "Here's the first thing you need to change for the American market. We like our chairs to roll around." He sighed. "Yes, we have heard that opinion. We prefer for the chairs to stay in place around the table. Much neater." He rotated his chair's seat, sat in it, and rotated back, without shifting it. With a graceful move, he showed the American how it's done. In Europe, anyway.

It underscored what I had been wondering: don't they have all their own products and operations worked out already? This is a very large, very old deep-pockets operation with a worldwide presence. What do they want from little Paul Downs Cabinetmakers?

Nigel had an answer. Eurofurn expected that a successful entry into the U.S. market would take several years. Eventually they would need a factory in the United States. Their manufacturing sites in other regions of the world were begun as joint ventures with local companies. When they moved into a new country, they identified suitable partners and worked with them to get the factories up and running.

For their American effort, they wanted a very small company, for whom even a low volume of orders would be significant business. It would take a while for the business to ramp up. If they went straight to a large, established company, they would not be able to provide enough work, initially, for the partner to treat the orders with importance. And they also wanted a company that understood the highest levels of craftsmanship. They would accept nothing less than work indistinguishable from the output of their German factory. At the end of this meeting, I was enthusiastic about the possibilities and flattered to have been chosen.

Back in the office, I found lots of information about Eurofurn on the Web. News reports put their sales at a hundred million dollars per year. Eurofurn's own site emphasized the partnership between factory management and the workers, their profit-sharing program, and their care for the environment. It especially emphasized the industrial designers who came up with the products, presenting them as heroes of creativity. It was clearly a great company.

The relationship developed throughout 2011. During that same time, we were running flat out on other projects, but I made sure that we responded quickly to Eurofurn's pricing requests and promised extra fast turnaround. In the fall, we got our first orders, totaling $8,111.

Our interactions with Eurofurn are oddly difficult. The drawings they send with quote requests are sometimes incomplete or make no sense. Even worse, they don't seem to have any uniform way of naming their jobs. We can't tell whether a given pricing request is a revision to a previous job or something entirely new. Sometimes a quote request has a customer name, sometimes just a date, sometimes what appears to be an invoicing number. There's no consistency, even on different items for the same customer. I've been sending Eurofurn inquiries to Dan Smolen—I thought that they would be relatively easy to sell—but the confusion drives him crazy. I wonder how they managed to keep track of orders going all around the world.

Despite these issues, Nigel seems to be happy with the way things are going. The New York sales staff found that American buyers demand more customization than the worldwide clientele, and some of Eurofurn's designs are not a good fit with American wiring practices. We've taken some orders for pieces that solve these problems.

At the end of February, I make another visit to New York. Since our very first meeting, Nigel has been dangling the possibility of a significant increase in order volume. Eurofurn wants to move manufacturing of its wood tabletops out of their home plant, and top management has discussed bringing that work into my shop. I have the space and see it as a way to increase my sales volume without ramping up ad spending.

Nigel and I discuss the prices we have quoted him for custom work. Why did we charge so much, he asks me, when he was getting much lower pricing for similar items from his factory in Asia? I tell him that there are two problems: we don't really have good information about exactly what the details consist of, because we haven't been provided with any engineering drawings. And we also get no opportunity to produce anything in volume, so we cannot operate efficiently. I assign our highest-skilled workers to Eurofurn jobs, as the look they want is difficult to build without some very sophisticated machines that we don't have. He admits that his Asia factories are actually running an assembly line and took several years to arrive at low prices. But he can't give us large quantity orders until we bring the price down. I can't bring the price down without more orders. I'm not going to borrow money to buy the extremely expensive machines we'd need without some commitment on his part. I ask him straight out: "What kind of order volume do you anticipate per year?" He answers: "I think we could be doing at least two hundred and fifty thousand dollars this year, and one million in 2013. Can you get your plant up to speed by then?" Frankly, I think his numbers are preposterous. I can't see how his office could even keep track of that many orders. But this isn't the moment to challenge him. He's bullshitting me, I'll bullshit him right back. "Of course we can do it," I tell him. "But I need to get better information from you." I want to see the engineering drawings for the work we are meant to produce. What I'd really like would be to get into his factory. I ask him, "Can you send me some pictures or video of what is happening at your home factory? Or can

I come over to see it in person?" That would be best. I'll see the machines, get a good look at their workers, and see what we're competing with.

Nigel agrees to ask his superiors about a visit. I leave the meeting in a mixed mood. I feel that his projection of sales volume is nonsense, and I know that without significant outside investment I won't be able to handle their million dollars in orders by the end of the year. I don't have the capital to buy the machines that I think we will need, or any good way to interview, hire, and train the additional staff. It would be a huge stretch for us. But now isn't the moment to put the brakes on. Neither of us has made any real commitment yet. I might as well keep going and see what happens.

MARCH

DATE: THURSDAY, MARCH 1, 2012

BANK BALANCE: $145,855.88

CASH RELATIVE TO START OF YEAR ("NET CASH"): $8,701.56

NEW-CONTRACT VALUE, YEAR-TO-DATE: $407,271

New orders arrived at a nice pace in February: twelve jobs worth $213,669. Nick continued as best salesman, closing six deals worth $150,104. Dan did four orders worth $37,768. I sold two, adding $25,797 to the total. Dan still trails Nick by a wide margin, but the total for the year exceeds my target. If current trends continue, I'll need to figure out what to do about Dan, as he's not producing at a rate that justifies his salary. The conventional fix for a slumping salesman is to pay him only with commission or get rid of him. Nobody would be surprised if I fired Dan—that's what bosses are supposed to do—but I just don't have the stomach for it. I can picture how unpleasant it would be to announce a decision that will probably destroy Dan's life. He's new to the area, with an unemployed wife and four small kids. He needs a stable paycheck. It's in my power to provide that or take it away. Nick is carrying the load for both of them, so I just let the whole thing slide.

Our cash position is solid. In the past four weeks, we took in

$232,475. Some of this included payments for jobs we did for the federal government in 2011. The government pays the whole contract amount thirty days after delivery, and we had shipped a couple of jobs to the Air Force in December. The rest is incoming deposits. We spent a good deal of money in that same period: $185,782, or $9,289 a day. More than I wanted, but the overall picture is good. We're ahead for the year.

Since we have cash, I decide it's time for the company to start making interest payments on the money it owes me. That number is substantial: $387,098. Most of that dates back to my years with The Partner and before. I would make loans to the company whenever the business ran out of money, once or twice a year. Incoming payments have always been unpredictable, but rent and payroll arrive like clockwork. I squirreled away as much of my pay as I could and usually had between ten thousand and twenty-five thousand dollars in a personal account, separate from the money I used for family expenses. I had no other financing options. Before The Partner, my books were in such disarray that no bank would lend me money. I remember well the humiliating day in 1994 when I dressed up in my best suit, sat down with the manager of my bank, and was told that I was far too risky for a loan. So I financed the company out of my own pocket. During the sixteen years I was sole proprietor, I loaned the company $167,650 and was paid back none of it.

The Partner brought some change. His wife sorted out my books, but she died before she could teach me to manage cash. Bookkeeping, which records what has happened to a company's money, and cash management, which looks forward to figure out what is about to happen, are very different. Bookkeeping and accounting are standardized. Cash management is not. Amazingly, it's up to each company to invent its own methods of predicting cash flows and planning expenditures. The Partner had no idea how to do this. He left it up to me, and my method was to watch my bank balance, make payroll first, let other bills accumulate, and hope for the best. We frequently ran short of cash and had heated discussions about how we had gotten into this fix, but we never came up with a solution. He didn't think that losses were unexpected for a growing company, and I didn't know any better. Our agreement was that we would each contribute equal amounts when the company needed more cash. Before the crash, we made twenty-one loans, averaging $31,776. We managed to repay ourselves just nine times, with an average repayment of $20,286. In 2005, we opened a bank line of credit for one hundred thousand dollars. In those days, banks handed out loans like candy to any company that showed revenue growth. They were eager to give us money, as long as we pledged our personal assets (my house, his money) as collateral. We used it all in eleven months. The Partner repaid the loan in October 2008 by raiding our cash (without asking me). He believed that we were about to fail and that his investment was gone, but he didn't want a bank default on his credit rating. His action left the company free of external debt, which turned out to be a good thing.

After the disastrous fall of 2008, I was forced to run the company without borrowing. It was painful, but I managed it—at least until the following summer, when I realized that our Web site was coded in a way that made it hard for Google to tell what it was about. Developers that we hired in 2004 to spruce up the site knew nothing about search engine optimization, so the source code for every page and picture was done without words, only letters and numbers. I was driving traffic to the site by paying for AdWords clicks, but we never appeared on the free rankings. I knew that as times got tougher, I would need better marketing or we would die. So I emptied my children's college fund ($31,251) and spent it on a new Web site. Development took seven months. The new site rolled out in early 2010, just as the economy and my fortunes began to recover. Coincidence? Maybe. Worth it? Definitely. If I hadn't spent that money, I'm sure we would have failed.

The debt is always in the back of my mind. If I had invested it in the stock market, I'd still have a lot of the principal available, and in some years it would have produced a handsome return. But I put it into my company, and since we were always broke, I have had no return, neither principal nor interest. But now, with cash on hand, I decide to at least make interest payments. As boss, I can structure them any way that I want. I can set the interest rate to my liking, as long as it conforms to IRS guidelines: the rate must be similar to what the company would pay on commercial loans from outsiders. And I can decide whether to repay principal, or pay interest only, or skip a payment if I want to. This flexibility is very useful as I manage cash flow. It's the main reason that I have dipped into my own pocket first when the company needed money. If I borrow from a bank or another commercial lender, I have no flexibility whatsoever. The bank will want its money, and if they don't get it, they will foreclose.

Having decided to make monthly payments, I choose an interest rate. Ten percent is on the high end of bank rates but lower than I might get from a lender who specializes in small, risky loans. I also decide not to make any principal payments. They're a further drain on cash flow. I write and sign a check for the first payment: $3,225.82. I can't bring myself to deposit it. Old habits die hard. I feel secure when the company has money, guilty when I take it out.

I CLOSED A DEAL on February 29 with Old Style Packing, who first called us the year before. They had a relatively low budget and wanted a set of tables that could be reconfigured on a regular basis.

We had been getting a good number of calls asking for a table like this and I decided to design one.

We had several modular tables in our portfolio, but all were large, expensive, and awkward to operate. A low-cost, easy-to-use version needed a compact and sturdy folding mechanism. We can't produce that ourselves. I found a company in Michigan that made exactly what we needed: a set with wheels that was inexpensive and looked good. I ordered a sample set in December and slapped together a prototype—I screwed the legs to a piece of plywood. It worked great. Easy to fold, sturdy, rolled around at the touch of a finger, and the wheels could be locked. I made a table design that incorporated this set, but also let us build in custom sizes and woods, and include wiring, at a reasonable price.

Shortly afterward, that call from Old Style Packing came in. It was a great opportunity to move from drawings to prototype, funded by a paying customer.

This is how I have always introduced new products. I love the challenge of designing useful items, but making things just for the heck of it is not smart. First of all, what to build? How do I know that some new design will succeed in the marketplace? And if it doesn't, what do I do with the prototype? Furniture is large, bulky, and hard to store. I don't want a perpetually expanding museum of failed designs. The solution to this problem is to listen carefully to what potential clients ask for and build that thing. Everybody wins: my R&D effort is funded by the client, who gets a useful finished product, and I can use the new design in my ongoing marketing efforts.

In the old days, it could be tricky to convince that first buyer to pony up some dough. Drawings of any design concept are bland and difficult to understand, but making a finished prototype before the sale was closed was hugely expensive and risky. That problem has disappeared. Modeling software shows the client exactly what the design looks like and how it works. I deployed this weapon in my proposal for Old Style Packing. Once I had a fully functioning virtual model of the leg mechanism, the complete table design was easy. I sent the proposal off, and a month later, the deposit check arrived. The job will be in production in the middle of March.

The first day of March is a milestone on another project. The Company S table is ready to go into the finish room. Making furniture from scratch has two phases: building and finishing. Building involves cutting lumber up and putting it back together in more useful shapes. Finishing is applying liquid to the wood surfaces, which then dries into a protective layer. Correctly applied, the finish coat makes the surface smooth, shiny, pleasant to touch, and protects the wood from dirt and water.

In our shop, we use a durable, water-resistant finish called a "catalyzed polyurethane." It is very tricky to work with, however. It consists of three parts: resin, solvent, and catalyst. These must be mixed in exactly the right proportion. Before the liquid finish hardens—about a fifteen-minute window—it must be sprayed onto the wood in an even coat. The spray gun and hose weigh about two pounds. They must be held out at arm's length, at the proper distance from the wood, and moved at the right speed. Spray too little, and the surface looks dry and blotchy; spray too much, and the finish will drip and run before drying. We often modify the natural color of the woods with stains and dyes. Stain mixes must be measured with the same precision as the urethane. And everything must be clean—dust in the finish is unacceptable.

The only way to fix a flawed finish is to wait until it dries, sand it off, and start over. Even if one tiny part of a tabletop is bad, the whole thing has to be redone, because a refinished section is never a perfect match for the rest.

Eye of an artist. Knowledge of math and chemistry. Physical strength and endurance. Meticulously clean. Performs under strict time pressure. It's unusual to find all this in one person. A good finisher is hard to find, and worth a lot.

Dave Violi, my finisher, has unleashed his superpowers on the Company S table. At the end of the first week of March, we reassemble it for final inspection. It is magnificent. Everyone in the shop stops to admire it. And, without exception, the first thing they do is run a hand across the top. A perfectly smooth, even topcoat, with no dust specks or other flaws, has been applied to each of the three oversize top pieces. Dave is a master of martial arts, and his strength and agility made the difference. We have eight days before our client's board members gather in their new headquarters. We need to get the table to the customer.

Back when we made dining room furniture, I did all the deliveries myself. I learned a lot from watching a buyer's first encounter with their purchase. Clients are very nervous on delivery day. Our sales process is designed to construct an image in the client's mind of what the finished item will look like. Their hope that we will do a good job will be confirmed, or not, by the actual product. When I was doing delivery, I could make sure that everything went smoothly and that the client was pleased. Happy clients make the final payments. Unhappy clients cause delay and distraction while their problem is addressed.

Google changed our market from local to continental. Our clients are now scattered across the United States and Canada. We have to ship a large, delicate product over long distances, as quickly as possible. Damage is a disaster. Our products are one of a kind, so we can't pull a replacement part out of inventory.

We have to trust strangers to transport and deliver our work without damage. Unfortunately, both truckers and installers vary widely in quality: some are careful and competent, and some are not. How can we find good people? How can we get them to take extra care? And what, besides paying them, could we do to make sure that they succeeded? I arrived at three methods: use middlemen to find the trucker and installer; redesign the tables for ease of shipment and assembly; and optimize packaging design. How does this work?

First: the middlemen. Our volume of business is too small to impress a large trucking company, and we need to hire installers in places that we have never been to. So we use a freight broker for trucking and an installation broker for installation. Both firms take the parameters of our job and get bids from interested vendors. It's their job to identify quality vendors and deal with them if things go wrong. The vendors get significant business from the middlemen, who represent lots of small companies like us, so they pay some attention. And we give significant business to the middlemen, so they pay attention to us. This is an instance where it is not in my best interest to shop around for a low price. We need to commit to our middlemen so that they act as our champions. This raises shipping and installation costs, but saves us a lot of time and trouble. I chose one freight broker and one installation broker years ago, and have stuck with them ever since. Our person-to-person relationship is as important as the money in making it work.

Second: the design. Traditionally, a person moving and assembling furniture is presumed to have specialized tools and some skills. Our clients have neither. Detailed instructions won't help. Our tables are all different from one another, so a universal instruction book won't work. We'd need a new one with every project. I tried this a few times, and it took huge amounts of time. The clients ended up calling me for help anyway. I decided to rethink our construction details with ease of assembly as a primary goal. All tables would henceforth consist of components small enough that one person could pick them up and move them, but big enough so that there weren't too many pieces. The parts would self-align so that they could go together only in the correct position. Hand knobs would join all the pieces together: no tools required. Even an untrained person could see at a glance exactly what to do. We adapted this system to everything that we built. As it turned out, this also speeded up construction considerably. In order to build a table, it needs to be put together and taken apart multiple times. So thinking about assembly from an ignorant client's point of view had benefits for our sophisticated workers as well.

Third: the packaging. This must do more than just protect the goods. It has to communicate to everyone on the path from our shop to client. We want to send a different message at different points in the journey. The packaging has to intimidate the warehouse worker, convert the installer from neutral actor to enthusiastic champion of our product, and delight the customer. After a lot of experimentation, we have settled on a two-layer strategy: wrap every part, crate the whole order. Every piece of the table gets wrapped in foam, then in cardboard, and is clearly labeled to show exactly what it is and how to open it. Then all the pieces are bundled into a custom-made crate with wood sides but no top, so that there is no temptation to stack another load on top of it. To the truckers, the shipment looks heavy, strong, and expensive—something that is worthy of extra care. When installers break down the crate, they find nicely packaged, clearly labeled, and easy-to-handle pieces that are a breeze to bring into the client's premises. We've heard numerous times from clients that the installers told them that we made the best table they had ever worked with. Good packaging converts the installers into our ambassadors and puts the client in the right frame of mind.

Designing tables for easy assembly ended up saving me money, but crating and wrapping is expensive. My shipping manager, Bob

Foote, needs a full-time helper to keep up with shop output. It's interesting to break my whole crew down and see what proportion of the workforce works in the different parts of the operation: out of fourteen workers, four are doing design and sales, six are on the shop floor building the furniture, two are in the finish room applying coatings, and two are handling logistics. In other words, the people doing the woodworking, which is what most people think is our primary activity, are outnumbered by people adding value at other points in the supply chain.

It takes two days to package all the components of the Company S table and to build custom crates for the oversize top sections. After it ships, I keep my fingers crossed, and the crate arrives safely at the installers, and a day later we hear from them that the install has gone well.

I send the final invoice, for $7,551, to my contact at Company S, along with care instructions. I don't hear anything back, which is slightly unsettling but not unusual. I presume they're busy with their board meeting. They have ten days to settle up. They've made all the previous payments without delay, so I turn my attention to other matters.

Emma Watson has been talking to the government. The U.S. Department of Commerce is eager to help us. She's also found that Pennsylvania has its own export assistance program and maintains trade missions in a large number of foreign cities. Both of them contract with a third outfit, the World Trade Center, to provide manpower. Emma makes an appointment with the WTC to come see us. Two guys show and give us three cards each.

Like everyone who visits us, it takes them a little while to wrap their heads around the concept of a cabinetmaking shop that makes nothing but conference tables. These export guys have been in lots of factories, and ours does not compare to bigger entities. In some areas we are very advanced—our robotic machines and our marketing on the Internet—but in lots of others, we look like what we are: small and undercapitalized. The government guys don't seem to care about any of that. Their job is to promote exports, and to do that they need American companies to work with. They wax ecstatic about our inevitable triumph on foreign shores, aided by their services. While they are gassing on, I'm looking at them and wondering what their day consists of. How hard do they work? Do they ever wonder if they won't get paid? (I suspect not, since the guys who print the money are issuing their checks.) Would I ever want a job like theirs, where I put on a suit every morning, do something entirely predictable, and then go home? Where I knew exactly how much money I would make today, tomorrow, and in the future? Would I be happier if my life had more security?

After the trade guys depart, we contemplate the pile of beautifully printed, expensive brochures that they left. Our first decision is whether to sign up with the federal program, run by the Commerce Department, or the state program, run by Pennsylvania. The local contacts are the same guys we just met with in either case, but the staff in our target countries is not. Emma has no doubt that the feds are the way to go. Her argument: every person on Earth will take a call from the U.S. ambassador, while nobody has heard of the Pennsylvania trade delegate. Go with the people who can open doors. I agree. That decision leads us to the various levels of services offered by the Commerce Department. We settle on something called the Gold Key Matching Service. (Who thought of that name?) For a couple hundred dollars, a Commerce Department office located in our target cities will call around to local merchants to see whether any of them are interested in meeting with us. The process starts with a questionnaire, in which we describe what we make and what kind of foreign business we are after, and continues with a phone interview with the trade rep. I'm still only half committed to the whole idea of exporting, but Emma is enthusiastic, so I agree to sign up for the Gold Key Matching Service. I have to spend money at this point—three hundred dollars—but I feel like that's not too much to see what happens next.

On March 9, our new folding tables are ready to ship. I take a number of photographs of one of them, both raised and folded, to add to our Web site. I can't get a good picture of it under our glaring lights, so I generate a nicer image with a rendering program. I only post renderings of pieces we've actually built and always include some shots of the table on our shop floor, even though those are often terrible photos. I want to prove that we actually do the work we show.

Photos are easy; pricing is hard. What should I charge for this new product? What should I charge for any product? It is a surprisingly difficult question. There are two ways to think about this: first, what is the customary market price? and second, what does it cost us to make it? The first approach doesn't work for us. We have almost no information on what our competitors are charging because they don't publish price lists. We have some idea of what factory-made tables cost, but that doesn't help us price a custom project. So we work from internal cost projections.

Our pricing spreadsheets predict the costs of each project, but when I check the actual build data, I find that the forecast was often wrong. Errors and differing skill levels of the workers on each project make for wide ranges in build hours, even for very similar tables. And the actual material costs are murky, too. The spreadsheet predicts how much wood we need to buy, but the area calculations are very imprecise, and we haven't updated our cost data for the different woods since 2007—I haven't had time to track down hundreds of (volatile) prices. I'm assuming that the recession has brought demand and prices for wood down. Given what happens on the shop floor, inaccurate cost data may not matter. Wood comes in random sizes, with some defects, so yield is inconsistent. Sometimes we can use scrap from earlier work in a subsequent project, sometimes not. Errors and rework require duplicate material orders and extra time. In order to give ourselves a margin of safety, we mark up the theoretical material costs by 40 percent to cover uncertainty. Then we add that number to our labor costs, calculated at $78 per hour, no matter which worker, with associated pay rate, is working on the project. The sum of those numbers is, theoretically, our minimum profitable cost. We then mark up that number by 7.5 percent as an additional safety margin and add 2 percent for the sales commission. That's our theoretical price for any of our products.

I have told Nick and Dan to get at least the calculated price out of the customer, but sometimes we need to cut a deal to make a sale. We might also change the price if the spreadsheet kicks out a number, say $10,032, or $40,151, which is just above an obvious pricing cut-off point. I'll gladly give up a couple of dollars to bring a number from five digits to four, or from one decile to its lower neighbor. I've read enough about retail pricing to believe that people really do respond to slightly lower numbers in those situations.

In aggregate, this system works. Our material costs are lower than what we charge for them, and we use about 5 percent fewer shop hours than the spreadsheet predicts. This system has produced positive cash flow and profit in the past two years. But in a particular case, I am wary of the time-cost predictions. They are wrong as often as right, sometimes in our favor and sometimes not.

Which brings me back to my modular table. I'm putting it up on our Web site and I want to put a number on its page. I have the build hours from the Old Style job. We had predicted that it would take sixty-nine hours to build four tables, and it had come in at fifty hours—28 percent under. The material costs were predicted to be $2,234, but we had ordered only $841 worth for that job. (But we might have used up materials we had on hand, so that $841 is not our actual cost.) Based on that data, I offer a lower price for future iterations than we charged to Old Style. They paid $9,210 for their set of four walnut tables, two of which had data ports. I rerun our pricing spreadsheet using the actual build times, and find that the new number is $1,594. Per table in a set of four, that is, and taking advantage of the efficiencies inherent in producing multiples. I expect that we will get orders for more than one table, and that the actual order size will be more than five thousand dollars.

I set up the product page so that you see a picture of the four tables arranged in a U configuration, with pricing per table of $1,594. If you read the body text, it's clear that I am talking about the per-table price in what will be a multiple-table order. I like the idea of featuring a low number, as I figure it will grab the shopper's attention. We'll sort out the particulars when a potential buyer calls us.

We now have 182 tables on the site, sorted by shape, features, and price. This makes it easier for buyers to find the kind of table they are looking for, and easier for Google to serve an exact match when people search for specific terms. We run different ads for a wide variety of table types: large, small, round, custom, boardroom, and so on. We haven't been pushing modular tables, so I write a new ad intended to drive traffic to that page. I check to see what kind of traffic the keyword "modular tables" will generate, and Google assures me that this is a heavily searched term, but without a huge amount of competition from other table sellers. I write a catchy headline, set an amount I'm willing to pay each time a viewer clicks on the ad ($3.50), and set a schedule. It will appear from seven a.m. to ten p.m. every weekday. This ad is just one of 126 we're running. Each is tightly targeted, so no single ad generates a huge response. In aggregate, they produce a steady stream of calls.

IN THE THIRD WEEK of March, I get a call from Nigel at Eurofurn. He has spoken to his superiors at the home factory, and they have agreed to host me for a couple of days. I have to buy the plane ticket, but they will pay all other expenses. The trip will cost me about fourteen hundred dollars. I'm happy to lay out that cash if I get a peek into their factory. I have never had such an opportunity before—my domestic competitors have no reason to let me see their operations, so I haven't tried to set up any visits. And, frankly, I'd think long and hard about letting any of them into my shop.

We settle on the last week of April. I'll fly on Monday and return on Friday. Also, he wants me to start design work on a table to be placed in their New York showroom. It's to be an upgraded version of their current table, which doesn't have up-to-date wiring capabilities. They won't pay me for my design time, but do agree on a reasonable price for the table itself: $6,523. This will be our first attempt at combining the Eurofurn look with our own design details. The table will be challenging: the top will be an equilateral triangle with radius corners, made in three identical pieces. We will be integrating power/data lids into the top, and the wood grain needs to run across the top and lids without disruption. I have a good idea how we will produce it, but I want to get a better sense of how Eurofurn would approach a project like this first, just in case they have some special tricks that will work better than our methods.

The next Wednesday, I get a call from my contact at Company S. My stomach drops. If we don't hear from a client after an installation, all is well. But if they do call, it can be good news, or bad. Sure enough, they're unhappy. After the board meeting, they found scratches on the table. Not big ones, the executive assistant tells me, but she could see them from a certain angle. She is convinced that there is something wrong with the finish. That seems unlikely; I carefully examined the top before it shipped and everything looked good. Sometimes clients scratch a table, but they almost always take responsibility for it. Anything other than laminates (commonly called Formica) and granite—including glass, marble, metals, and wood—can be easily scratched if a sharp object is dragged across the surface. Every wood table eventually picks up a lot of tiny scratches, mostly from users' jewelry and laptop bottoms. It's an unavoidable consequence of normal use.

I ask her to e-mail me photos of the damage. They arrive the next day. They're terrible, taken at very close range with a shaky cell phone, but I think I can see something. In the universe of scratches, they rank about 1.5 on a scale of 1 (undamaged) to 10 (chewed by wolves). In other words, marks that are normal for any table in actual use. Meanwhile, I asked Dave Violi: did anything go wrong? Not as far as he knew. He built up a very thick layer of finish to get the look the client wanted, but the process had gone well.

It looks as though the client is overreacting to something that they did, but they don't see it that way. They still owe me more than $7,500. Blaming them isn't going to make them happy or get me paid. But it's impossible to repair a finish like this on-site. The chemicals in the sprayed finish are noxious, residue would end up all over the room, and if you don't recoat the entire top, the newly sprayed section will look different. If I am going to respray it, we will have to ship the top segments back here. Despite the logistical headache, I'm leaning toward agreeing to respray. Any alternative is likely to turn into a Stalingrad—an endless, damaging battle, most likely ending with bad feelings from the customer and an unpaid balance.

A respray will cost a little bit less than the balance due, but at least I will have satisfied the customer. Unless, that is, they damage the table again. I really need to figure out what happened out there.

I make the trip on March 27. My journey begins at four-thirty a.m. For the convenience of nobody, Philadelphia TSA has decided that all travelers from four terminals will have to go through one security line. That's an extra forty-five minutes that I didn't plan for. I end up jumping to the head of the line and sprinting to make my plane. Two flights and a long drive later, I walk into the board-room, the executive assistant at my side. From the doorway, the table looks perfect. "You have to look from a certain angle," she says. I look from a certain angle: nothing. "You have to get up close." I get up close. When my head is inches off the tabletop, I can see some fine scratches. Normal wear. But I make sympathetic noises. "Do you think the finish is defective?" she asks. The honest answer is "No, you did this and it's your fault." Instead, I ask her what had been on the table. She goes through the inventory: glassware, place-mats, folders with notepads. She's been very careful. I ask about unglazed mug bottoms—common culprits—and she tells me she thought of that and sent their mugs to a local potter to be reglazed. At this point, the CEO comes in. He says he's disappointed that this happened. He really loves the table; in fact, one of his board mem-bers even asked who made it because he's interested in having us make him one. And as soon as we fix this, he will tell me who it was. (CEOs of billion-dollar companies don't get there by being stupid.) I surrender. I agree to retrieve the pieces in mid-April and return them three weeks later, before their next board meeting. The boss offers to pay for a rental truck, but we have to fly out my ship-ping manager to manage the packing and loading process and drive the truck back ourselves. It will be a huge, expensive pain.

I am still mystified as to what caused the scratches. We take out all the dishes and identify the culprit: it's the mugs, after all. The local potter didn't reglaze the bottoms, only painted them with varnish. I dragged one of the mugs around on the table, and voilà! Tiny scratches.

I'm back by midnight, exhausted. I feel like a chump for knuckling under, but arguing would have resulted in a much bigger mess. When I get home, I find a surprise. On our front door, my wife has taped up one of her drawings—a cartoon showing me with my arms raised in triumph over a kneeling businessman, who is handing me a large stack of dollar bills. It didn't turn out that way, but it's nice to have some family support.

This is a business book, but you can't understand a boss without knowing what he goes home to. I have been blessed with a happy family life. I met my wife, Nancy, in college, when she was eighteen and I was nineteen. Immediately after graduation, we moved into our first apartment together and I opened my shop. Nancy has been my bedrock during many turbulent years. She grew up in a family with intermittent income and she can deal with a life of financial uncertainty. And she has proven equal to the challenge of raising a child with special needs.

We have three sons: eighteen-year-old fraternal twins, Peter and Henry, and a younger boy, Hugh, who is sixteen. Hugh and Peter are typical kids and attend the local high school. Henry is severely autistic. We knew something was wrong quite early, as his twin brother developed normally. Henry lagged behind in every way. He received an official diagnosis at the age of two. After that came years of therapy, special classrooms, speech therapists, and behavior experts. Nothing cured him.

At age eighteen, Henry still has the mental development of an infant. He cannot speak—he tries, but the brain development that allows the tongue and lips to form a full range of words never happened. He cannot read. He has little interest in other people. He won't watch TV. He likes only a few things: to be driven around in a car, to listen to a particular Beatles CD over and over (turned up as loud as the boom box will go), and to eat. He is 6-foot-3, 205 pounds, and still growing fast.

Henry is volatile. Since he can't talk, he has great difficulty communicating what he wants. We've learned to anticipate his needs, but sometimes he weeps with frustration, or slaps his own head repeatedly, or jumps up and down bellowing at the top of his lungs. And if someone gets too close while all this is happening, he will attack them—grab them around the neck and try to throw them to the ground.

Before age twelve, Henry was usually very calm and cooperative. When he started puberty, the violent behavior appeared. By age fifteen, he would attack my wife out of the blue, once or more a week. Now, at eighteen, the hormonal surges are abating and the tantrums becoming less frequent. But he is much, much larger. The episodes are harder to handle. Nancy is wary about being alone with him, but even so she'll take him with her in the car as she does errands, and he behaves well. He likes driving and going to the grocery store— it's like a food museum for him.

At first glance, he's a tall, handsome teenager. It takes a moment to see that something is off. Fortunately, people are quite tolerant of him. Even if he bellows or bursts into tears, they take their behavior cues from us. If we treat whatever he's doing as normal and expected, everyone stays calm. It's embarrassing, though, to be in public when he's difficult. It doesn't keep us home all the time—he gets bored, and so do we. Not to mention that two hundred pounds of autistic boy jumping up and down has cracked our plasterwork and loosened our stair treads. So we take him out, and take our chances.

Henry's twin, Peter, is a direct refutation of both astrology and the notion that Nurture is more important than Nature. Born two minutes ahead of Henry, he couldn't be more different. He's been accepted to the Massachusetts Institute of Technology on early decision and has inherited his mother's gregarious nature and easy charm. Our younger boy, Hugh, has different interests, but he is smart and a very diligent worker. Maybe we've been compensated for the difficulties of raising Henry with these two.

I'm not a hero for running a business while raising a special-needs kid. Everyone has some kind of trouble in their life. Every boss needs to make a decision as to how to deal with pressure. Work all the time, drink, cheat on your spouse, yell, road rage? Or more benign choices? Take your pick. If you can. High levels of stress drive you to your worst behavior.

I had some tough days before the twins arrived, but in retrospect those years were a lark. The day you have children, you enter a different world. Mix parenthood with the problems of a business that doesn't actually make money, and stress is a much bigger issue. I've tried to keep the work problems at work, but sometimes I'd bring the stress home and would suddenly explode over some stupid thing. It was usually an innocent request made by my wife, assuming that *of course* I would be able to supply the money or time required. Then the fight would start, with me shouting that she had no idea what was going on at work, and she replying with equal vigor that I was always promising that someday the business would go well and I would have more time and money for the family, and it never happened. Every couple has a fight that just keeps coming back, and this was ours.

When the recession arrived, and I was struggling every day to keep the doors open, the stress returned to unbearable levels. I decided that the only way I could deal with it would be to tell Nancy everything that was happening at work, good or bad, every day. She hated hearing it at first, as it reminded her of difficult times in her childhood. But we ended up getting along much better. Keeping a barrier between my work and home lives was a mistake. When my wife had a clear picture of the situation, she became an ally instead of an adversary.

My kids are old enough to take care of themselves now, and Henry is away from home much of the year. When he comes back, life is harder. But as long as the business does well, I'll be in decent shape.

ON THE LAST FRIDAY of the month, I review our sales numbers and they aren't good. We end up selling just $135,732 in March, drastically undershooting my $200,000 target and leaving us well short of our quarterly target of $600,000. Sales for the first three months are just $543,003. Nick had the worst month, booking only $25,502 in orders. Dan did better than January and February, closing deals worth $49,783. Neither of them sold anything after the eighteenth. I am the champion of the month, with $60,447 in orders. "Best Salesman" is a prize I didn't want to win. Watching Nick and Dan falter makes me feel very uneasy.

The sales pattern for March is odd. The number of orders hasn't decreased—it's actually grown from eleven in January and twelve in February to sixteen in March. More customers should be a good thing, but in this case, the additional orders don't amount to much. The value of the five smallest orders adds up to $5,854. Peanuts. And the remaining eleven average just $11,807. This is well below our average order for the first two months of the year, which was $17,688.

The size of our orders varies widely. The majority of our jobs fall in the five- to twenty-thousand dollar range, but their aggregate dollar value is less than half of our total. Big jobs are important, and the biggest—more than fifty thousand dollars—have a disproportionate effect on our fiscal health. Land a few whales, all is well. Catch only minnows, and it's hard to make our target. And March brought us only little fish. Nick and Dan assure me that they are working on some jumbo orders that will arrive soon. We could be back on track any day now.

One thing is undeniable: undershooting our sales target has affected our cash flow. If we'd hit our goal, we'd have another thirty-two thousand in cash right now, from deposit payments. A couple of months of strong sales followed by a weak month is not unusual— I've seen that pattern many times. But I have also seen sales shrink for several months in a row, and that's a disaster. The shop is staffed for a certain production level, with all the attendant costs of payroll and machinery. If we fail to bring in work at the same rate we produce it, we get hit two ways: incoming cash falls below our spend rate, and eventually we will run out of work to do. Then come layoffs.

I'm not sure what I need to do right now, but my confidence that I could back out of my sales role has evaporated. I can't rely on the other two, and don't want to take a chance that they muff a deal when we are behind our quota. I am going to work more deals myself, starting with sucking up to Eurofurn. Maybe they'll throw more business my way.

APRIL

Date: Monday, April 2, 2012

Bank balance: $136,260.92

Cash relative to start of year ("Net Cash"): -$893.40

New-contract value, year-to-date: $543,003

This is the twenty-fifth April since I opened my doors, and the weeks before tax day have always been quiet. But Nick and Dan, who haven't experienced this swoon, are confident that something will arrive soon. The phone rang steadily in March, and we have a lot of solid proposals out there. And there are always clients who say they'll place an order if we'll revise our earlier quote.

Nick is preparing his twenty-third proposal for a buyer at the Kaiser Family Foundation—a new record for us. His first quote went out a year ago, and now he's racking his brains to come up with another variation. He's stuck with the same basic design, a ten-foot round table with some combination of wood and marble on the top. Every couple of weeks, the buyer in Manhattan calls back, swears that his bosses are about to make a decision, and asks for one more change—a different wood, or a different number of data ports, and always a lower price. It isn't a cheap design and it won't be a cheap delivery. We've bottomed out at twenty-two thousand dollars for the whole thing, but the buyer won't stop. Nick has asked me repeatedly if he really needs to send another proposal. Patience, I tell him. I have been through this before. Usually they disappear, but sometimes they end up buying, and we can't let any potential jobs slip away through our own laziness.

Nick has been on the same merry-go-round with an Air Force facility in Virginia. They've been very specific about what they want, and it looks like a forty-thousand-dollar order. Again, he's submitted multiple designs and spent significant time responding to requests for small changes. The flyboys tell us that they are *very* impressed with the proposals. Using their photos and our modeling software, Nick has made a perfect simulation of their room and finally come up with a table they love. They reassure him that he's doing great, but that they need to put the job out for bid—federal contracting rules. I tell Nick that this won't be an issue if we can persuade them to let us help write the bid specifications. That way we can make it very difficult for anyone but us to fulfill the requirements. This trick has worked in the past. Not this time. When they post the job on the federal contracting Web site, the table is described in generic language. And there's a requirement that bidders must attend a public briefing at the base—a six-hour drive from our shop. I tell Nick to make the trip. He's done a ton of work, and we don't want to lose the opportunity by not showing up.

Dan is working on his own big order, worth more than thirty-five thousand dollars: three tables for Cali Heavy Industries, a large engineering firm in California. Along with the designs, we have provided the buyer with a complete plan of our tables and offered to help him lay out the floor drillings for all the power and data wiring.

I've been communicating with the facilities manager at a local bank. They are renovating their headquarters and trying to decide whether to repair their existing table or replace it. Of course I have an opinion about which of these would be the wisest choice, but I can't even get the guy to respond to my e-mails.

I do have one potential buyer ready to get started. A good friend of mine wants me to make him a bedroom suite. I am not eager to accept this order. I have built a fair number of beds and dressers over the years, and they are surprisingly complicated. I've warned him that I will have to charge a high price—about as much as a new car—just to cover costs, but he's persisted. I didn't tell him that I really, really hate working for friends. I have done it on a few occasions, without any problems, but I don't like the exchange of money tainting what should be a purely social relationship.

He's been after me for almost a year, and I recently sent him the designs for review, but I haven't given him numbers yet. He's asking for a lot of work—a large sleigh bed with matching nightstands, two large dressers, and a bookshelf, all built of solid cherry with details in anegre, an exotic veneer from Africa. Aside from the materials, this is a job that only my foreman, Steve Maturin, can complete in a reasonable time, so my labor costs are going to be very high. I ran the pricing and, even cutting him the best possible deal, I've come up with a shocking number: $28,797. I'm worried that my friend will be horrified by the price, but also too embarrassed to back out.

Signing any of these jobs would bring us back to where we need to be for the year, and signing two or more would put us ahead. And these aren't the only prospects. My gut tells me that something is bound to come in. Eventually.

I hope that orders arrive sooner rather than later, and not just for the cash injection. I'm also starting to worry about our backlog. That is the amount of work that we have lined up to produce. We don't start building a job the day it's ordered. It would be very bad to rush ahead and build a table before the client has stopped making design changes. So we have a procedure: we send a final set of drawings and images to the client with the warning that these documents show exactly what we intend to build. We accompany this with finish samples: pieces of wood of the species and color that the client had discussed. Then we wait for them to either confirm that everything is correct or suggest alterations. Sometimes it takes weeks while their company goes through whatever internal decision making is required. It always takes at least two weeks after order placement before anything hits the shop floor. And if the client is slow, it can take a month or more.

At the beginning of April, our backlog is just over five weeks. That's a rough calculation—my formula, which I run each Monday, doesn't make any compensation for jobs that are burning more or fewer hours than we estimated. It's an approximate view of reality at best. But I've found that flawed measurements, if performed consistently, can be helpful—it isn't the result itself that matters, but rather the change from week to week.

At the start of the year, our calculated backlog was a little under four weeks. We sold enough in January and February that we now have more work than we started the year with. But the trend is down—we had maxed out at seven weeks at the beginning of March. Our sales slowed down and the shop started working faster.

At least I think it did. I can easily see the total value of the jobs shipped each month, but not how much of that amount was labor, as opposed to materials. It looks as though we're building at a $40,000-a-week pace. If we have a week where we sell less than that number, we are eating backlog. With a little more than five weeks of work queued up, and assuming the shop runs at the current rate, we will run out of work in early May.

A shrinking backlog also means that incoming cash is drying up. We aren't getting any deposit payments. The total amount of cash we can expect in the future is dropping as well. At the end of the first week of April, the cash we will collect by completing our entire order book is just $107,410. It will take us five weeks to fulfill our commitments, and that will generate only three weeks of funds. In the other weeks, we'll need to pay for materials, rent, advertising, and electricity just as we always do. How can I cut our spending?

My biggest expense is payroll. Payday is every second Tuesday. The amount varies depending on the exact number of hours worked, but it has been averaging $36,000. This covers hourly wage, pension contribution, and payroll taxes for fifteen people, including me. It doesn't include the cost of health insurance, which is $10,140 a month (to cover nine of the fifteen workers and their families, including me). The pay rate for each worker ranges from thirteen dollars an hour to thirty-six dollars an hour. Add them up and the cost to employ all those people for one hour is $317. (That number excludes my own salary.) That's before payroll taxes, workmen's comp insurance, and unemployment insurance, which vary in complicated ways but add another 18 percent or so to the cost.

Payroll is a very difficult number to reduce, unless I get rid of some employees. I can't simply have everyone work fewer hours—not at this point. We lost a lot of time with Company S, and we are behind on our other work. And if we don't complete jobs, we won't get the preship or final payments, which is the only cash I am sure to receive.

I cannot ask people to work more hours without pay. That is illegal for unsalaried workers. And a reduction in pay rates is a drastic and morale-crippling move. In the fall of 2008, I cut my workers' pay by 15 percent, and it was not popular. I got away with it because it was obvious to everyone that we were in serious trouble, and they had no place better to go. In 2012, the woodworking economy is still rocky, but it's a lot better than it was. If I cut everyone's pay again, some of them will leave—most likely, my best guys. We still have work to do, and I'm hoping that we will turn this thing around, so I don't want to risk defections.

Fortunately, there's one worker who will never quit. He's getting a good-size paycheck, too, so stopping his income will have an effect. I know from long experience that this guy will put up with anything I give him—work longer hours, do multiple jobs, reorder his personal finances, even loan money back to the company if necessary. Who is this patsy? You already guessed: the boss.

Over the years I have raised and lowered my pay countless times, using it as a throttle to increase or decrease our cash burn rate. Do I have enormous piles of gold coins in my basement, a vast store of personal wealth that I can tap when needed to fund my business? Not at all.

I'm not broke, but my business has not generated much wealth for me. Manufacturing custom furniture is not known as a lucrative profession, because it isn't. For example, take a look at how my company performed from 2003 to 2011. Sales for that period totaled $16,352,367. The profits? The total for those years is negative. The vast majority of those losses happened before the crash in 2008, when The Partner and I were doing a very bad job of trying to grow the company. From 2003 to 2008, our losses totaled $1,086,648. The Partner ate much of that when he left. My father, my brother, and I—the remaining shareholders—made emergency loans in those years just to keep the doors open. Since 2009, I have managed to stop the bleeding, and the company has made profits totaling $210,114. That still leaves an accumulated loss of $872,084.

I have managed, during some very rocky years, to pay my bills. First and foremost, all the employees who have worked for me got paid, on time and in full. All the taxes were paid, on time and in full. All the vendors and my landlord were paid in full (not necessarily

on time, but I used most of the post-2009 profits to gradually eliminate the debt). While the company owes my partners and me a pretty
good pile of cheddar, it owes nobody else.

Between 2003 and 2010, my annual salary averaged $78,484.
That number includes the amount I had to pay for health insurance—
taxable compensation for a company owner. My cash wage was
lower. Each year I loaned, on average, $29,363 of that back to the
company (after I had paid taxes on it). That left me an average of
$49,121 a year. I'm hardly one of those predatory CEOs making mil-
lions while my workers starve.

I have a lifestyle to match my income. My wife and I live very
modestly. We don't travel much. Even if we wanted to, Henry's unpredictable behavior keeps us from anything but family visits. I
own two crappy cars: a 1992 Toyota Camry and a 1999 Honda Odyssey. Nancy is very frugal and gets most of our clothes at the thrift
shop. And we don't eat out. Nancy is a very good cook, so we eat at
home every night.

I'm not destitute, though. Leaving aside whatever the business
might be worth, because it's not in any shape to sell, my net worth
is a little less than $400,000. The equity in my house is worth about
$165,000. My cars are worth nothing. I have $92,356 in a retirement
account that I have been contributing to since 1998. I have $48,525
in emergency cash in a Vanguard account. And I have $78,525 in my
checking account, as a result of my success in 2011.

That windfall came right on time. My oldest son starts college in
September, and my wife, in preparation for the empty-nest experience, is getting a master's degree so she can teach. Her schedule
will match Henry's so that she can be at home when he is, and I can
continue to work myself. Tuition bills for both of them will start in
September. The first year will eat through all my savings.

I'm not complaining. I am doing better than the vast majority of people in the world. But I do not feel secure. I have pledged my personal wealth to cover debts that the company has incurred. Aside from the $387,098 that the company owes me, the lease on our shop space requires payment in full, even if we fail. I currently have twenty-six months left to go before I renew. At $9,250 a month, I am committed to shell out $240,500. The business has two credit cards with a $65,000 line of credit—we generally have about $30,000 a month in outstanding charges. If I get behind, they will come after my personal assets. And, realistically, there is a minimum level of spending just to keep some employees on staff and the lights on. If I have to lay everyone off, and there's nobody to do the work, I am done. I have too much overhead to start as a single-man operation again. I need to spend $5,000 a day to be in business. If I have to reach into my pocket to do it, after sixty days I will have lost all my cash, and my house will be heading into foreclosure.

So owning a business, even one with millions in revenue, has not made me rich. I feel a great deal of shame at my lack of success. I can't tell you how many times I have attended parties and felt humiliated when doctors and lawyers describe fancy trips to Africa, rounds of golf, and nice cars. If I had joined my contemporaries who went to law or business school, and stepped onto the corporate treadmill, I would at least have a high salary to show for my efforts. Sure, you can live that life and fail in any number of ways, but you also don't have to invent the profession as you go.

Do you know any wealthy woodworkers? I didn't think so. If they exist, nobody is talking about them. I'd really like to know how to convert my business into one that does great work, and pays its people well, and makes its owners rich. I haven't figured out how to do this on my own. I need to look elsewhere for guidance.

Where can I get good advice? This has been a problem for me from the start. I opened my doors when I was fresh out of college, back in 1986. I didn't even know anyone in the business. And there was no Internet back then, no magic universal library that answered every question. My nature is to try to figure things out on my own, which, in retrospect, has been bad for me. I stumbled on the most basic business problems: Where do I buy materials? How do I keep records? How do I pay taxes for my employees? How do I advertise? It was very hard to find answers. There were books about running a business, but none about *my* business. I never imagined that anyone would be interested in helping me, so I never asked for help. And I was always so strapped for time that I would implement the first idea I found, even if it was bad practice. I just muddled along for years and years.

When you get right down to it, nobody cares how I run my business, or whether I am competent or not. As long as I pay my taxes, my workers, and my bills, I am free to be as good or bad at business as I wish. This is the main reason that I took the risk of entering a partnership in 2002. I was desperate for some guidance. I presumed that The Partner, since he had money, knew a lot about business. It didn't turn out that way. He had been successful with previous companies, but we found out the hard way that what had worked for him previously would not necessarily work for my business.

The Partner was my sole source of advice for many years. He taught me a lot, and also led me astray. Not because he was malicious, or dumb, but because his experience didn't match the problems we were having. He was not good at identifying situations where the old ways wouldn't work. And we never found a way to identify the issues he had overlooked entirely—if he didn't focus on a problem, I would not do anything about it. This caused a lot of cash flow issues and management problems on the shop floor.

Fortunately, The Partner is an honorable and reasonable man, so our relationship did not descend into personal animosity. But our ideas as to how to proceed diverged, particularly in the fall of 2008. He wanted to shut us down, take his losses, and move on. Without telling me, he used most of our operating cash to pay down a line of credit in order to limit his liability. The company owed him a lot of money, and from his point of view it made sense. But I was counting on those funds to keep the doors open. Without my company, what would I do? We came to an irreconcilable difference in opinion. After that, I stopped listening to him.

During the years that I was getting advice from The Partner, the world was changing. With the arrival of the Internet, barriers to finding basic information disappeared. Now we are drowning in content. Unfortunately, quantity does not imply quality or relevance. I have found the business press to be useless. Pick up a magazine or paper, or read a blog, and you see one story repeated ad nauseam. Success! How this guy got it, how that gal got it, how this huge corporation got it, how you can get it. These stories are long on results and short on techniques, and almost always omit the really interesting details. There's an overemphasis on software start-ups and way too much emphasis on outliers, like Steve Jobs or Mark Zuckerberg. I've read a lot about those two, but never anything that stated the obvious: they were really, really lucky.

I have never seen a thorough, detailed account of a small business like mine. I'm looking for specific techniques for dealing with my particular problems. Many of those are complicated and technical and revolve around the personalities of the people involved. Given the format limitations that confront business reporters, and their own lack of technical knowledge, it's not surprising that everything we get is brief and vague. Nobody wants to write about the multitude of challenges that a boss faces every day, in a way that captures the difficulty of dealing with everything at once.

My biggest problem is finding numbers. I have to make most of my financial decisions without a good idea of what's normal. My competitors, like me, are all small, privately held companies. There is no single place where I can find any information on the size of my market, who the largest players are, or even what my competitors charge. We produce roughly $140,000 per employee each year. Is that good or bad? Is my second-best bench cabinetmaker worth $18 an hour or $21 an hour? What would this person be worth to another shop? The difference is substantial, both for me and for the employee. My AdWords campaign costs me $10,000 or more a month. Is that too much or too little? I'm paying a 2 percent sales commission to Dan and Nick, on top of a decent salary. I decided on that arrangement because it seemed reasonable. Was I wise or not? Would a different split be better? The cumulative cost of this uncertainty is hundreds of thousands of dollars each year—far more than I have ever taken out of the business. I'd love to know whether my spending decisions are high, low, or on target. For most of these issues, no information is available. For some, like the AdWords question, I can get vague answers from sources of questionable objectivity (Google itself, or consultants whose answer is always self-serving).

I miss The Partner because he was always willing to listen, and he knew the people who I was talking about, and his advice, even though flawed, was intended to help. It's been lonely since he left. Sure, my employees and I discuss the technical issues that arise every hour in a small factory—materials, jobs, broken machines, whatever. But on the larger issues, particularly the thorny intersection between the particular personalities of my workers and money, I have nobody within the company who would understand my perspective.

There are certainly small business owners out there whom I would enjoy knowing, but I haven't made their acquaintance in social settings. My wife arranges our social life. We go out regularly, but Nancy is an artist, so the vast majority of people we meet are in the art world. And from a business and manufacturing perspective, nothing they do makes sense.

At the end of 2011, I found a possible solution to my problem. It came in the mail: an invitation to join a group of business peers, organized by Vistage. They arrange regular meetings for groups of small company owners. Each group is vetted so that there is a similarity in company size but some disparity in business type—manufacturers, retailers, professionals like architects and accountants, software guys—enough variety to bring a broad viewpoint and avoid direct competitors in the group. Some of the members of each group are start-ups, some are multi-generational family firms, and some are like me—in business a long time, but stuck. A minimum yearly revenue requirement ensures that every member is a viable business. Each group is led by a trained leader. There's a group meeting and an individual session each month. I could bring up my own plans and problems for analysis by the leader and the other members, and I would hear about their companies in return.

I liked the concept. If it worked, I would have a chance to interact with people who are like myself. I also liked the focus on taking each business to the next level. It would cost me twelve thousand dollars a year and some hours of my time—cheaper and easier than trying to get an MBA.

I responded to the invitation, and Ed Curry, the group leader, scheduled a meeting at my shop. We met in December 2011. Ed is in his mid-sixties. He was raised in a small coal town in Pennsylvania, went to Vietnam for a year, and then worked for many years at a manufacturing company that made precision measuring equipment for auto manufacturers. That company had a couple thousand workers, and he worked his way up to a high management position. When they were bought by a German competitor, he went to Ernst

& Young, the accountants. After retiring, he got involved in Vistage. For several years, he had been the leader of one group, but it had grown and he was splitting it up and putting together another. We ended up talking in my office for about an hour. Ed asked smart questions and listened carefully to the answers. A week later, I went to the introductory meeting, thought it was good, and signed the contract.

As of April, I have attended three meetings with the group. It's an interesting mix of businesses: an accountant, a software start-up, a trucking company, a coffee roaster, a house painting and repair company, a document storage company, two software firms, and three manufacturers. One does precision grinding of metal components, one makes prefabricated metal stairs, and one makes custom conference tables. The group is all male. Ages range from late twenties to seventy. Three businesses are multi-generational: the precision grinding company is run by the son of the founder, and the trucking and coffee companies date back to the nineteenth century. Every other company is run by its founder.

I'm particularly interested in learning more about the staircase manufacturer. It's owned by Sam Saxton. He is the youngest member of the group. He graduated in 2003 and then went to South Dakota to make his fortune. He bought farmland and put up tract houses, and prudently saved his profits. After the crash, he came back to the East Coast and looked for a company to purchase so that he could get richer. He purchased an outfit that manufactured prefabricated staircases, and then bought out a smaller competitor and folded both into one operation. He borrowed a couple million dollars from a bank to do all this. He needs to grow his companies quickly in order to service his debt and build equity.

Unlike me, who wanted to make things and ended up with a business, Sam wanted a business and ended up making things. He looks at the manufacturing part of his operation from a more neutral perspective. To him, it's just a cost center, like every part of his business. Administration, marketing, sales, manufacturing, shipping: they all need to pull their weight. If they don't make him money, and he can't repay his loans, the bank will foreclose.

Sam projects energy. He's a tall, strong-looking guy. He talks fast and with absolute assurance. Everything he has done since high school is aimed at business success. He studied entrepreneurship at Babson College, made his first small fortune before he was twenty-five, and since acquiring his factory, the sales have doubled. He has positive cash flow and is paying off a significant amount of debt every month. His biggest problem is operations—a couple dozen workers in a good-size factory are a challenge to manage under the best of circumstances. Sam has weak operational systems and doesn't have a complete grasp of how his product is made. He wants to get the manufacturing under control so that he can grow the company even faster. Or so he has told the group.

Since our operations are very similar, I approached Sam after our January meeting and suggested that we exchange shop visits. At the end of March, Sam and his shop foreman, Dean, came out to see my operation. They expressed polite interest as we toured the shop floor. Visitors are usually blown away by the action out there. Sam and Dean, having been in factories before, just weren't as impressed. Then I took them to the office and showed how we produce our proposals, how we make shop drawings, and how we use Google Docs for spreadsheets that we all needed to see at once. None of this elicited any comment. What got them excited was our database software, where we track our manufacturing activities from contract to delivery. Every day, my workers enter the number of hours they work on each project. We can see where each job is in our production stream and how many hours have been used at each point. And we can see all the jobs in each link of our production chain. It performs a bunch of other functions as well. It's an incredibly useful tool.

The Partner's daughter spent two years writing it for us. Her wages cost me about sixty thousand dollars, a bargain. Comparable packages from Microsoft or other vendors would cost hundreds of thousands of dollars and then require modifications to fit our processes. So I got an exceptionally well-crafted piece of software for very little money. Sam and Dean don't have anything like this, and their operations suffer as a result. They have a hard time figuring out exactly where each job is in their pipeline and how much labor they are using on each order. They're still using paper tickets to follow each job. Those get lost or damaged, and generate a lot of data entry work.

I tell them that fancy software doesn't solve all my problems. In particular, our estimates of the hours required to build each project aren't very precise, and there is a fair amount of error in entering data—my guys will often choose the wrong job from a drop-down list. Then their hours get charged to the wrong project. On a computer, bad data looks just like good data. It can be very difficult to tease out whether the numbers are a good reflection of actual operations. But I never want to go back to paper. We did that for many years, and it's much worse.

I make my visit to Sam's place in the first week of April. He's a few towns over, in the most non-descript building in a non-descript industrial park. There's no sign, just a couple of doors on a long, blank wall. The first one I try is locked. The second one opens into a small room with an unused reception desk. Behind it I see a dimly lit kitchen space, and then another door. Nobody in sight. I open the door and find myself out on the factory floor. It's very large and gloomy. There's a steady roar of machinery. A couple of guys are packing a spiral staircase in cardboard off to my right. "Sam Saxton?" I shout. One stops wrapping and leads me to a staircase. "Go up there, through that door. They'll help you." I climb and find myself in a small room with six cubicles. Each holds a person wearing a headset, looking intently at a small screen, focused on their conversation. Eventually one of them looks up. "Sam Saxton?" "Sure, follow me," he says, and takes me to the other end of the space. He knocks on a door, then opens without waiting for an answer. The inner sanctum, at last.

Sam is behind his desk, on the phone. He waves at me, holds up one finger: wait. I sit on the sofa and take a look around. Sam's office is dark—only one small window overlooks the dismal parking lot. Walls painted light gray. The carpet is dark gray. There are a couple of large holes in the drywall. No art. No photographs of family. All the furniture is cheap, old, and well-worn. Sam's desk is covered with paper, in a semi-orderly fashion. His computer dominates the space.

The phone call ends and Sam springs to his feet, coming around the desk with a big smile and hand extended. "Sorry about that—consultants!" Short pause. "Sorry about my office. Not so nice as yours." He gestures to the holes in the wall. "Sometimes I get mad and need to punch something. How about we tour the shop and then talk?" Sam stops at one of the cubicles and tells the woman there where he's going. We descend to the shop floor.

I take in the expanse. It's a large space, with eighteen-foot ceilings. Sam answers my first questions before I ask. "Thirty-eight thousand square feet. I have twenty-nine guys right now. I'm hoping we do four-point-two million dollars this year." It's the beginning of a very informative tour.

Sam's operation is very similar to mine. He uses machines to cut parts and workers to do assembly. There are a lot more welders in our economy than skilled woodworkers, so he pays his workers three to five dollars less than I pay mine for comparable jobs.

Metalworking isn't as dusty as woodworking, but it's grimier—there's a thin layer of black sludge on every surface. Once you get beyond that, though, the shop is neatly arranged. The workers move around at a decent speed. Sam knows everyone's name and tells me a little about each one. Half of them are American citizens, of all colors, and the rest a grab bag of immigrants from Eastern Europe, Mexico, and Central America. No women. Sam tells me that some have been in the military, some to trade school, and some just picked up skills at other jobs.

We head back up the stairs and pause at the cubicle cluster. We have been discussing AdWords, which Sam also uses to connect with far-flung customers. Sam says, "Those proposals you e-mail to the client? They're very nice but we would never do that. We always make an appointment to review our proposal with the client. We get them on the phone, make sure they are in front of a computer, and then fire up a program called 'Glance.' Clients can see on their screen whatever is on our screen. We go through their quote line by line, show them the proposed design and the numbers. Then we ask for a credit card. They don't get the document unless they buy." I think about that for a moment. It seems very aggressive. "Who designs the stairs?" I ask. "Does the client see any drawings, or an image of what they are going to get?" Sam tells a young man to bring up a quote. The stair set is shown in a simplified drawing. There are clear photographs of similar stairs, but not an exact representation of this particular one. The numbers in the quote are in a large font, easy to read. This approach is very different from ours—the design itself isn't highlighted as much as the numbers. It doesn't sell itself. The salesperson is doing the actual persuasion. I'd like to see a screensharing session, but nobody has one scheduled until the evening.

Over lunch, I focus on the question of who designs each custom staircase. Do the salespeople do it? Do they actually know enough about building staircases to do a good job? Sam tells me that this isn't really a problem. Staircases are not that complicated. Even a spiral staircase can be worked out using simple algorithms, as long as the height to be traversed is measured correctly. All the construction details are simple and are deployed the same way in every job. It's similar to our approach—a limited set of construction details used to make a wide variety of items. But the overall complexity is orders of magnitude less than ours. A much smaller set of choices will satisfy the vast majority of his buyers. On the few occasions that he gets a request for something complicated, one of his people with an engineering background can solve the problem.

I ask how he finds salespeople. "We put ads on Craigslist." That works? "You get a lot of bozos. But I get a few who have done some sales before. I do phone interviews first—you can tell a lot from that. If they sound good, we bring them in for a face-to-face. And if that's good, then we start them training here, and also send them out to be trained. I have a consultant—he's great—Bob Waks. He's been working with me for a year now. Our sales have doubled. You should meet him." My first instinct is to recoil at the mention of a consultant. Doubling my sales would be good, though.

Sam tells me that when he bought the company, "There were a couple of sales guys here, not very good. Just stuck in their way of doing things. After I brought in Bob to train them, they weren't happy with new ways. I had to get rid of them." I'm sympathetic; firing people is difficult. Sam shrugs. "Had to happen. I can't have people selling who don't sell. I'm constantly going through them." I'm curious about pay. What's the split between salary and commission? "I give them a monthly draw at first, two thousand dollars. Then it's a hundred percent commission." What if they don't cover their draw for a couple of months? He gives me a look: you really need to ask me this? "I get rid of them, of course. I give them three months after training, and if they aren't hitting their numbers— goodbye! They can't do the job, I'm going to find someone else." We finish lunch and he comes back to the subject of the consultant. "Look, you should call this guy. He's good. He'll help you." I don't know. We have our way of doing things, and it has worked well. Things are bound to turn around. I'm afraid that any changes will make things worse. But I keep thinking about it on my way back to work. Why am I so afraid to fire people when they don't perform? Why do I put their interests ahead of mine? Is that really what a good boss does?

ON THE SECOND SATURDAY of April, I pick up my son Henry from his school. He'll be with us for two weeks. Until he was twelve, he lived at home and attended the autism classroom at our local schools. In seventh grade, as puberty kicked in, he became very aggressive. We were lucky to find a residential school near us, Camphill Special School, which can handle him. The cost, $65,000 a year, is covered by our local school system until Henry is twenty-one years old. Then we're on our own.

It was an amazing change to get Henry out of the house. Until then I hadn't realized how much energy he was sucking up, and how it distorted my relationship with my other boys. The timing was also good for my business. Henry left in 2006. I was doing all the design, selling, and administration for a company of eighteen workers. I can't imagine how I would have managed with Henry at home. It would have been a perpetual emergency for me and my wife as he battled with the storms of puberty. I strongly believe that without the federal legislation that forces the local school board to pay for appropriate schooling, my business would have failed. Having Henry home all that time would have broken me.

Henry's school is part of a farm. There are easy chores for him to do. He is very well cared for, well fed, and kept busy. We can't replicate that. The school runs on a normal school calendar, so he's home for Thanksgiving, Christmas, spring break, and summer vacation. While he's back, our lifestyle changes. Like all teenage boys, he's always hungry. We have to keep our kitchen cabinets and refrigerator under lock and key. Henry will not wake himself at night when he needs to pee, so I get up at two and six a.m. and take him to the bathroom. When Henry is not eating or sleeping, he listens to music. He likes to hear the same disc over and over at top volume. When he eventually gets tired of that, he throws the CD player across his room. Henry also demands to go for a drive at least twice a day. It doesn't matter where, but anything shorter than an hour, and he has a huge tantrum.

It's an exhausting regimen. My wife runs the day shift; I step in when I arrive after work. Long office hours are out of the question. He'll return to school on April 22. And the next day I fly to Germany to visit Eurofurn.

With Henry home, I have a good excuse to delegate more work to others. Emma takes up the urgent administrative tasks, Dan and Nick decide who will take each incoming lead. While I'm out driving Henry around, I can stop at the shop. He can tolerate a short visit, but he has figured out that the fridge is not locked. If I lose track of him, he helps himself to sodas and sandwiches, and then I have to buy someone's lunch.

WHILE HENRY IS HOME, I'm watching our bank balance, contemplating the dollars that are not coming in as we fail to collect deposits, and the amount going out to fund operations. My projections predict a zero bank balance early in May. I can delay that day only by slowing expenditures. It's time to stop paying myself.

I set my pay depending on how much I think the company can afford. No employee would put up with this, but I am used to it. From 1999 to the beginning of 2008, and in 2010 and the start of 2011, my salary was $70,000 a year. In November 2008, I had cut my pay by 50 percent, while cutting my workers' wages by 15 percent. I restored my people's wages a year later. I only restored my own pay in March 2010. That's thirteen years without a raise.

We pay biweekly, twenty-six times per year, so $70,000 a year works out to $2,692 per paycheck. Adding on taxes, each of my paychecks was draining $3,230 from our working capital. Not too expensive for a worker who was producing all the sales and designs, running HR, doing all marketing, answering the phones, and covering any administrative tasks. By the middle of 2011, which was a good year, I decided that I could afford to give myself a raise. I bumped my pay rate to $140,000 a year, or $5,384 every two weeks. Add the taxes, and now each of my paychecks removes $6,461 from our working capital. If I went out and hired someone who could do everything that I do, it would cost me at least this much.

At the end of 2011, we suddenly found ourselves awash in cash. I decided to pay all my workers a nice bonus and give myself a much larger one, a small compensation for all the lean years. So my last paycheck of 2011 included a $70,000 year-end bonus. I decided at the beginning of this year to raise my salary again. I wanted to see whether we will still have positive cash flow if I pay myself the same amount as in 2011 but at a consistent rate, not a small regular check with a giant bonus at year-end. So I increased my pay rate from $120,000 to $180,000 a year, or $8,307 per check. This put my pay at 7.5 percent of our target revenues of $2.4 million a year. That's on the low side of what $2.4 million should produce for the boss. Ten percent would be a decent yield for the owner of a business of this size. Reasonable or not, my salary costs more than $16,000 a month. If we make our sales targets, it's not a problem. But if we don't, it hastens the day when we run out of cash.

Well, we have not made our sales target, so I decide that April 9 will be my last payday for a while. Our biweekly payroll for the whole company, including myself, had been in the $34,000 to $39,000 range, depending on overtime worked. Stopping my pay will buy some time by bringing that down into the mid- or upper twenties.

Now I have to consider whether to stop the interest payment to myself as well. I wrote the first check, for $3,225, just last month, and it was two weeks before I could bring myself to cash it. I decide to continue for a while so that I can at least cover my mortgage. Outgoing interest payments incur no additional taxes on the company, and I won't have to pay personal taxes on interest income until next year. And I can cut them off at any time. I don't want to do that, though—it feels like the beginning of failure. As long as I'm taking something out of the company, I haven't hit rock bottom.

I'VE BEEN FOLLOWING Emma's ongoing e-mail exchange with the Commerce Department guy in Kuwait. He's lined up five companies that would like to meet me, and he wants me to commit to dates and an itinerary. I'm horrified. I never thought that he would get much of a response. Emma is excited and presses me to schedule the trip. I don't want to go. I've already missed a lot of work, watching Henry, and I'm about to go to Germany for a week. But Eurofurn and Middle East exports have the potential to fill our schedule when domestic sales are slow. I start looking for tickets. I can't fly directly to Kuwait, I'll have to pass through Dubai. I may as well see what that town has to offer. I have Emma get in touch with the Commerce Department again, and she sets up a Gold Key for Dubai. I will be in the Middle East for the entire first week of June.

MY SON PETER has decided to look for a summer job. When I was his age, I went to the local Roy Rogers and filled out an application. A week later, I was making French fries for $2.65 an hour. Times have changed. Peter knows how to write computer code. He's posted some of his projects to a coders' forum, and now he's getting job offers, from start-ups desperate for programmers. An e-book publisher in San Francisco has offered to fly him out for an interview. He leaves on Friday the 13th and returns on Sunday with a job offer in hand: summer work, and a permanent position if he wants to defer school for a year. The pay is, to my mind, stunning: $54,000 a year. This for a kid who hasn't even graduated from high school yet. Apparently his coding is pretty good. He'll never need to make French fries for a living.

Peter is very excited. It's an amazing opportunity. Nancy is not happy. She wants him to go straight on to college in the fall. She's worried that he'll get caught up in the start-up lifestyle and abandon his college education. Wasted youth, twenty-first-century version.

I'm not worried. I have two sisters in the Bay Area, so he won't be alone in a strange city. Next week we go up to check out MIT. Peter already knows some people there, and they plan to put him up and show him a good time. I think he'll have enough information to make a good decision about whether to work or study next year.

———

SALES HAVE BEEN SLOW. Nick has sold three jobs totaling $30,665. Three orders from Eurofurn come in, another $16,297. Dan has been told that his bid for the California engineering firm, worth more than $35,000, has been accepted, and the purchase order will be issued soon. But we can't bank or build on promises. At the end of the second week of April, we have added just $46,962 to our total.

At the beginning of this year, I set up a Google spreadsheet to record our calls and e-mails every day to see if there are any patterns. It appears that we get about the same number of inquiries each day until Friday, when the rate drops in half, and on the weekends, when hardly anyone calls. We have been averaging 16.25 inquiries per week through the end of March. In the first week of April, we have chalked up twelve inquiries, and the second week of April, just nine inquiries. We have only had one week so far with as few as twelve inquiries, in February, and that included both a federal holiday and a big snowstorm. Nine inquiries is the worst week we have had all year.

This conforms to my theory about the April Swoon, but seeing it play out in real time is distressing. A steady stream of incoming calls is required for healthy sales. I can look back at orders from the past three years and see that we close a large number of small jobs, a decent number of jobs in the ten- to thirty-thousand-dollar range, and a few whoppers. It stands to reason that more calls will yield more of each type of job. If there are fewer of them, it is less likely that we'll make our sales goal.

ON THE FOLLOWING DAY, I make it in to work for a few hours, and Bob Foote updates me on the Company S situation. The CEO's assistant told him that he can pick up the table any time after April 18, but it has to be back for their board meeting on May 9. This is a tight window for us.

Bob has looked into various options. Our regular shipper quotes us $2,955 for a single truck, including driver, who would pick up the tabletops and drive straight to us. I would still need to fly Bob to Company S so that he could supervise packing. The total cost of that option, including hotel and wages, will be close to four thousand dollars. Returning the table will be cheaper, but it will still be in the range of $1,000, and we have to pay the installers to put the top back on the table. Any option will eat up much of the $7,551 that Company S still owes us. The job has been running over budget from the minute it hit the shop floor.

Bob thinks that it might be cheaper if we rent a truck in Milwaukee and drive it back ourselves. And he offers to take his wife along. She doesn't need to be paid, she can do a little driving, and they can stay in one hotel room. I'm convinced. They depart on Tuesday and return on Thursday. When we unwrap the tops, they look perfect until you get up very close. Everybody is disgusted that I knuckled under, but nobody can think of a better way to deal with it.

On the twentieth, I pack the family into my '99 Odyssey van and drive to Boston to attend MIT's new-student weekend. I'm hoping to get at least another two years out of this vehicle, but there's a worrisome hesitation between first and second gears. This is the second tranny in a car with 145,000 miles on it. I keep my fingers crossed, and we arrive without a breakdown.

The lowlight of the weekend, for once, does not come from Henry. Instead, a financial aid officer provides unpleasant news. My income last year, $260,992, disqualifies us from any aid. It was the one spectacular year I have ever had. In the preceding twenty-five years, my total income added up to $888,331. Assuming a 2,200-hour working year, that's $16.15 an hour. In 1994, when my twins were born, I took home $6,200 in wages. We qualified for welfare: WIC vouchers to help us feed the kids. We used those benefits for the next three years. And as recently as 2008, if you subtract the money I loaned the company to keep the doors open, I made only $8,357, or $3.79 per hour.

Financial aid calculations take none of that into account. As far as the aid officer is concerned, I'm a prosperous business owner with a substantial income and savings. He's not interested in the fact that my income is very volatile or that Henry (who is in the meeting with us) will most likely be living with us for the rest of his life and will require expensive care. He doesn't care that I have just stopped paying myself any salary. He considers only the numbers from 2011. When I paid out the big bonuses at the end of last year, I set aside enough cash to pay for Peter's first year of college. Right now, I have $78,525 in my checking account and $48,525 in another account for emergencies. MIT will cost about $65,000 (!) each year. We'll need the rest to live on. And in two years, my youngest son will be looking at colleges, too.

I suppose I could do what everyone else does and borrow Peter's tuition. But that presumes future income to repay the loan, and I have no confidence in my ability to make steady money. I'm terrified by debt that can't be discharged through bankruptcy, like student loans. No matter what happens to Peter or me, we could be stuck with that millstone around our necks for years.

I was very fortunate to start my adult life without student loan debt. School was a lot cheaper back in the 1980s, but my father and mother worked hard to put five kids through school without loans, and I'd like to give that same gift to my own children. If I had been saddled with loan payments, I would never have started my own business.

Driving home, I mull over all the numbers that don't add up: the sales we have not made, the cash on hand, my income for the next year, and the cost of putting two children through school. The one redeeming feature of having an autistic son: he won't be going to college at the same time as his twin. He will never need to go to college. He will be expensive in the future, but not right now.

I STAY HOME on Monday, since I am flying overseas after dinner. The long flight gives me plenty of time to reflect. Nick and Dan have sold a few jobs, but we're still far behind our target. My bank balance is down to $115,229. On the other hand, this trip holds some promise. At the very least, I'll see how an established company makes conference tables. And maybe this trip will initiate a flood of orders from Eurofurn.

I arrive in Hannover early Tuesday. Nigel told me that Eurofurn would make all arrangements for my stay. Sure enough, in the line of drivers holding cards, I see my name: "Herr Downs." I am staying in Hildesheim, about fifty kilometers from the factory.

When I was in high school, in the fall of 1978, I visited West Berlin. It was the definition of "grim"—cold and foggy, and with plenty of war damage. Hildesheim couldn't be a greater contrast. It's a charming town with medieval walls and old half-timbered houses. My hotel is a restaurant with a few rooms on the second floor. I fire up my iPhone and find a text from Nigel. We will be joining Peter Baumann, Eurofurn's worldwide head of marketing, for dinner.

Nigel and Milosz, who's also here for the week, pick me up at seven. I am looking forward to real German food, but the sign on the restaurant says "Pizza." And it's packed. A mention of Peter Baumann's name makes a table magically appear, along with some bottles of wine. We start drinking. About an hour later, Peter Baumann appears. He's young, cheerful, and fit, with a shock of blond hair. Nigel has prepped me on Peter's attempt to bring fresh air to the hundred-year-old company. Peter has led the expansion into Southeast Asia and the Middle East and is behind the move to start up in America. Everything has worked out well so far, but continuing economic weakness in Europe is raising questions about the wisdom of more expansion. The meal stretches on until midnight, but we don't talk business, just soccer and politics. I get the feeling that the real purpose of the evening is for Peter to get a look at me. I hope he likes what he sees.

Nigel and Milosz drive me to the factory the next morning. It's deep in the countryside. We'll be taking a tour with two new hires from New York, both in their mid-twenties: Jeff, in charge of shipping, and Pamela, who tells me, to my relief, that she will implement a new IT system. We're still having trouble with confusing job names.

The tour starts at the headquarters building. The walls are covered with large black-and-white photos of Eurofurn's designers. The message: product design is a heroic struggle, performed by geniuses. The company's head of design, Gerhardt, suddenly appears among us, dressed entirely in black. He talks for twenty minutes, explaining Eurofurn's philosophy: the company exists only to make superior design. How lucky we are to be able to participate in bringing these precious objects to the masses! He's mesmerizing. I'm both impressed and jealous. I've been designing furniture for twenty-six years, without much fuss. I take pride in my work and I hear from my customers that they like my designs, but nobody in the outside world has taken any notice. Will I ever have my own heroic black-and-white picture on the wall? Will I join the pantheon of form-givers? Maybe my relationship with Eurofurn will vault me from obscurity, and I'll become better known as a designer. Gerhardt's speech has inspired me to dream big.

Gerhardt leaves us—I'm surprised when he just walks out the door and doesn't disappear in a puff of smoke—and we are joined by Jens, an engineer who oversees Eurofurn's manufacturing sub-contractors around the world. His job is to make sure that their products are identical to the work that comes out of the German factory. Jens is young and seems like the guys in my own factory: careful, diligent, and intelligent. He tells us the rest of the day's agenda. After the group tour and lunch, the others will see another facility. Jens will spend the afternoon with me answering any questions I might have about making tables.

The tour starts with the upholstery facility, where leather is cut and sewn into chair seats. About half of the work stations are occupied. The workers appear to be in their late fifties or early sixties. Their skilled hands guide laser-cut pieces of leather through the sewing machines. The finished product is beautifully made, consistent, and precise. Modern craftsmanship: machines and people, each doing what they do best.

Next we see the office. It's large, but the thirty-four people I see don't fill all the desks. I peek over one person's shoulder and see room plans with a table in the center. Jens explains that the tables are designed to fit the client's space, just as we do. I see a printout with a 3-D drawing tacked to a wall. Jens confirms that this is what the customer will see after placing an order. The model is not all that detailed, isn't in color, and doesn't show the wood grain or the room. Our presentations are much more impressive.

Eurofurn gets work from furniture dealers and architects, and through an old-boy network. Its CEO and other top managers sit on the board of other companies and influence purchase decisions.

In contrast, Google allowed us to grow without any relationships with the mainstream furniture industry. We bypass the normal sales channels and still have a very prestigious clientele. But our sales tend to be one-offs. We work with a client and then move on. We have no network of allies in the market. When I ask Jens whether Eurofurn sells direct to clients over the Internet, he looks as if he has never heard of such a thing. "You sell something to a total stranger? Why would anyone want to do that?"

I ask him how they keep track of the variations in a job. Pamela, who has been hired to solve this problem for New York, overhears and says that the whole company uses an enterprise software package. She will be getting special training in it later today. I hope she masters it soon, and that it's actually capable of solving their naming problems.

We move into the woodworking facility. I can barely see the far wall. This building looks at least four times the size of my shop floor. Our first stop is a veneer cutting station, where a single worker, a middle-age woman, is fixing a manufacturing error. She is trying to replace the damaged section of a tabletop. That makes me feel better. We're not the only ones who make mistakes.

We walk for an hour as Jens explains how tables are built. I recognize every machine. This plant is larger, better lit, and neater than my shop. Every step of the process has its own logically arranged area, full of the very best German machinery, and special assembly jigs to speed production. There's a huge investment here. I see at least a hundred special lifters, to help a single worker move tops. They cost fifteen to thirty thousand dollars each. In the veneer glue-up area, there is a glue application machine. Last year, I looked into getting one, but was stunned by the price tag: sixty-five thousand dollars. It might make sense if we were doing thousands of panels a day, but we do only a couple at a time, using paint rollers that cost seventy-nine cents each. Three workers are hosing the machine down. I ask Jens how long it takes to prep the machine for work. Twenty minutes, and more than an hour for a three-man crew to clean it. "And we only had one order today. Fifteen, tops. The machine ran for less than thirty minutes."

Jens's comment leads me to ask how busy the factory has been. As it turns out, most of the workers have been laid off. The recession in Europe has been brutal, and even in 2012, the market is very soft. My business grew steadily from the beginning of 2010 until March. Is the weakness in Europe starting to spread to America? We continue for another hour, and everywhere I see the same thing: beautiful machines, spacious work stations, but very little work being done.

Before I left for Germany, I asked Nick and Dan and Andy Stahl, my engineer, what they wanted to know about a modern factory. We came up with eighty-three questions. After lunch, Jens answers most of them but can't comment on build times, labor rates, or overhead costs. It turns out that, except for a couple of automated processes, we use similar machines, glues, and finishes. We are capable of producing most of Eurofurn's tops in our shop. How much we should charge is another matter. We won't know how long it will take us to make tops in quantity until we do it. And we don't even have cost targets to aim for. We need those numbers.

Jens and I spend our last hour in the production engineers' office. They receive plans from the sales office, check them, and then send them out to the shop floor. We have some difficulties doing this ourselves. Andy Stahl produces detailed drawings from our proposals, and Steve Maturin passes them to the guys working on the piece. These often have small errors that get caught only by chance, and I often see my workers taking the long walk back to Andy's office with a question. Is there a better way?

Jens sits me down with the only engineer on duty that day, an older gentleman named Martin who does not speak English. He's clearly uncomfortable, but I'm not sure whether he's shy or he dislikes the idea of a foreign stranger learning his company's operational secrets.

I start asking questions. Each results in a very long exchange between Jens and Martin, and then a very short English answer back to me. But I'm able to work out their process. Because they have only twelve standard designs, they send a single paper sheet listing the type of table, size, wood to be used, edge detail, and quantity desired. This would not work for us—our tables vary too much. We cannot avoid making a full set of drawings for each table, even though they are very expensive to produce.

I conclude the day with another long meal with the New York contingent, and a good night's sleep. I return to the factory the next morning and head to Jens's office to thank him for being so helpful. "I would not do this normally," he says, "because I am the one to tell the outside partners what they must do. But I was told that you are special, and that I am to give you all the assistance that you require. And now you must excuse me, as I have spent more time with you than I can really afford." How about that? I'm special! But what does that mean?

At lunchtime, Nigel introduces me to his friend Johann, whose job is to arrange financing for Eurofurn's operations. We make a short drive to a nearby restaurant: pizza again. Johann makes it clear that this is not in honor of an American guest, but just because he really likes pizza. While we eat and chat, I'm thinking: since I'm special, maybe the steady stream of orders is going to begin. If they plan to keep me busy, it would be worth buying some equipment to do their work. All that will cost money. I ask Johann whether there's any chance that Eurofurn would help, and he holds up his hand. "No, no, no. We are having enough trouble financing our own factory. We bought a lot of equipment before the recession and now we need to be very careful."

After lunch, while we're driving back to Hildesheim, I ask Nigel straight out what Jens meant when he said I'm special. Is Eurofurn going to commit to me? Will there be any contract specifying levels of production and investments required? Are we engaged, or just dating?

Nigel is evasive. Eurofurn is excited to have found me. Eurofurn wants us to work closely together. Eurofurn needs the highest quality, and we can do that. Eurofurn needs the lowest prices, like it gets from its other foreign partners. Eurofurn would like me to show my commitment by assuming the costs of the next phase of our relationship by myself. Maybe Eurofurn will formalize the relationship at some point in the future. Eurofurn is also, as an organization, not sure that it wants to work with foreign partners at all. The Eurofurn management team is not entirely behind the decision to send work overseas.

The rest of the drive to my hotel passes in silence, and I eat dinner alone. My flight out is very early the next morning. I'm watching TV in my room when a text arrives from Nigel. Peter Baumann would like to take me out for a drink. Can I be ready at nine? Peter picks me up and we head to a non-descript bar in town. It's crowded. I'm introduced to a bunch of Peter's friends, local farmers. After a couple beers, I'm given a sinister-looking concoction: a wineglass half full of vodka. Perched on the rim, a slice of lemon is topped with a pile of dry instant coffee. "Luftwaffe Special!" exclaims the man. "My grandfather drank these in Russia! Keeps you happy, but not sleepy!" He demonstrates. You fold the lemon around the coffee, eat the whole thing in one bite, then chug the vodka. I master it on the first try, to applause from the guys. Then I have another—they're tasty.

Peter has been drinking, too, and we lean close to each other. "I love your factory," I tell him. "Very clean. Very good machines. Nice people. Very impressive." He drapes an arm across my shoulder, very friendly. I decide to ask him the question that has been bothering me all day. "What do you want from me? Why don't you do the work at your factory?"

He answers slowly. "It is not so good there. Business is very, very bad. Everyone is old. We cannot get young workers to move to the country. We have too many machines. We are losing money. We need to move the work to places where it is cheaper and where we can grow. And it takes too long to ship product. Many weeks on a boat does not work. We need to be close to our clients." I can see the sense of this. My biggest doubt is whether I'm the right choice for them. We will never be as efficient as a factory. Can we create an assembly line and deliver work at a lower price? It would be a drastic change in our operation.

I'm home on Saturday after a hellish, hungover flight. Can't sleep. I go down to my kitchen and log in to Dan's and Nick's e-mails to see what they've been up to. They've been busy. We have a lot of potential work hanging out there. If even half of it comes in, we'll be swamped.

We each sold one order while I was away. Dan finally scored with a sixteen-footer worth $9,106. Nick sold a smaller table for $7,413. Emma sold some power/data units for $453. And a purchase order worth $24,111 came in from a local insurance company I've been working with. Sales for the month so far: $88,045. And for the year, just $631,048. There are two business days left in April. We need a miracle: $170,000 in three days to put us back on track for the year.

Our cash is melting away. I started the month with $136,261, and today I have $105,294. Cutting my pay has slowed down our weekly expenses, but we've averaged $34,440 a week for the past two weeks.

That might be OK if we were making a book profit. I have explained at the weekly meeting that we need to keep production up, to collect cash from final payments as soon as we can, but the shop guys know that this speeds the day when we run out of work and I lay them off. They're slowing down production, maybe unconsciously, maybe deliberately. And we've been distracted with the Company S debacle. So far this month, we've shipped $145,236 and built just $125,036. Both of those are far below my target of $200,000 a month. And far below our cash outflow.

Inquiries are jumping all over the place. The first two weeks of April were slow, but the third week was higher than average: twenty-one people contacted us. The next week, when I was in Germany, was the worst I have seen in years: just seven incoming calls. The total for the month so far is just forty-nine, far below the totals in January (seventy-nine) and February (sixty-six). The missing inquiries give me a very bad feeling. As the number of possible buyers shrinks, we're less likely to hit our targets.

Well, there's one deal ready to go. I e-mail my friend who wants the bedroom set. If I can see him this weekend, I can review the final designs with him and hopefully get a deposit check. A $28,797 order will help. My friend is happy to meet me late in the afternoon. I go upstairs to tell my wife that I'm leaving. I need to go to the shop to pick up some checks and then go see my friend. "Well, be careful," she says. "The van has been acting funny."

I back the Odyssey out of the driveway and shift into drive. The engine revs up, but the car doesn't move. Shit. The transmission has finally given up. I let the van roll to the curb, then I try the Camry. The engine runs very ragged, and I see to my horror a huge cloud of white smoke behind the car. I turn it off. Peter normally drives the Camry. I go upstairs and shake him awake. "What happened to the Camry?" He shrugs. "I don't know. There's a lot of smoke coming out the back, but I got it home from school yesterday." "When did that start?" "I'm not sure, I just noticed it yesterday on the way home." We have an excellent auto mechanic a block away, and a car rental shop within a short walk, but both are closed on the weekend. I ride my bike out to the shop, and on the fifty-minute trip, I try to figure out what to do. The Camry is twenty years old, has 135,000 miles on it, and just two months ago, I spent $2,800 replacing the power steering. The mechanic told me then that I was most likely throwing money away. I've had the Odyssey for thirteen years, but it has even more miles. Neither car is worth more than the repair costs.

I bike out to my friend's house and show him the latest version of the designs. He takes the news that his new bedroom set will cost as much as a car without flinching and asks me what he can do to get onto our schedule. That's easy: hand over some money. He writes me a check for $12,500.

On Monday morning, I pull the Camry into the mechanic's lot. White smoke is billowing from under the hood. The diagnosis: "Head gasket, maybe a cracked block. Junk it." And I'm not throwing more money at the Odyssey. I'm carless. I coast the Camry back home, park it in my driveway next to the van, then walk up to the rental place and pick up the cheapest car that will fit my family of five (tall) people, a purple PT Cruiser.

The last day of April brings a surprise: two more orders. The first is worth $29,835. The buyer is a woodworker in Maine who was asked to make a very large table for a local company, but realized that it was beyond his capabilities. It's an easy job for us. The next is smaller, $15,301, for a company that makes tools for auto mechanics. We've been dealing with their general contractor. We were initially asked to price five different tables, but the job has been whittled down to just the top of the largest table. The design calls for a mostly metal top, with some wood. I'm pretty sure that we'll lose money at the price I quoted. The metal work will be a challenge, but I'll take anything at this point to keep the guys busy.

Dan and Nick have a long list of jobs that they hope will come in. Dan is still waiting for the purchase order from the California engineering firm. Nick has sent off his formal submission for the Air Force base. And there are still other proposals out there. I feel discouraged at their report. They are so hopeful. And they are selling almost nothing.

I spend the rest of the day doing administrative work that should have been done the week before. I review the bills the bookkeeper paid, the payroll that Emma submitted, make a local tax submittal, and walk through the shop to review work in progress. Everyone asks about Germany. I took a lot of pictures and some movies of Eurofurn's factory. I should put some kind of presentation together so that they can see what I saw. No time, though.

As I walk through the shop, the contrast between us and Eurofurn is stark. We can do most of Eurofurn's work, and do it well. Our products are well made and appealing. But our shop is a mess. Not by American standards—it's one of the cleanest shops I've ever been in—but compared to Eurofurn, it's appalling. There's no particular order to our machinery. We just set it down here and there as we acquired it. A decade's accumulation of dust frosts unused horizontal surfaces, and there are heaps of scrap everywhere. The only bright spot is the finish room. Dust in there causes finish defects. Dave Violi keeps it spotless.

One other difference: my whole crew is working. Our backlog is shrinking, but it isn't gone. I think back to Eurofurn's unoccupied work stations, and Peter Baumann's gloomy prognosis for that factory. Is that our future? How long before I have to lay someone off? Is the recession in Europe spreading to America? Is it 2008 all over again?

MAY

Date: Tuesday, May 1, 2012

Bank balance: $105,203.90

Cash relative to start of year ("Net Cash"): -$31,950.42

New-contract value, year-to-date: $704,981

May starts on a Tuesday. Cash reserves are down. Sales? My last-minute surge brought our April total to $161,978. Not what I wanted, but at least better than March.

The production numbers aren't so good, either. We built projects worth $125,036, with shipments totaling $145,236. I try not to be too discouraged. Considering these statistics on a monthly basis can be misleading. We add a job to the "Built" list on the day it enters the finishing room, and to the "Shipped" list when it goes out the door. A large job can skew the numbers if it's mostly completed in one month and tallied at the beginning of the next. It's more meaningful to look at the numbers across a three-month span. Our build for the first quarter, January through March, averaged $207,819 per month, which is better than my goal of $200,000 a month. Shipments averaged $194,418, just short of target. Costs during that period averaged $181,736 per month. We were making a profit, on an accrual basis, of about $12,400 a month, even though our cash position didn't reflect this. Uncollected balances and the deposits that never showed up in March made our cash balance decline.

As I look at the jobs in our database, it looks like our ship number for May should be much closer to our average. How much will we build? That depends on whether things go well in the shop. Whether workers are moving jobs out the door, or fixing mistakes, or drowning in misquoted, difficult projects. And whether we can keep the shop occupied by adding more work to our queue. I run the calculations for our backlog and it shows four and a half weeks. We'll be out of work in June. Better get back to selling.

How much time do I spend each day thinking about things? It depends on what else is happening. Aside from my primary job—making sales—on any given day I might have to: review incoming bills; sign outgoing checks; call a customer to find out when they will send us the money they owe us; check bank balances; monitor our credit card accounts; file taxes; photograph a completed table; edit a photo or write content for the Web site; write an ad; change the ads in our AdWords account; evaluate a change in shop operations; move a machine or a worker to a better location; buy new equipment; fix a broken machine; call the landlord about the plumbing, heating, or neighbors; negotiate a new lease; evaluate and purchase health and dental insurance, and general liability, workmen's compensation, and auto insurance; contest an unemployment compensation claim; do the payroll; decide whether to give a worker a raise; deal with a worker's request for emergency leave; perform annual reviews; respond to credit checks for my workers; verify employment for former workers; shoot a bird that has found its way into the shop; figure out why a printer stopped working; restart the server; add a user to our network; purchase a new software program; vacuum my office for visitors; get the truck inspected, on and on.

Some of these tasks are interesting. Tinkering with machines is fun. Marketing decisions, especially how to manage the Web site and AdWords, are an intellectual challenge. Some are unpleasant but lead to a satisfying conclusion, like nagging customers for past-due payments. (They've always paid me, eventually.) Some are frightening. I can change an employee's life with my decisions about pay rates and whether to hire and fire. And many are just aggravating: the taxes, insurance purchases, legal issues, and some of the employee interactions. Each layer of government, each enormous and indifferent private bureaucracy, requires its own special knowledge: the right form filled out the correct way and filed at the right time. Learning how to complete one type of tax filing tells you nothing whatsoever about how to fill out the next form. One health insurer presents a quote one way, another in an entirely different way, and both require extensive study to determine the best choice. It's like stepping back to an old, old world where every tree, every rock, every stream is inhabited by its own resident spirit, and each needs to be mollified in the correct manner. Or very bad things happen.

I didn't start my company to do any of this. I had no idea, when I decided that I would make furniture in exchange for money, that this was in my future. And the strange universe of administration expands as the company grows. I can push some tasks onto Emma and Pam, our bookkeeper, and we can outsource some payroll functions. The rest is still my responsibility. The company has fifteen employees now, and takes in more than two million dollars annually. If I spread out a year's worth of administrative tasks evenly, they take about three hours a day.

Please keep in mind, as I tell my story, that the narrative has been extracted from a year's worth of days that were actually a mix of selling and dealing with this other stuff. Not one single day presented itself neatly arranged, like a book or a movie.

———

WEDNESDAY, MAY 2, brings a bonanza—three large checks, totaling $32,820. Big mood lifter! The first is the deposit for the Maine table, worth $14,918. The second is for $3,300, a preship for a single table that we sold in January. And the last is for $14,602—another preship, for a group of tables going to a local software developer. This cash injection offsets payments totaling $25,304 that I sent out yesterday.

The downer is seeing how much cash we could possibly collect in the future, if, and only if, we finish all jobs and collect all balances. It's down to just $53,008. Add that to the $127,601 I have, and there are about five and a half weeks before the money is gone. If our output is as low as it was in April, we will run out of cash before we can expect to collect the balances due.

At home that evening, dinner discussion focuses on Peter's job offer in San Francisco. He's decided that he wants to commit himself to a whole year of working before starting school. I ask him whether it will be difficult to get permission to defer from MIT, and he tells me that it's as simple as checking a box on their Web site.

Nancy is strongly opposed. She has a long list of worries that boil down to: young man on his own in a big city, with money. She thinks that he will be lonely. She thinks that he will hate working. Or that he will love working so much that he will skip college entirely. My reaction to all this is—so what? He's going to grow up one way or another. Take a chance! Go West, young man! If it doesn't work out, he can always come home.

I have a less noble reason to back his plan: it solves a financial problem for me. When I stopped my salary, I knew that my personal cash would cover Peter's tuition. Then the cars died. If he defers for a year, I'll have enough money to buy two decent cars without borrowing, enough to live frugally until the end of the year, and another fourteen months to round up more money. I won't have to actually write a check to MIT until fall 2013. I'll be able to reapply for financial aid in the winter of 2013 and show a more pitiful financial picture to the aid officers. I'll have very little cash on hand, and my income is likely to be much less than one hundred thousand dollars. So the cost of Peter's next year might come way, way down from the sticker sum of sixty-five thousand a year.

I don't mention this line of reasoning to my wife. Instead, I point out that my two sisters live in San Francisco, that Peter will always have someone to call if there is trouble, and that he can come home at any time. Her great-grandfather said goodbye to his parents in Minsk and left for America, without cell phone, e-mail, waiting family, or a job. He was brave and his parents let him do it. Are we too weak to let go of our children anymore? He's going to head out the door one way or another. Why not let him do what he wants? She agrees that he can give it a try for the summer.

THE NEXT DAY, Thursday, I design the Eurofurn showroom table. The order arrived in March, but I didn't want to start until I had seen their factory. I'll be using a drafting program on my computer to make a drawing. This is how information about an object is normally conveyed from the designer to wherever it is manufactured. The drawing portrays an object, but it actually consists of a bunch of lines and text on screen or paper. It has its own existence, independent of the qualities of the item that is being drawn. If the drawing is unclear, or riddled with errors, production is difficult and inefficient. Drawings look nothing like completed pieces. It takes a great deal of skill and experience to look at them and visualize what the object will look like, and even more to tell how it will work.

In our shop, the sales team does the initial drawing of each table. We modify it as the design is worked out with the customer. When the job is finalized, we send the file to Andy Stahl, our engineer. He will transform our concept into two different formats: one detailed set of drawings for the workers in the shop, and one set of instructions for our CNC machine. His job requires a deep understanding of what happens in the shop, as well as the skills required to convey complex information clearly, both to people and to a machine.

If you studied the drawings that Andy makes for the shop floor guys, you might eventually notice what isn't there: no indications of what machines to use, no instructions as to how to build the table, or in what order the subassemblies should be built, and nothing at all about how it will be assembled, finished, and shipped. All that knowledge is elsewhere, much of it in the heads and hands of the craftsmen. Our drawings contain about 5 percent of the information required to produce the object they depict.

Andy determines the details of what will be built, but the big decisions have already been made. Dan, Nick, and I do what most of us think of as design—the creation, from nothing, of a new object. How do we do that?

The mental and physical parts of the task are done simultaneously. We think, and we draw. We try to identify what object will function per the customer's requirements, look good, can be built efficiently in our shop, can be assembled and disassembled with ease, will fit into a shipping container that we can handle, will be durable, and whose cost doesn't exceed the customer's budget. And just to make it trickier, the best solution for any single requirement usually means a suboptimal approach to another. Fortunately, we've been solving these problems for years and have identified effective strategies for each of them.

I have designed every kind of furniture for home and office and learned that there are many issues beyond durability, looks, and price. Designing a bedroom requires tactful questioning about how it will be used. Designing an individual's office should include some consideration of how the proposed design will look to colleagues and underlings. Chairs need a great deal of structural knowledge. In contrast, a conference table is pretty simple: a flat surface and something to hold it up. The top should be thirty inches from the floor, with at least twenty-seven inches underneath for legroom. We know that eighteen inches between the perimeter of the top and any vertical structure provides enough knee room, and that we should allocate at least thirty inches of perimeter for each chair, and that the table should be no closer than forty-two inches to the wall or other furniture.

We determine the size of a table by asking the client how much space they have and how many people they want to seat. If their answers contradict each other, we show the biggest table that will fit in the room. Since size is easy to determine, most of our design thinking is about how the table will look, how to build it, and how to integrate the audiovisual equipment.

Eurofurn is more sophisticated than our typical customer. They've told me what size, shape, woods, and special features that they want. The table will be a modified equilateral triangle, seventy-seven inches long and seventy inches wide, with gently curved sides that become much tighter radii at the corners. Any object based on a triangular geometry presents difficulties, because our materials and equipment are designed for a rectangular world. My machines default to 90-degree cuts. Our wood comes to us in rectangular chunks. And clamps, which we use to hold pieces together while glue dries, don't work on triangular shapes—as pressure is applied, they slide toward the vertex and then fall. Since clamps are heavy and bulky, this will usually ruin the work.

The top is also too large to cut out of one piece of plywood. It must be made in pieces. I could cut it into two sections, but a single seam running across the triangular top will look arbitrary and clunky. If I make it in three identical pieces, then the seams will reflect the triangular geometry better. Each piece will have its own power/data hatch. In the center, where the three pieces meet, I'll put a circular hole down into the base. This will allow a wire to be run from a telephone to the floor without going through the hatches, and it will also eliminate the awkward spot where three pointed pieces meet.

I spend some time working out the radii of the two curves on each top edge. We'll have to bend a piece of solid walnut around these curves without cracking it. We can steam the wood to make it flexible, or we can use several layers of very thin wood and gradually build up the required thickness with multiple glue-ups. I want to avoid either of these techniques, as they are both very slow and extra build hours mean extra cost. I came up with my selling price, $6,523, by estimating how much a production version of this table would cost to build if we have everything worked out. But we don't have everything worked out, and it will likely take more hours than my estimate suggests.

I complete the drawing of the outline of the top and the seams in a couple of minutes. Then I paste in a drawing of the power/data hatch that I took from an earlier project. Copy and rotate the hatch two more times, add explanatory text and dimension lines, and the drawing is complete (see page 117).

The next step is to design the base. I know that they don't want to see any of the wires connecting the power/data units to the building wiring. They'll want it to look very restrained, very clean, very simple. Very Eurofurn.

I decide that the base will be the same shape as the top: a trian-

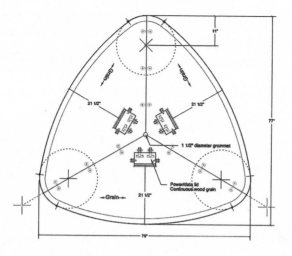

gular drum with rounded corners. I'll make it out of walnut with a stainless-steel accent. But how big should it be? I want to maximize the distance between the edge of the table and the vertical face of the base, to give users as much knee room as possible. People really, really hate it when their feet or knees hit a table base. But if there's too much overhang, and too little base, the table will be tippy. And more overhang means more top flex. Eurofurn wants this tabletop to be very thin, just one inch thick. In many of Eurofurn's designs, a thin top is no problem, because there are legs at the corner of the table, but in this case much of the top is unsupported. So I should make the base bigger, to minimize top flex.

Good reasons to make the base small, good reasons to make it big. I also have one last reason to minimize the size. I want to cut all the structural parts for the base out of a single sheet of plywood, four feet wide and eight feet long, and one and a half inches thick. This will minimize the material cost and reduce the amount of labor, as we will have to put only one sheet onto the CNC bed.

I settle on an eighteen-inch overhang. In my mind, I've been visualizing all the parts required to make the base. I draw each of them, and then start dropping them onto a single sheet of plywood, arranging and rotating them so that they all fit. The final layout looks like this:

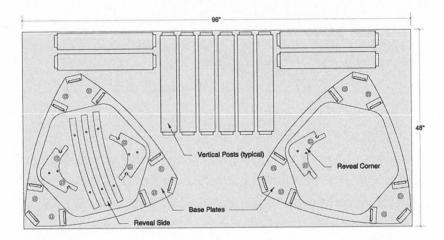

That's it. I'm done. Andy will use my drawings to make another set of drawings, fleshing out my design ideas, formatted specifically for the client's perusal. These are called "shop drawings," or "shops." If the client doesn't like something that we build, and we haven't shown or mentioned it in the shop drawings, then it's our responsibility to fix it. If the point of contention was explained in the shops, and the client either missed it or didn't understand what was shown, then they have to pay for any fixes. Theoretically, the Eurofurn guys should be able to look at the shop drawings and understand what the table will look like. But I decide to put together a quick 3-D model and use it to generate some renderings. Adding this type of image greatly reduces the chance of disagreement down the road. They show what most people care about—the look—in a way that's easy to understand. Here's one of the images that I'll send:

As you can see, this is much easier to comprehend than my design drawings.

Andy completes the shop drawings and sends them on Friday. Nigel approves them by e-mail later that day.

By the end of the week, Germany is a memory. I'm back to doing paperwork, talking to clients, and worrying about sales, cash, and marketing. The week I was in Germany, we received only seven inquiries. That was the worst performance since I started keeping records in 2011. This week was higher than average: twenty calls and e-mails. The pattern since the beginning of April looks like this: 12 : 9 : 21 : 7 : 20. These are wilder swings than I have ever seen. What does it mean? Is our advertising working, or not?

Sales for the week have been weak, totaling just $30,779. They're all Dan's jobs. Each one is near the $10,000 mark. If not productive, he's consistent: he's sold fourteen jobs this year, totaling $146,130. That's an average sale of $10,438. This is lower than Nick's total, $397,495, and average, $17,282. I have sold $200,110 and averaged $12,506.

Neither Nick nor I sold anything this week. Even worse, my last sale of April, to the tool company, is canceled, via a very short e-mail with no explanation. Take $15,301 off my total, and the sales for April are now just $146,677. A cancellation is unusual. We never got a deposit and haven't done any drawings, so it's easy to strike this job and move on. But what happened? Since we've only dealt with the general contractor, I have no idea who made the decision and whether the job was canceled or went to someone else. I could e-mail the contractor and see if he has an explanation, but if he wanted to tell me why, then he would have. Another mystery to contemplate over the weekend.

I SET OUT on Saturday with a mission: to buy some cars. I'm assuming that this will be a horrible experience, but since I'm in sales myself, I'm interested to see how they deal with me. My dream vehicle is the newest version of the Prius, both for the mileage, to lower the cost of driving Henry around in circles, and for the room. Everyone in my family is six feet or taller. The Prius V is much larger than the standard version. I've already decided that it will be perfect for me.

My wife will use the second car. The Camry wagon she was driving had three rows of seats. When I told her that I wanted to get a Prius, she asked how well it would handle the five of us on long trips. I had no answer, never having been inside one, so we agreed to look for a used minivan.

I check prices for a new Prius V and a used Sienna. The Prius is going for list ($27,600) or more. I find a nice used Sienna at a local dealer—I'll call it Urban Toyota—and head over to check it out. When I get there, I find that the office is being rebuilt and they're doing business from construction trailers. I enter. The room is full of cheap desks and chairs, some occupied with salespeople and cus-tomers. There's an office to my right where I can see a bunch of young guys, all dressed in suits and clip-on ties. I'm standing there, but nobody greets me. After a couple minutes, I stick my head in the office. "Are you the sales guys?" A man behind a desk confirms that this is the sales department. "Can I get some help?" Desk Guy points to a young man sitting on a stained sofa. He heaves himself to his feet and sticks out a hand. "I'm Chet. How can I help you?" I explain what I'm after—the Sienna—and that I am also in the market for a Prius V. I would like to test-drive them both. And if I like them, I'll buy them, today, cash on the barrelhead.

Chet has other plans for me. "OK, here's the first thing. We need to prep the Sienna for the test-drive. And I only have one Prius, and that's going to need prep, too. Take a seat." I sit and wait. And wait. And wait. Almost half an hour later, he comes back with the keys to the Sienna.

I take it for a spin—very nice, quiet, roomy, runs fine. This car has 63,000 miles on it, and they want $19,600. Pricey, for what it is. I tell Chet that I'd like to try the Prius and then we can talk. Back in the trailer, I start waiting. While I'm parked there, I can't help overhearing a deal being closed to my left. A salesman is sitting with a family of six—husband, wife, and four small kids. The hus-band and wife are speaking to each other in Spanish.

Their salesman is busy with his computer. He's a one-fingered, look-for-every-key typist, so it takes him a while to write up the deal. As he types, he explains what he's doing, slowly and loudly. This deal is all about the monthly payment and the trade-in value. The couple is nervous. The salesman promises that "you can drive home in a *Brand. New. RAV-4. Today.*" He slides a pile of papers over, and the husband starts signing. The wife has a stricken look, but the husband and kids are very excited, and the salesman sports

a broad grin. What am I seeing? Is this a good deal? A happy purchase, mutually beneficial to both parties? Or something more one-
sided? That's a whole lot of paperwork that the guy signed without
reading any of it. Good luck, folks.

It's been forty-five minutes. I'm just about to bail when Chet
comes back in. "Here ya go," he says as he hands me the key. "It's
out on the lot, I'll follow you out." The car is pulled up near the
door. This is my first look at the Prius V. I get in and find, to my
surprise, that there's nothing on the dashboard: no dials, nothing
analogue, no information at all. My old cars predated digital read-
outs. There doesn't even seem to be an ignition switch. Chet climbs
in. "Put your foot on the brake," he commands, then he leans over
and pushes a round button in the center of the dashboard. The display jumps to life, but there's no engine noise. Is it running? "OK,
this car is kinda weird. Watch how the shifter doohickey goes. Ya
push it over into D, then just let her go, and she'll spring back to
where she was. Keep your foot on the brake. Same thing with re-
verse. OK, let's get this over with."

I gingerly press the accelerator and we move forward, gently,
slowly, out to the street and through a five-mile test ride. When I
accelerate, I can hear the engine spring to life, but there's not much
pickup. We return to the lot. I sit in the backseat—plenty of leg and
headroom—and I can see from the digital readout that I was getting
mileage in the high forties, just as I wanted. But in all my research,
nobody mentioned that a Prius V can barely get out of its own way.
I'm wondering whether I'll learn to live with such an underpow-
ered car. But I'm already sick of car shopping. I decide to proceed to
a deal.

Back in the trailer, I tell Chet, "OK, I'd like to take both cars. You
want nineteen thousand six for the Sienna and how much for the
Prius?" Chet types a bit on his computer and looks back to me.

"Twenty-eight seven fifty." That is $1,150 over the sticker price on the car. I decide that he must just be playing to see if I'm stupid. "How about I give you forty-four five for both of them? I'll write you a check right now." He thinks about this for maybe a quarter of a second and then stands up. "Nah. I think we're done here. Good luck with your search." He heads back to the holding pen. I'm stunned. Did he really just walk away from someone who was ready to hand him money? Was my offer some kind of insult? I puzzle over the experience on my way home. Chet treated me like garbage, but why?

MONDAY, 8:58 A.M. I can see the crew gathered at the square table, ready for the meeting. There's no chatter. They wait. For me.

What will I say? I normally do the numbers, then some commentary about how things are going. Our cash position is worrisome. We have $135,782 on hand, less than a month's worth at our present spending rates. We don't have much of a backlog. We are far, far behind my sales targets. It seems like things are slowing down, although I can't put my finger on exactly why. I don't want to confess that the situation is bad, that I don't know what's going on, and that layoffs will arrive next month. But that's how I see it. Can I lie to them? Should I cancel the meeting? Or would they prefer a warning?

Before our last disaster, in the summer and fall of 2008, The Partner insisted that I not talk about our financial situation with the employees, that it was too much for them to handle, and that the good ones would jump ship and look for other jobs. Our partnership agreement said that we both had to agree on a course of action—each had veto power over the other. I still trusted The Partner's judgment back then, so I followed his orders and kept quiet.

I never felt good about that policy. There were days when my longtime, trusted employees asked me directly whether the company was in trouble, and I had to keep mum. It was an enormous mistake. I found out later that all the workers knew it was very bad, and in the absence of any real information from their bosses, wild rumors were spreading. Morale was in the toilet. On the day that I laid off half the staff, I was surprised by how happy and relieved everyone was. Hearing the truth, even when it's dreadful, is comforting. I promised the remaining employees that I would always tell them what was happening from then on.

Which brings me back to my Monday meeting. I drag myself out of my chair. Chin up. Shoulders back. Walk out there like a boss. Stand and deliver the truth. "Sales are not where I want them to be. Dan and Nick and I are doing everything we can to close some deals. Think back to 2009. Even in the worst year ever, we sold a million and a half. Something is going to come in soon. We have almost as much cash as we started the year with, which is not so bad. We need to finish the jobs we have on hand efficiently so that we can collect the money they owe us. Does anyone have any questions?" No. "OK, that's the meeting." They rise and return to their benches, machines, spray booth, desks, and broom.

TWO DAYS LATER, mid-morning. I'm working on a proposal when Bob Foote, my shipping manager, comes through the door. "Do you have a minute?" He has that look on his face that I recognize from years of interruptions. Something is wrong and I have to deal with it. He continues, "There's a thing—Sean and I want to talk to you, if you have time. If it's OK. If you're not busy. I don't know. Maybe after lunch."

"What's the issue?" I ask. He doesn't respond. I lead him to my private office and shut the door. "OK, what's up?"

He hesitates. "I don't want to be a jerk, or anything." Another pause. "Sean and I have been keeping track, and we think that Eduardo is cheating on his time sheets. He's turning in hours when he's not here." Shit. I didn't need this at all. I have things to do. But now I have to fire Eduardo.

Firing a worker is the most unpleasant thing I have to do as a boss. Fortunately, I haven't had to do it often. The first time was shortly after I opened my doors. I (stupidly) hired a temporary worker even though I knew she was a junkie. She showed up and did some work. While my back was turned, she stole a check out of my checkbook, forged my signature, and then used it to buy cigarettes at the corner store. The grocer knew her well so he called me to make sure it was OK. Of course it wasn't, so I told her not to come back. But the agony of that confrontation—I was twenty-four years old, had no idea what to say, and had no idea how she would react. Fortunately for me, she wasn't surprised, she didn't make a fuss, and she left. (What was she thinking, using the check on the same block she stole it? Junkie logic.)

It was eight years before I had to do it again, but the second time was even worse. This was a full-time employee, Nate Morgan, who had been with me for four years. His work wasn't great and his attendance was spotty, but I liked him and kept finding excuses for his failures. Finally, he didn't show up one day, even though I had emphasized that he was needed for a critical delivery. No phone call, no nothing. When he rolled in the following day, I was furious and told him it was over. He was astonished—apparently all the little talks I had given him about what was expected had made no impression. Or he thought that I would never go through with it. He begged me for another chance, tears rolling down his cheeks. But my other workers were sick of his failures and one guy told me that if I didn't fire Nate, he would quit.

So I steeled myself and fired him. I knew that he would have a hard time getting another job, but I did it anyway. After he left, I broke down myself. Depriving someone of employment is no joke. But the mood of the other employees improved immediately. And that taught me a valuable lesson: bad employees make good employees feel bad. It makes them wonder why they should follow the rules. If the boss doesn't care, why bother? My workers are craftsmen and have their own standards for behavior: show up, work hard, and try their best to make a good product. Seeing a coworker get away with sloppy work and laziness is a slap in the face. They hate it.

For all the bad advice that The Partner gave me, he was correct about firing people. Shortly after another termination, he told me, "It's not your fault. They do it to themselves. When you need to fire someone, just do it." This worker was ruining projects with errors and hiding the faulty work under his bench. Which might not have led to immediate termination, but he was also falsifying his time sheets. The problems didn't come to our attention for a number of months, by which time we had written an employee manual, at The Partner's insistence, that listed acts that would lead to instant termination. These included showing up under the influence of alcohol or drugs and falsifying time sheets. Every employee is given two copies: one they keep, another they sign to indicate that they have read and understood the provisions. My expectations are crystal clear.

Which brings me back to Eduardo. I know what I have to do. But it's still an effort to switch gears, to go into Crusty Boss Mode, to become the guy who will pull the trigger.

Eduardo has worked for me for seven years. When we needed a floor sweeper to empty dust bags and keep the shop clean, The Partner asked the groundskeeper at his country club, an acquaintance, if he knew of anyone who was looking for work. What followed was surreal. The groundskeeper showed up on the following Monday with six guys, ranging in age from about twenty to forty or more.

"Take your pick," he said. The Partner turned to the youngest—Eduardo. "Do you speak English?" Eduardo said yes, although we would later learn he could barely speak the language at all. "This one," said The Partner, and that was that. I felt bad for the others, but The Partner waxed philosophic. "They were all OK, or the groundskeeper wouldn't have brought them. But the young one will be the cheapest."

Eduardo was a good worker. Eventually we decided to see if he could do some woodworking. With training, he was OK at the simpler assembly tasks. He was reliable, worked hard, and followed directions.

Being an immigrant with brown skin caused him difficulties outside the shop. On January 21, Eduardo did not show up. As our company policy requires, he left a message saying that he was unexpectedly held up in New York and would be back in two days. When he came back, I asked him what had happened. He had been driving his cousin's car, and for reasons he couldn't or wouldn't explain, had been pulled over by the police. They looked inside the car and saw a plastic toy pistol that one of the cousin's kids had left on the backseat. Apparently this is a felony in New York. So Eduardo was arrested, released on bond the next day, and given a court date about a month from then. He showed me the court documents, which confirmed that the problem was the toy gun. I could picture what would happen next—defenseless Eduardo, who barely speaks English, becomes a pawn of the New York criminal industrial complex. I called a friend of mine, a criminal defense attorney in Brooklyn, and asked for help. When Eduardo showed up in court with competent counsel, all charges were dropped. It cost me a thousand dollars to set this up.

But now Eduardo has broken *my* rules, and in a way that I can't ignore. I have to fire him. First, I call Bob and Sean into our small conference room. They're nervous, as you might imagine. I open by telling them that I'm going to be firing Eduardo within the next hour and thank them for having the courage to come forward with this. That it is a testament to their value as employees and their faith in the company that they wouldn't tolerate theft. That it is entirely proper to act in the interests of the company, as the company is the foundation of all our prosperity. And that the problem is not their doing, but Eduardo's. And I ask them to repeat what Bob had told me earlier, with details.

Their story is detailed and believable. They show me their written notes and the discrepancies with the reported hours. I check my records, and they confirm the story. And then something curious comes out: it turns out that the week before, they took the problem to Steve Maturin, the shop manager, and showed him the same evidence. Steve Maturin heard them out—and then did nothing. Fantastic. Now I should fire Steve, too. Can I continue to employ someone who would ignore a case of theft from the company?

But I need to sort out Eduardo first. I write a description of the problem, a summary of the dates involved, and a quotation from the company handbook referring to the policy violation, and the consequence (immediate termination). The document concludes, "The undersigned, Eduardo Lopez, admits that these events occurred and understands the consequences of his actions," with a signature line and a date. I have Emma review it and tell her that she will be sitting in on the firing as a witness. And it will be recorded on video. This helps me keep up my resolve and provides evidence in case Eduardo files for unemployment compensation. If he is fired for stealing, he is ineligible, but if it's lack of work, or even incompetence, I have to pay fifty-two weeks of benefits. It's also incentive for everyone to behave civilly.

I set up the camera and tell Emma to find Eduardo. When he

comes in, he sees the chairs and the camera. He knows that this is trouble. I motion him to the chair across from me, and Emma sits down next to him. I begin. "Eduardo, I'd like to record this meeting. Do I have your permission?" He agrees, barely audible. "It has come to my attention that you have turned in time sheets for hours that you were not in the shop. This was witnessed on April seventeenth, April nineteenth, and April twenty-fourth, and reported to have happened on other occasions. This is a violation of company policy. Here is the handbook with your signature on the cover. You acknowledged that you read it and understand the policy. Here is the page with the causes for immediate termination. Look at number three: falsifying time sheets. Your employment here is now ended for violating this policy. I'm sorry, but you have to go now." His face has turned bright red. He has tears in his eyes. "Eduardo, do you have anything to say?"

After a long pause, he asks me, "Can I pay you back? Can I pay a little every week? I will never do this again." It's tempting—my resolve weakened when I saw his tears. But then what? What about Bob and Sean? Will they think that stealing from the boss is acceptable, at least the first time you try it?

"I can't have you here anymore, Eduardo. I can't have the others see you working here after this. This is the choice you made. If you needed money, you could have asked me. I've helped you before. You made a different choice. You did this repeatedly. It's not something I can tolerate. Now you have to go. Please sign this acknowledgment that you understand what happened. And if you file for unemployment I will contest it. But if you want to use me as a reference, I will never mention this. I will tell them that you are a good worker and that you left because of the long commute. I want you to have another chance, and I'll help you with that. But you can't work here anymore."

Neither of us have any more to say. He signs the paper and walks out. I turn off the camera. Exhale. "Well, that sucked." Emma looks a little upset but shrugs and says, "He had to go. You had to do it."

Now I have to deal with Steve Maturin. This is a more complicated problem. Since he ignored theft, I should fire him. But he's in charge of the shop, so removing him will cause a lot of disruption. I will also have lost a third of my production capacity—two out of six workers—in one day.

Steve Maturin is like a machine. He arrives exactly at five-thirty a.m. every morning and works steadily and efficiently all day. His completed projects are immaculate. He never wastes time with small talk. He won't even speak unless spoken to. He eats lunch at his bench precisely at noon and leaves at exactly two-thirty p.m. During his nine hours, he will complete more work than anyone else in the shop. My records show that he has consistently been the fastest, highest-quality worker I have had. I've never hired a new person who didn't tell me that Steve is the best cabinetmaker they have ever seen.

Steve has been around forever. I hired him in the fall of 1993 and made him the shop floor manager a few years later. At that time, I had three guys building furniture and I did everything else: sales, design, engineering, administration, finishing, delivery, and overseeing the shop floor. I needed to push some of that load onto someone else, so I put Steve in charge of the shop. I chose him because he was my best craftsman. Shouldn't that person be in charge? After promoting him, I heard from the other workers that he was very fair, didn't play political games, had no favorites. They accepted him as a leader.

Nineteen years later, he's still building stuff and running the shop. He has performed this job even as we got much larger, moved twice, switched our products from furniture to conference tables, downsized after the recession, and rebuilt the business. He has never complained or asked for help, even during the worst crisis. His management responsibilities—reviewing drawings with Andy Stahl, assigning the jobs to different workers, monitoring work in progress—seem to get done in very little time.

We rarely speak. He seems to avoid interactions with me and I don't stop by his bench unless I have something specific to tell him. When that happens, he'll listen to whatever I say without comment and answer direct questions with as few words as possible. I would go so far as to say that Steve dislikes me, except I can't think of a reason why he should. I've always gone out of my way to praise his work to the others, and he is the highest-paid guy in the shop. Over the years, I have seen him laugh and joke with some of the other guys. He's never even cracked a smile with me. Frankly, his silence intimidates me. I know that I should have a better relationship with him, but I can't figure out how to get past his defenses.

Aside from a frosty relationship with the boss, Steve has one other weakness: he is not innovative. I can't rely on him to look at operations, identify possible improvements, and implement them. I don't know whether he doesn't care enough or isn't capable of it. He doesn't seem to spend any time making sure that the other workers do things the best way. I often see workers making choices on how to build a project that will get them into trouble, and I wonder why Steve doesn't set them onto the right path. He clearly doesn't like to interact with anyone beyond the bare minimum to divide the work up. So the shop is stuck. We don't identify best practices, don't make sure that everyone does things the same way. I'm too busy trying to deal with customers and administration to take over shop management myself. I'm mystified. Does he already have too much work to do? Does he have plans that he can't implement for some reason? I have no idea.

I think that he's unhappy that the shop has shifted from making a range of furniture items to just conference tables. I sympathize to a certain extent, but we can't make any money doing this and that. It's not efficient, in either marketing or production. If all my people were willing to work for ten dollars an hour, maybe we could survive. When everyone wants a high wage, and they all need to make mortgage and car payments, we have to face reality. Conference tables work as a business. Fine furniture does not. I've never heard him comment on whether he likes making conference tables but his demeanor speaks for itself. Always grim. The jokes and smiles have disappeared. He arrives, does his job, and then goes home.

The firing of Eduardo brings his failings into sharp focus, but I have to take some responsibility as well. I have done a very poor job of managing Steve. His resistance to any interaction with me has kept me away from him, but I have not put any effort into teaching him what I think a manager should do, nor made much comment on his style of running the shop. I have been lazy, or intimidated, or maybe overwhelmed by my other duties. And now I face the consequences.

First thing: I decide that this is not going to be Steve's last day. But I still need to talk to him. I send Emma out to find him, and he arrives a few minutes later. He sits and looks at me, silent.

"I just fired Eduardo." No reaction. "He was falsifying his time sheets." Silence. "Apparently this was brought to your attention? And you did nothing?"

He shrugs and replies, "I was busy." Pause. "Getting work done."

Now I'm getting angry. "Do you realize that in any other company, you would be fired for this? You are in charge out there and you ignored an incident of theft? I should fire you right now." I wait for a few seconds, but he just stares at me. Unbelievable, but, as usual, I fill in the silence.

"I'm not going to fire you today. I'd love to, but I have to take some responsibility for your weakness as a manager. I never told you what to do when something like this happens. I didn't think I would need to tell you, but apparently I do, so it's on me. So here's what you do: you have a problem you don't want to deal with, just bring it to me. It's not so hard. I have to be the one to fire someone anyway. From now on, when you have an issue, I want to hear about it. You got that?"

His only reply: "Yes." Then he sits like a stone.

"OK, we're done here," I tell him. He stands, turns, and heads back to his bench without a backward glance.

My thought as he walks away: Why didn't I fire him? Why not do it and deal with the consequences? Do I need him that much? Maybe. Probably. I don't actually know. What happens if he's gone? How does that affect our deliveries? Who will replace him? Can I run the shop myself? Can one of the other guys step in? Or am I just being weak? Why do I always let this guy get away with disrespect? Why didn't I give him a better speech? You did the right thing—don't act out of anger. You're a fool—taking the blame for his failures.

I'm furious with myself for losing control of the situation, for being such a coward, furious with Steve for his attitude, with Eduardo for being so stupid and causing all this mess. And it's not even noon. For the rest of the day I can't unsee the look on Eduardo's face when he realized he'd been caught. What would I do if it were me? How would I explain it to my family? Would I even go home? I've never been fired. Could I wake up tomorrow and start looking for a job? Was I too harsh? What else could I do? My pity is accompanied by a less compassionate line of reasoning. Eduardo has done me a favor. He adjusted my workforce to fit a falling sales scenario. Our biweekly payroll will drop about fifteen hundred dollars, but over the course of the year it will yield about twenty-five thousand in savings.

The next morning, I steel myself and ask Steve who will be building bases. I don't mention Eduardo. I just want to put yesterday's mess behind me. Steve tells me that he's going to have Will Krieger do it. That's a good decision. Will is very fast, and his bench is right next to Eduardo's, so he'll be able to jump right into the work. Since I agree with the choice, I say nothing more. Steve has already turned back to the project he's working on. It's like nothing happened.

AT THE MEETING on Monday, I go over the numbers, then I pause. I need to say a few words about Eduardo. I've been dreading this moment all weekend. Here goes nothing: "Some of you may have noticed that Eduardo hasn't been in for a few days, and you might have heard what happened. Eduardo was fired for falsifying his time sheets. Honestly, I didn't expect this from him. I don't know why he did it. I don't care why he did it. When I find out that someone is stealing from me, I will fire that person on the spot." I look at everyone—everyone's paying attention, even Steve. "Falsifying your time sheet is stealing from me, and stealing from all of us. If we're spending money on payroll and not getting work done in return, it weakens the company. It makes it harder for me to pay the rest of you, and to pay my bills. Not a good thing. I'd like to thank the guys who brought this to my attention. You did the right thing. I want this company to provide for all of us, and to do that, we can't have thieves here." I pause, trying to figure out how to wrap this up. "I don't think, with this crew of guys, that we will have this problem again. I hope not. If we do, I'll fire that person, too." Speaking off the cuff is not going well. I'm not finding a way to turn this into an inspirational address. "Anyway, we all have work to do. That's the meeting." It's the worst pep talk I've ever given. I turn and walk away. One of my special powers as boss: when I stop talking and leave, the meeting is always over. And the flip side is that when I go, I can't see what I'm walking away from. I'll never know what my people really think about Eduardo. I hope that I did the right thing.

AFTER LUNCH I take a break from spreadsheets and e-mails and go out to the shop. Ron Dedrick has started building the Eurofurn prototype table. All the parts have been cut on our CNC, and he is gluing a strip of solid walnut to one of the top pieces. As I anticipated, this is a very complicated clamp setup. Ron sets each clamp in position, then tightens the screw handle to just the perfect amount of pressure. When he's done, I ask him how long it took. "With prep for clamping? That took a good hour. Milling walnut took about half an hour. This is the second top blank, and it went better than the first. The edge on the first cracked and I had to rip it off and start over. All morning, and I just have two done." I take a good look at the first top piece, which is still in clamps. It's going to take him much of the day to do this operation. I saw a machine at Eurofurn do a similar operation in a couple of minutes. I should qualify that statement. A machine that Jens told me cost $740,000 did it in a couple of minutes. And if I borrowed the money to buy that machine and paid it back over time? Ron is still cheaper, per hour. For that much money, I can employ Ron for more than fifteen years. And he can switch from one type of product to another very easily, and make sure that the wood on every one is beautifully arranged. What he can't do is turn out hundreds of tops a day. If we need to build tops that fast, I'll have to find a better method than the one he's using right now.

Over the next couple of days, Ron completes the prototype. The removable panel in the base is very tricky. It needs to fit precisely into the opening in the base. Even a tiny fraction of an inch too wide, the latches won't work. Ron completes it in two days after the top is finished.

My shop drawings show a hole in this panel that can be used to get a grip on it. Without the hole, there's no indication that the panel comes off, and no place to grip and pull it. Ron has cut the panel to exactly the right size. He has mounted the hardware and pressed the panel in place. Then he comes to get me. All three panels—two permanently glued, one removable—present a smooth, unbroken surface. No gaps anywhere between the panels and the solid pieces that make up the sharper corners of the base. A triumph of craftsmanship. But I can't tell which panel will open. The hole at the top of the removable panel is invisible unless I get down on my knees to look for it. Hmmm. Nobody is going to do that. You should be able to look at this base from a standing position and, at a glance, know what to do and how to do it. I ask Ron how well the latches work. He smirks. "Try it." I have to put a lot of oomph in exactly the right place to pop the panel off. And when it finally releases, I have been pulling so hard that I nearly fall over backward. Ron's smiling with his special "this is a stupid design, even though I built it perfectly" face.

"OK, we need to make this easier to operate. I'll get Andy to find different hardware. I want enough of a gap to show that the panel is removable. And we can add a notch to the base behind the panel so that we can get fingers behind it to pull. That should do it." These modifications make it much easier to remove the panel. It would work even better with another hole or a knob at the bottom of the panel, but that will clutter up the clean surfaces that Eurofurn loves.

The hatches that cover the power/data ports on the tabletop are also problematic. In Germany, they use a small, sleek, precise hinge and have custom machines to cut the special holes required. Those hinge cutters cost fifteen hundred dollars each, and you need two of them to cut left and right holes. The hinges we've chosen don't require special equipment and they are invisible when the hatch is closed, giving us that very clean, very sleek Eurofurn look. But when opened, the hinges are quite prominent. Our solution isn't as elegant as the German hinges, but we've shown what we intend to do in our shop drawings. And they approved the design. Ron builds these hatches exactly as shown in the drawings. They work fine.

I'm tired of paying good money to rent a PT Cruiser, so on Thursday I head to a local Toyota dealer—I'll call them Automall Toyota. I got an online quote for a Prius at five hundred dollars under list price, but the dealer that sent me that quote is a hundred miles away. I thought that I'd stop by Automall and see whether they would match it. My experience is a stark contrast to Urban Toyota. A receptionist greets me immediately and a salesman is at my side within a minute. He's about my age, about my height, slim and professional looking. His name is Steve. I tell him that I want to see the big Prius. He returns with keys within three minutes. Once we are in the car, he insists on going over the controls and draws my attention to three buttons between the two front seats that change the driving mode. Driving mode? Yes, this car can transform instantly from an eco-friendly fuel sipper to a howling rocket sled, with an intermediate step in between. We head off in the eco mode, and I recognize the sluggish golf cart that I drove the week before. Steve leans over and punches the power-mode button, and suddenly it's an entirely different car. It handles a steep highway on-ramp without difficulty. We take it out onto the local expressway and it drives very well.

Back in the showroom, I pull out my price quote. "Here's an offer from WayFarAway Toyota, for the car at $27,100. I'd rather not drive a hundred miles, so if you can match this, I'll write you a check right now." Steve checks with the manager, and a couple of minutes later, he's back with the paperwork. Deal.

Automall Toyota seemed to know exactly how I wanted to shop: they clearly explained the product, showed some flexibility on the price, didn't waste my time, and got my money. I picked up my new car the next day. Could I have gotten an even better price? Maybe. But I like to buy things, enjoy them, and not look back. I'm still wondering why Urban Toyota didn't seem interested in my business. Oh well, their loss.

My sister solves the minivan problem. She's selling her 2009 Sienna. My nephew is just starting college, and she can't handle tuition bills and a car payment at the same time. She wants $14,000. Done. Solving my car problem cost me $44,000. I still have $34,000 to live on for the rest of the year. As long as Peter doesn't start college in the fall, I'll be OK.

MY MONTHLY VISTAGE meeting falls on Tuesday, May 15. We all start the session at a whiteboard, giving scores for both our personal life and business prospects. We're using a scale from 1 (suicidal) to 10 (euphoric). I can give myself a reasonable personal score, but how should I rate my business?

It's a tough question. I'm trying to organize an unruly set of facts into a coherent story. This narrative needs to be both an assessment and a prediction, combining recent events with what I think will come next. I have all kinds of material to work with, but my mind returns consistently to a number of distressing trends. Inquiries seem to be drying up. Halfway through May, and we have booked just $71,321 in new orders. We stand at $787,550 for the year, far behind my target of $900,000 for this date. The Germans think I'm special, but they also told me that Europe is suffering from a dismal economy. And the newspapers tell me that the United States might be headed for another recession. We sell to a very wide range of customers, and every day Google tells me that thousands of people search for our product. Where are they? Who are the people who might have clicked, might have called, might have bought, but didn't? What changed their minds? Am I about to become victim to another crash? As in 2008, I don't have a lot of money on hand, and can't expect much more in the near future. I don't have a pipeline full of orders. I survived the last crash by laying off workers and cutting everyone else's pay. I'm not sure that I have the stomach to go through it again, and I'm not sure that we'll survive another down cycle. I rate my business prospects: three out of ten. My score is by far the lowest one on the board.

We're all sitting around one large table. Ed Curry asks each person to give a brief statement about the score they have given themselves, adding whatever detail they wish. As it happens, I'm one of the last to speak. Business scores for everyone else range from seven to nine. Orders are coming in. Nobody else is crying doom or seeing sales slowing down. When it's my turn, I give a recap of my situation and explain my theory that, as a broad indicator of business confidence and activity, my business is the canary in a coal mine. Inquiries are falling because fewer people are shopping. Sales are falling because those who do shop are choosing cheaper options. Everyone's pulling back on spending. Get ready! Rough water ahead!

No heads are nodding in agreement. Keith DiMarino, who owns

a company that stores and shreds documents, raises his hand. Over the months, his advice has been blunt but intelligent and on point. "Let's start with one thing," he says. "Whatever is going on here is your fault. You did something. I don't want to hear any more whining about the big world collapsing and poor me being a victim. I don't see it. Nobody else sees it. *You* have done something to make things slow down. Even if your story is true, and we're all doomed, it doesn't matter. You have to fix it. It's your problem. You. Stop complaining and get started." This is not what I want to hear, but nobody else has different advice. Further discussion focuses on what I might have done to mess up my marketing. I don't know what to tell them. I haven't made any changes since early March. Our Web marketing is working fine—page views are steady, within the same range that they have been for the last year. But incoming calls and sales are collapsing.

As I leave, Sam Saxton pulls me aside. "You have to call my sales guy. He'll help you. Just call him, have a meeting, see what you think." I remember that Sam had urged me at the last meeting to call the consultant, but somehow, between Germany and everything else, I haven't done it. I've never hired a consultant before. But Keith told me to start fixing things. The next morning, I call Bob Waks. We arrange for him to come out to the shop on the twenty-third.

I don't find time to look at my marketing until Saturday. On the weekends, the shop and office are quiet. I want to think everything through, and this requires focus.

OUR MARKETING EFFORT, in its entirety, consists of four interacting efforts. First is product development, the group of things that we offer for sale. Second: the Web site, which presents our offerings to the world. Third: Google, both free search results and AdWords, which directs people to our Web site. Fourth: the sales department, which responds to each inquiry with a proposal. I've made no changes to this overall structure since 2009, when I launched a new Web site. So if I did something to degrade our marketing, it must have been on a smaller scale. So which effort is the most variable? Where should I start looking?

The problem is that I've tinkered with all of them for years. I constantly develop new table designs, photograph them, and put them up on the Web. Google makes note of these changes in some mysterious way and then shows our site in a better or worse position. We have settled on a basic game plan to respond to incoming calls, but Nick, Dan, and I each have different design ideas, writing skills, and graphic sensibilities. I don't always have time to review what they send out. And nobody looks over my shoulder. Any one of us could be losing sales without knowing why.

I decide to start with Google. I have access to enormous amounts of data, in both AdWords, which looks at my paid search results, and in Google Analytics, which looks at all aspects of site performance. I log in and start looking through both sites. They are bewildering. Google's interface allows me to examine every possible aspect of my campaigns in multiple ways. There are statistics, graphs, change records, hundreds of links to rearrange the view this way and that, pop-up screens with more information, little warnings and suggestions, modeling tools to game alternate scenarios, et cetera, et cetera. If there's a malfunction hiding in all that, it's not obvious where and what it might be.

AdWords serves my ads each day, at a wide range of costs for each click, until my daily budget—$450—runs out. It's not clear exactly what time that will happen, as the cost of each click is dependent on a bunch of variables. Google shows my ads about sixty-five hundred times a day, and from that we are getting about a hundred clicks. Only a couple of the clickers contact us—our average for the past two weeks has been two calls a day. A year ago, the same inputs were producing 3.2 calls a day, and our sales were much better. Nothing I can see tells me what's different this time.

I have fifty-eight ad groups, each serving a different ad tailored to a set of similar keywords, 403 in all. Each of these ad groups behaves differently. Some get a lot of traffic, but a very low percentage of viewers click my ad. Some are the opposite. I can't tell which ad groups prompt the most calls, e-mails, and sales. When I've asked people which ad they saw initially, nobody seems to remember. And since we don't sell directly from the Web site, the answer to this question isn't in any of this data. I can see that I'm spending a lot of money on clicks and that this seems to be producing the same number of views and clicks as it did a year ago. And yet our calls and sales are dropping. Why?

I spend a couple of hours clicking this way and that, getting more and more frustrated. There is only one consistent message from Google, delivered in a variety of ways: I should be spending more money. I am missing clicks that are available with a larger daily budget.

What to do? If I make a bunch of changes at once, I won't be able to tell which ones worked. And I could make things worse. I don't put much stock in the messages recommending an increased spend. Of course Google would say that. It's their business. If they were really trying to help me, the interface would be more user-friendly. They seem to be drowning me in facts without providing any way to make sense of it all. I head back home, still worrying.

MONDAY ARRIVES AND I give another honest/discouraging speech. It's a repeat of the past two weeks: sales slow, cash disappearing, but we aren't out of work yet, so keep going as fast as you can. After lunch, I receive a curious phone call from an office furniture dealer in California named Jim. "I've got your proposal for Cali Heavy Industries here," he says. This is Dan's job, the one his contact at Cali Heavy told him we were getting. Jim tells me, "I really like what you guys have done in this proposal and I want to find out more about your company." I tell Jim our story, and he says, "I love this. We could use somebody like you. The big manufacturers can't handle really large custom tables. I get stuff like that all the time, and I have to pass on it." He promises to be back in touch if any of his projects include custom work. This could be another outlet for us, like Eurofurn, but we wouldn't have to copy another company's style. We could do our own work, our own way, and just sell more of it. The dealer would get a healthy cut, but if they were selling a huge amount of other furniture at their normal prices, they might accept a smaller markup on the custom jobs, so that they can offer a spectacular table as an extra incentive to their customers. This could work out well. Between Eurofurn and dealers, I could decrease my reliance on Google.

Dan's happy, too. "I've done a ton of work for Cali Heavy. I just sent them complete plans of our table. My guy says the purchase order is coming any day now." He's been saying that for more than a month, but sometimes it takes these big companies a while to do the paperwork.

AFTER EVERYONE HAS LEFT on Monday, I log in to AdWords again. Inquiries have slowed to a trickle: twelve last week, eight the week before. Then I take another look at my Google budget, the maximum amount of money that they can take from me each day. I determine this amount, along with the ad schedule. I run my ads from eight a.m. to ten p.m. Eastern time, so that they are showing on the West Coast after the end of their business day. Google shows the ad when it receives a search string that it thinks is a good match for one of the keywords I have chosen, and charges me if somebody clicks on the ad. The cost for each click varies, depending on how much I offer to pay for it, how much other advertisers want to pay Google to show their ads, and whether Google thinks my content is a good match for the original query. When the summed cost of all the clicks I receive each day exceeds my budget amount, Google stops showing my ads.

Like Saturday, Google is telling me that my budget is too low. They promise that spending more money brings in more clicks. They have a helpful tool where I can punch in different daily budgets and see how many clicks they think I will get. For instance, it might cost me five hundred dollars to get a thousand clicks, a thousand dollars to get fifteen hundred clicks, and two thousand dollars to reach 1,750 clicks.

Google tells me that I could be getting hundreds more clicks per day if I bump my daily budget up to seven hundred dollars. But the additional clicks may not be of sufficient quality to result in additional sales. AdWords doesn't promise that they will come at the end of the day from some previously untapped group of eager table purchasers on the West Coast, just that I will get more of them throughout the day. So who are the extra clickers? I presume they come because Google shows my ads to more people, even when the search strings aren't such a good match for my keyword. Some number of viewers will click on anything, often by accident. That doesn't mean that they have any interest in buying a big conference table. Google's definition of a success is a click. They have no way of knowing if I make a sale from that click or not. Because I've always had concerns about whether more spending will actually get me more income, I've set my daily budgets at numbers that I feel I can afford, which is about 30 percent less than Google's maximum recommended amount. That worked fine for years. But now, maybe, it doesn't. So I decide to roll the dice and do what Google has been nagging me to do. I increase my daily spend from $450 to $650. That should get me 90 percent or more of the available clicks each day.

THE NEXT MORNING Nick has bad news. The Air Force job in Virginia has gone to another company. Forty thousand dollars that we had been counting on. I sympathize: "Those assholes," and ask the obvious question: "What happened?" He tells me that he has had a bad feeling ever since he went on the site visit.

"It was a big meeting, with a bunch of companies. They showed a slide show of what they wanted—it was the proposal I sent them with our name removed. I thought it was a lock for us. After the meeting, I went to introduce myself to the officer who presented. He was standing out in the hall, talking to a guy from another company. They were laughing and joking, and they kept going on and on, so eventually I left."

"You drove twelve hours to the meeting and back and you didn't even talk to them?"

"I've been e-mailing them proposals for months. They know who I am."

"You should have talked to them so they would put a face on all those e-mails."

"Yeah, I probably should have. I thought we had this one for sure, though. They kept telling me how awesome the designs were and thanking me for doing all that work."

"Give them a call, see what happened."

Later Nick tells me that he'd heard back from the guy: our price was too high. On the Air Force contracting Web site, I see that the job went to the outfit whose salesman had been joking with the officer. The winning price was three hundred below our bid. We'd sent pricing along with our proposals, and the officer probably showed it to the company they really wanted to work with. We've been played.

The next day we ship the three Eurofurn orders that we received in early March. We haven't received any new requests for quotes since I came back, so we only have to finish and deliver the prototype table. I presume that their sales are slow, just like ours. Or maybe they are waiting to see the prototype before committing to more orders.

At three-thirty, I have my appointment with Bob Waks, the sales consultant. He has a couple of inches on me, and I'm 6-foot-1. Blue blazer, golf shirt, tan slacks, tasseled loafers. Leather briefcase. Silver hair, neatly trimmed. Firm handshake. Laser-beam eye contact. "We finally meet! Sam has told me so much about you." I take him out to the shop floor for a tour. Bob shows polite interest and then asks to see the sales office. He meets Dan, Nick, and Emma, and I show him a couple of proposals. Again, a polite but muted response. I'm expecting him to be amazed by our software models; I'm a little insulted by his lack of enthusiasm. We retire to my private office for further conversation.

"Why am I here?" is his first question. I describe our situation: falling inquiries, falling sales. I don't know why the inquiries are drying up. I'm not sure what's happening with sales. I've been through dry patches before, and they always corrected themselves eventually, but I'm afraid that this is going to be an especially rough ride. I'm almost out of work, and I can see that my cash will dry up soon as well. I tell him that Sam Saxton thinks he can help me. I hope that Sam's right.

"I'm not sure that I can," is his surprising response. "I'm a little worried about you. Whether we are a good fit together. Guys like you can be good to work with, or very, very bad. You are a classic boss, Paul. You make quick decisions, and that's good. I don't have to fight my way through layers of an organization to get to the decision maker. If Paul Downs says it's a go, it's a go. The problem is when I tell you something you don't like. You might agree or you might fight me. If you fight me, we're wasting each other's time. I don't need the hassle. I have lots of customers. And I can see that Downs is a smart guy, you can think on your feet, and you can talk your way into anything." Yup, that's me. "But you aren't going to like what I'm going to show you about how your sales 'organization' isn't working. Your first instinct will be to figure out how I'm wrong about you. Then you'll start fighting me. Pushing back. Telling me how I've got it wrong."

I think about this for a second. It's true that I make quick decisions and that I'm used to having my own way. And that I can debate with the best of them. All my employees know this and never argue with me about anything. If I feel like it, I explain my decisions. If I don't, I don't. I'm not used to any push-back. Sometimes I wish I did get a fight from my workers. I know that they are smart people. They must have some good ideas. I must be wrong fairly often, or my business would make more money. But they don't challenge me. Am I that intimidating? Possibly. I think that this is why I was interested in joining Vistage—to get someone to criticize me when I needed it. And this is why I called Bob. I want someone to take a hard look at how we sell.

At the same time, I'm not so sure that Bob Waks is the right guy. He is the classic salesman—tall, groomed, confident, articulate, and he gives off a sales-y vibe. Ice to Eskimos. Anything goes to close a deal. There's nothing to dislike about him—he seems like a very

friendly, smart guy—but he's 100 percent sales. And this rubs me
the wrong way a little bit. I'm used to selling a thing, and I close the
deal by making the thing so good that it speaks for itself. No fancy
double-talk required. We are craftsmen, and we fade into the background as soon as the job is completed.

I have to put my prejudice aside. I have Sam Saxton's testimony
that Bob is effective, and his numbers back that up. I want my sales
problem fixed. I don't know whether Bob is the solution, but I have
to try something. So I reply, "It's true that I make quick decisions.
It's true that I push back when I'm challenged. So what? That's who
I am. I'm also good at change. And so are my people. We don't get
hung up on yesterday, because yesterday usually sucked. I'm willing to take criticism. And I believe Sam when he says that you are
good. So let's presume that I'll be good to work with and that you
will help. What's the next step? What do you actually do? When can
we start? And how much will it cost?"

Bob tells me that he's going to need a couple of days to put together a recommendation and a contract, but he'd like to set up the
meeting to review them now. Am I available next week? I'm going
to be in the Middle East the following week, but we set a date for
Thursday, the thirty-first. I think I've been maneuvered into doing
something, and I don't like that. On the other hand, I'm heading in
the direction that I wanted to go. I have nothing to complain about,
other than a vague sense that I haven't been in control.

On Monday, after another dismal set of numbers, I tell the crew
that I'm doing everything that I can think of to turn things around.
I tell them about increasing the AdWords budget and the consultant. After the meeting, I ask Dan and Nick whether any of their
clients are likely to place orders this week. They don't know, but
promise to reach out to the most likely prospects. They are busy
with outbound e-mails all morning.

Discouraging replies start arriving after lunch. The worst is from Cali Heavy Industries. Dan thought that it was a lock. Now Dan's contact writes, "We have chosen another vendor to move forward with this project. Thanks for your hard work and good luck in the future." I call Jim, the dealer. He's "in a meeting." Send him an e-mail. No response. That's a thirty-five-thousand-dollar job, gone. Add that to the forty thousand in Air Force work, and we could have been in much better shape for May.

Thursday is the last day of May. First thing in the morning, I go over to Bob Waks's office. His coy protest that he might not be able to help has been replaced with a multi-level plan of attack. First, evaluations. The fact that I have been making sales for twenty-six years notwithstanding, I will need to take a series of tests to see whether I am psychologically suited for the job. Dan and Nick will take the same one. It's called DiSC Profile and is commonly used in business. I've never heard of it. I will also take another set of tests to evaluate our company sales practices and culture and my own performance as sales manager. Sales manager? Is that what I do? I never thought of my job that way. Bob will also come out to our office to observe us at work, so that he can better understand how we approach our job.

After the evaluations, training. Dan, Nick, and I will take a ten-week course on the basics of the Sandler method of selling. I haven't heard of this either. I didn't realize that selling comes in different systems, but it makes perfect sense. Every company makes sales and wants to make more. And some people are bound to develop a theory of how it should be done.

During the training, and continuing on for the next twelve months, we will also receive two monthly counseling sessions with Bob himself. These sessions will allow us to discuss the ongoing development of our skills and to get help with challenges that come up.

It takes about an hour for Bob to go through this. In the end, I have one more question: how much? For the whole package, $37,000. Holy smokes. On the other hand, I could continue doing what I'm doing, even though it isn't working well. Sam saw his sales rise by 40 percent in the first year after the training, and he attributed all that to Bob's work. If my sales rise 40 percent, I will have an additional $800,000 coming in the door. Spending $37,000 for that result is a bargain. I have to pay Bob $8,000 right away and the rest in monthly payments of $2,416.

The eight grand is 8 percent of my working capital. The payments don't seem that bad. I ask Bob if I can put it on a credit card, and he says yes. That will help—I can give him the deposit, wait thirty days before I have to pony up cash, and retain the option of rolling the card balance if I'm still short on funds. I can't do that for very long, but it will give me some time to see whether the program is working.

I asked Bob whether he would be willing to include Emma for the same price. She's smart, and I want her to keep our clients' point of view in mind. Nick, Dan, and I have a lot to win or lose, and that might cloud our perception of what we are being taught. Also, if the rest of us go through the program, she would be the only person in the sales office who hasn't learned the new methods and the new lingo. I don't want to have to explain it all to her while we are learning it ourselves.

Bob agrees and I sign the contract. I decide that I'm going to approach it with an open mind and do my best to learn something. After lunch, I give Dan and Nick an overview of the training and the cost. They look very worried. "This worked great for Sam Saxton," I say, "and I'm sure it's going to work for us. Look, I just bet thirty-seven thousand dollars that we can be better at selling than we are now. Sam's sales jumped forty percent. If we sell forty percent more than last year . . ." I take them through the calculations I've performed to convince myself that this is a good idea. I need them to buy into the program or it will be an expensive waste of everybody's time.

At the end of the day I take stock of the month. As usual, there's no clear message to be assembled from the jumble of data and events. Things that seemed important at the beginning of May have faded in my rearview mirror and been replaced by fresh concerns.

The numbers for the month are mostly bad. Total sales: $114,042. We shipped the Company S job back to them on the first, and they paid me what they owed in the middle of the month. Inquiries for the past four weeks have been consistently terrible: eleven per week. Increasing my AdWords budget has bought us more clicks, but so far they haven't translated into more calls. It's also been another month of low build totals: $137,086 moved from the shop floor into the finishing room. If that's all we have to ship next month, we're in trouble. Surprisingly, our cash position did not deteriorate. I started the month with $105,203 on hand, took in $182,594, and spent $175,113. That means an increase of $7,481. Stopping my own pay made a difference. I will end the month with $112,684 on hand. At our current rate of spending, that's enough to operate the shop for fifteen working days.

An increase in cash is better than the alternative, but it doesn't mean that all is well. I'm still down $24,470 from the beginning of the year. And I need to figure out why cash held steady and whether it can be sustained. Four factors are working in my favor. First, we shipped a lot of the jobs that we sold in January and February, with a total value of $198,496. That effort yielded $91,035 in preship and final payments. Some of these jobs had been sitting for a month or more, waiting for the client to get the site ready. And a few have been ready to go since last year. The shipment total, being higher than the amount we spent, results in a theoretical profit for the month of $23,383. Not all of that magically appears in my bank account, but it's better than a loss.

Second, we booked the deposits for the last sales of April in May because I deposited $27,418 on the afternoon of Monday, April 30. Third, one client surprised me by paying for an entire job up-front. That table cost $24,111. We had been expecting a check for $12,506.50, and instead we got one for $25,557.66—the table plus 6 percent sales tax. I won't need to pay the sales tax until the middle of the month after we deliver, so we got a nice thirteen-thousand-dollar loan from a customer without even asking.

The last factor is easy to overlook. May 2012 had twenty-two working days. The extra days can make a difference when there's a thin line between good numbers and bad. We shipped two jobs worth $15,833 on the last day of the month, which helped to boost the month's numbers at the expense of June's totals. Overall, my month has been puzzling. I'm doing everything I can to fix things, but I don't know if I am doing the right things or if any of them will work.

JUNE

DATE: FRIDAY, JUNE 1, 2012

BANK BALANCE: $107,096.18

CASH RELATIVE TO START OF YEAR ("NET CASH"): -$30,058.14

NEW-CONTRACT VALUE, YEAR-TO-DATE: $803,722

I come in early on Friday. There's an e-mail from Bob Waks with a link to the personality test and sales self-assessment. He says these will provide an objective measure of how I am performing. He ends with a warning: answer the questions honestly, or you are wasting your time and money. OK, I think, an unbiased evaluation would be useful. My visits with Sam Saxton and my strolls through the Eurofurn factory have been eye-openers. I'd like to know how my sales efforts measure up. I've never taken a personality test before. The questions don't quite make sense. I come to the conclusion that there are no right or wrong answers, just choices. It's liberating. I rip through the questions and press Send. Now for the sales self-assessment.

There are two sections: one about selling, and another about being a sales manager. The first questions aren't hard:

Do you know how to generate leads?

Yeah. Pay and pray. I give Google a ton of cash for the top AdWords spots and hope they show my organic results in a good position as well. And it's been working great, at least until recently.

Do you know how many potential jobs are in the pipeline?

I'm keeping a tally of the leads that come in, and about half of them get proposals.

After a few more process-oriented questions, they take a different tack:

Do you want to succeed?

Of course. I'm sick of failure. Who doesn't want to succeed?

Have you written down a list of your goals?

No, why would I? I just want to sell more; do I need other goals? I have a million e-mails to do every day; I don't have time to write anything down.

Do you control your own emotions and behavior?

Absolutely. At least in front of my employees. And my wife and kids. Keep it all inside, locked down tight. I have to be strong.

How do you make major purchases yourself?

I do some research, make my choice, and slap my money down on the counter. Is there a better way to shop?

What is your definition of "a lot" of money? A hundred? A thousand? More?

I'm spending eight grand every day, selling tables that can

cost fifty thousand dollars. A hundred dollars is a rounding error. It's what the scrap in one trashcan costs me. A thousand dollars? Not much. A hundred thousand is a good pile of cheddar. A million dollars is a lot of money.

Do you have a system for selling?

Yup. Write a great proposal. Put a bunch of them out there, and some will come back.

Do you track your selling activity every day?

Nope. I'm sitting in a small office with Nick and Dan, so I know what's going on.

When do you send a proposal?

As soon as I can! I want to put my info into my client's hands before my competitors can even raise their pencils. The buyers always say how impressed they are by our speed. I'm sure we'll score highly on this question—we can hardly do any better.

Do you know whether the person you are dealing with is a decision maker?

Sometimes, when they tell me. And I can always tell when it's a boss on the other end of the line. But the others? We'll give anyone a proposal, so that they can pass it up their chain of command.

Are you sympathetic toward your clients?

Sure, they're nice people, mostly, and they want us to help them. Sometimes they get to be irritating—Eurofurn—but that's just the way it is.

Do you want your clients' approval?

Who doesn't? Having them disapprove is hardly the path to success.

Are you willing to accept their excuses for delaying a decision or ending the project?

Sure. What else can I do?

Do you try to get them to make a decision?

Not really. Our proposals speak for themselves. If they appreciate good work, they'll realize that we're the guys to go with.

What do you tell yourself when a sale is lost? Do you blame external factors or accept responsibility?

Well, the economy has been pretty bad the past few years, and it looks like it might be getting worse again. And our product is good, our prices are fair. We're doing the best we can. We're not the cheapest guys around, and so we can't be a good fit for everyone. Sometimes it's just not meant to be. Everything I'm doing has worked for years; we're just going through a bad patch right now.

Do you hold regular sales meetings?

Like, sit-down-with-an-agenda-and-watch-the-boss-bloviate meetings? Why bother? We're all in the same room. It's like a continuous meeting already.

Do you provide coaching and feedback for your salespeople after every proposal?

I should definitely do that. I told the guys to cc me on

every proposal they send, and they've been pretty good about it. I don't always have time to look through them, though.

Are you a good listener?

Of course I am. I have a unique ability: I can listen to a person talking to me and type an e-mail at the same time. It's the only way I can get work done when my workers keep interrupting me. And I'm considerate. If they start to tell me something, and I'm still thinking about something else, I'll very nicely ask them to start over.

Do you constantly look for new salespeople?

You mean someone who understands how to make our product, and knows our software, and can zip through a couple proposals a day? They aren't out there. It was enough trouble to get Nick and Dan up to speed. I don't have time to start that process over.

Do you use reasonable hiring criteria when choosing salespeople?

I think so. Nick was the only guy working for me who could talk on the phone, so he was the obvious choice. Dan had dealt with clients in his previous job, maybe not selling, but at least he had spoken to them. And he showed up at the right time.

Do you need approval from your salespeople?

Like letting them veto decisions I make about the company? Or are you asking whether I feel good when they respect me? I'm not sure what this means. But I don't think those guys see the big picture, and I don't have time to explain everything to them before I make my mind up. So no, I guess not.

Do you accept mediocrity from your salespeople?

Look, sales is chancy. Success and failure come in clumps. I don't know why those guys can't make a sale every day; it's probably the same reason I can't make a sale every day, not that I actually know why that is. I don't like picking up the slack when they don't sell, but that's what the boss has to do sometimes. And what am I going to do anyway, fire one of those guys?

Have you ever fired a salesperson for poor performance?

I've only had two salespeople. I'm not sure that Dan has what it takes, but firing him would be pretty harsh.

Why not?

This question isn't on the test, but the other questions lead me directly to it. Dan is lagging way behind Nick in sales. He hasn't even passed the two hundred thousand mark, and we're almost halfway through the year. I was hoping for at least eight hundred thousand from him by December, but it looks like I'm not going to get it.

I submit the results. Dan and Nick have just rolled in. I don't feel like discussing the test with them—the line of questioning has been disturbing, to say the least. I e-mail them the link to their own assessments, asking them to complete them as soon as possible. As for my own test, I wonder how I'll score. It's strange to answer a bunch of questions about how I do my job and whether I'm heading in the right direction. I'm not used to being challenged in this way.

SATURDAY EVENING I FLY to Dubai, which is the last thing I want to be doing, not least because the trip will cost more than four thousand dollars. I arrive on Sunday afternoon. I have three meetings on Monday in Dubai. In the evening, I fly to Kuwait City, where I have four meetings on Tuesday and one on Wednesday morning. After lunch, I'll fly back to Dubai to catch an early-evening flight home.

That's a lot of meetings, especially considering that I'm not sure whom I'll be meeting or whether the PowerPoint I have prepared will be impressive. I hope that my client list will be enough to show that we're legitimate.

I'm also painfully aware of my company's limitations. We're not large, we're not profitable, and the business seems to be collapsing. How can I be confident that I'll survive long enough for this effort to pay off? How do I walk up to strangers, shake hands, and make a convincing promise of a prosperous and profitable future? I have no choice. I'll put my problems at the back of my mind. I'll just do it.

The next morning, I meet Bahar O'Brien. She's my Commerce Department contact in Dubai and she'll be accompanying me all day. She's cordial but reserved. Just her tone of voice is enough to put me in my place: today's American businessman, come to Dubai in search of riches. And, she seems to imply, not a particularly impressive specimen. Now I'm wondering about my suit—a summer-weight wool affair, in an attractive sand color, perfect for the Middle East. Or so the salesman had assured me back in Philadelphia.

Our first meeting is at the Al Reyami Group, a local conglomerate that does a little bit of everything, including design and construction. When we arrive, our contact doesn't remember making the appointment, but he tells us he has twenty minutes. I pull out my laptop and start the show. The first slides show the table we made for the World Bank, an enormous oval forty feet long and twenty-four feet wide. One picture shows the finance ministers of the G20 countries sitting around it. Instant credibility. Our contact leans back in his chair with a smile. "I think we have something for you. I need to check with my boss. Give me a minute." He's back in five and takes us to see the head of the design department. I run through the slides again, and he calls one of their project managers. Twenty minutes later, we meet him and two designers. He tells me that they are renovating the local office of a multi-national petroleum company that I'll call BigOil, and that the client wants a very large boardroom table. By chance, they are having a meeting to discuss this at two p.m. Can I attend? Absolutely. I never expected a shot at an actual project on this trip. Home run on the first pitch.

The second stop is an architectural firm. The receptionist takes us to their boardroom, which is dominated by a large walnut table. We could have made it. I'm on my knees examining its underside when my hosts walk in. I scramble to my feet and shake hands with the firm's owner and his general manager. After my slide show, they comment, "Very nice work. We could have kept you really busy ten years ago. Now there's not much going on. The recession is still bad. We're barely surviving ourselves." Why did they take a meeting with me? Curiosity: they've designed a lot of boardrooms and wanted to see somebody else's approach. We chat, and I learn more about the local market. Nobody in the area specializes in boardroom tables. The local custom furniture market is dominated by much larger firms that offer a full range of products, from upholstered furniture to wall paneling. They promise to contact me if a job turns up, but I don't think I'll hear from them again.

Our last stop is half an hour away. During the drive, Bahar

confirms that Dubai's boom has passed. We drive by stubs of roads that terminate in empty desert and the skeletons of partially completed structures covered in dust. Bahar's descriptions are a variation on a theme: "This was supposed to be a [luxury shopping mall, luxury hotel, luxury international business hub], but the owners went broke." Even so, we pass small gangs of workers, their heads wrapped so that only their eyes are visible. The forecast today is for a high of 115 degrees. And it's not a dry heat. They wear pants and long-sleeve shirts, buttoned to the wrist. I wonder what brought them here. I've heard that local pay is, by my standards, abysmal. If working in a foreign country under a broiling sun for peanuts looks like a good idea, the other choices must be truly awful.

Our third meeting is in a strip mall. It's a store selling residential furniture, but there's no one visible inside. In a back office, we find a middle-age man leafing through a magazine. Bahar tells him that she's arranged to see Mr. Bubbedin. Unfortunately, Mr. Bubbedin has gone to Chicago. Would this gentleman like to see my presentation? He shrugs. I rip through the slides. He compliments me in a perfunctory way and tells me that I should have been here ten years ago. It was crazy back then, money flowing like water. I take his card, but there's nothing for me here.

We return to Al Reyami, and in their boardroom we meet representatives from BigOil, Al Reyami, an interior design firm, and the audiovisual equipment contractor. The project manager announces to everyone that they have found someone from America to build the table. I run through the PowerPoint and show them a nifty 3-D model of the World Bank table. Then we start discussing details. The schedule is a potential problem. They'd like delivery in late August but it is already the first week of June. (Shipping from America to Dubai takes about thirty days.) But nobody seems too worried about schedule, so we move to other technical issues. We close by agreeing that I will prepare a complete design after I get back home.

As I'm leaving, the project manager introduces me to a young man who has been sitting quietly in a corner. I'll call him The Manager. He is in charge of Al Reyami's woodworking facility, which builds custom furniture and millwork, including all Al Reyami's conference tables. We will be direct competitors for this job. The meeting was set up for him to present his own ideas for the table, but he was never asked to speak. I apologize to him for taking the limelight. He is very gracious and says that he is quite impressed with my work.

With a few hours to kill before flying to Kuwait, I ask The Manager whether he would be willing to show me his factory. I half expect him to say no, since a tour will reveal the strengths and weaknesses of his work, but he's flattered to be asked and says that we can go there immediately.

The factory is thirty minutes away. The Manager arrives just ahead of us and dashes inside. We scurry from our car after him— every second in the blazing sun is torture. The office we arrive at is tightly packed with cubicles, each with multiple workers. The Manager explains, "Engineering staff area. All are working on projects." I ask The Manager how many workers he has, and he tells me about two hundred, give or take a few. Two hundred! That's a pretty big operation. He tells me that he has 3,750 square meters, about 40,000 square feet. My own shop is 33,000 square feet. I have fifteen workers. Sam's factory, similar in size to Al Reyami's, has thirty-six workers.

He runs through a long list of their products: millwork (woodwork that is attached to a building, like custom paneling, doors, and

trim), furniture (chairs, accessory pieces, and cabinets, some upholstered), and tables (dining and conference). It would be tough to find
a comparable operation in America, producing such a wide range of
products under one roof. Our factories tend to be much more specialized. If someone asked me for upholstered work, I would sub it
to an upholstery shop, and they would send table work to me. This
specialization means that my workers get really good at a narrow
range of tasks, which helps amortize the cost of their training. It's
difficult to make money in America if your workers are switching
gears all the time. They can never develop a competitive level of
skill and efficiency. So you must compensate with low wages, which
don't buy you a worker who knows several trades. It just doesn't
work.

The Manager's workers all come from India and are hired on a
contract basis. He pays a competent bench hand about a dollar an
hour. A typical skilled cabinetmaker in the northeastern United
States will make about forty-five hundred dollars a month, not including taxes and benefits. For that money, I could hire at least ten
decent Indian laborers. I currently have five bench cabinetmakers, who together (should) build between $180,000 and $200,000 a
month worth of product. Replace them with fifty good guys for the
same price and we'd churn out huge amounts of work.

We arrive at a balcony looking down on the main shop floor, a
space as large as my entire shop.

I can see many workbenches, relatively few machines, and a lot
of guys out there. I count them: forty-six workers visible. There
might be more, as I can't see all the first floor. Compare that to how
many people I have in a comparable area: five. The Manager tells me
that they're producing all the furniture and millwork for an em-
bassy in Ghana. We descend to the shop floor. It's easily 100 degrees

there. Many workers have towels wrapped around their heads to catch sweat. They move at the measured pace of workers accustomed to a long day of physical labor.

The machinery is simple and cheap but of decent quality. The number of tools I see is maybe a third of what's on my shop floor, and they have at least forty-six workers, and we have only five. I have multiple copies of all my tools so that none of my people have to waste a second waiting for someone to complete an operation. My yearly labor cost would buy me a new shop full of tools every six months, so having extra machine capacity is well worth it to me.

Their work quality is good, but they're doing it in a different way than we would. They're using cardboard templates, and all the parts are being hand cut and assembled. We used to do things this way ten years ago, before we got our CNC machine. This factory doesn't have one.

I notice that lots of workers are just standing around, doing nothing, generally near someone who is doing work. Are they apprentices? Helpers? I give the phenomenon a name: the Stand-Around Guy. An example: three workers surround one who is cutting a part with a hand saw. As the end of the part swings near them, the Stand-Around Guys gently touch it, as if to steady it. When it moves away, they drop their hands back to their sides. They're pantomiming real work, adding no value whatsoever. Sometimes the ratio of primary worker to Stand-Around Guys is astonishing. I see six guys using a jointer to trim a panel that weighs less than a hundred pounds. One worker could do this, but in my shop, our CNC machine would cut the panel to exactly the right size, and the whole operation would be unnecessary.

We pass through different areas: assembly, sanding, finishing, a carving station, and an upholstery shop. I see Stand-Around Guys everywhere. I also see some very skilled workers—one guy is cutting intricate veneer patterns with a knife (we use a fifty-five-thousand-dollar laser to do this), and another is carving beautiful flowers (we buy carvings from Indonesia). The upholsterers are doing a nice job, and the finish on the furniture pieces is of good quality.

I can't ask The Manager why so many of his guys are unproductive—it's kind of a rude question. I'm also afraid to ask whether this factory is profitable. I have one number to consider: The Manager told me that he'd charge about thirty-three thousand dollars for the BigOil table. We can make it for about forty-five thousand, but it will be a very different product. With our CNC cut parts, assembly and installation will be much faster and easier. The Manager's table will require a lot of fussy handwork. Before we got our CNC, we had spent huge amounts of time fitting top pieces to each other. After we got the CNC, our time for making complex tabletops dropped by more than 40 percent. Adding a sophisticated sanding machine dropped build time another 20 percent.

It's time to go. We thank The Manager and leave. What a nice guy. I would hire him in a second. Instead, I have to compete with him. His willingness to show me his operation tells me two things: first, that he's proud of it, and second, that he's not worried about me as a competitor. He has some huge advantages. He's local, so he doesn't have to sprint to meet the deadline. And he'll be around after delivery to take care of any problems.

On the way to the airport, I consider what I would do if I were running his factory. I'd identify the fifty most productive guys, double their wages, fire the rest, and spend two-thirds of the money saved on better machinery. That sounds pretty brutal, but it's what has happened in every factory in America—the ones still operating, that is. The alternative for American managers is to take production overseas. And many of them have done that.

The Manager was a smart guy, so he must be aware of the

American manufacturing paradigm: buy fancy machines, use skilled workers, and operate with as few of them as you can. Why doesn't he do it this way? One advantage of his model is lower initial investment. His machines didn't cost much. And he can lay his guys off whenever he feels like it, cutting his operating costs drastically. That's a nice option for riding out slow patches, as long as he's sure of getting a new set of workers whenever he needs them. He told me that his guys get their training in India and that there's no shortage of people with the skills he needs.

Another thing his model has over ours: lots and lots of jobs. His factory gives two hundred workers a place to go every morning, a way to feed their family, and the pride of making good work. I would guess that the Stand-Around Guys are his B- and C-level performers, who wait for the moment the factory needs a large number of workers, irrespective of their skills. What does the future hold for B- and C-level workers in America? I don't have any on my shop floor. And the next generation of robots may take out all my A-minus guys, too. The end point of our trajectory is the elimination of people in factories. My biggest marketing struggle is convincing people that our product, which incorporates a lot of hand labor, is worth the extra money. I could come up with tables that require less labor, and sell them for less money. They would be crappy and cheap. A lot of companies have already taken that route, so I'd be entering a mature market where my product is a commodity. Without very deep pockets, I can't compete that way.

I'M IN MY HOTEL in Kuwait at midnight, but too jet-lagged to sleep. At eight-thirty a.m., I meet my minder from the Commerce Department in Kuwait. He's a short, cheerful man named Fordham Mathai. He was born in Kuwait to Indian parents, which means he is forever barred from Kuwaiti citizenship. He's a great admirer and now employee of the United States of America. In contrast to Bahar O'Brien, he's delighted to see me and makes me feel confident that I will succeed. Over breakfast, he reviews our schedule. The firm whose inquiry started my odyssey, back in February, is missing. Fordham says that he could not establish whether they are reputable, so he has left them off the list. Not to worry; he has found many companies eager to meet me.

Approaching Kuwait City from the south, I see its striking, futuristic skyline. We pass a commercial district that Fordham tells me dates to the 1960s. Companies selling similar goods are clustered together: tire shops, auto repair, fabrics, vegetables. It's a pattern that predates the Internet and presumes that all shopping is done in person. Customers can walk away from one deal and quickly find another. Merchants live and work as neighbors and agree on appropriate price ranges. It works as long as they all have similar costs and are selling to local people. When I started my business, there were several similar districts in Philadelphia. North Third Street was dominated by machinery dealers, and South Fourth Street had a long row of fabric dealers. The Internet and rising real estate prices decimated both clusters. Suddenly these businesses were forced to compete across a national market. Machinery is pretty much a commodity— one can buy the same tool from any number of dealers. The ones who prospered mastered the Internet, carried large inventories, and had easy highway access. The Philadelphia businesses were stuck with cramped, expensive real estate, in a neighborhood that couldn't accommodate full-size tractor-trailers. They couldn't carry enough inventory, and shipping was difficult and expensive. Only a single sandpaper supplier remains on North Third, surrounded now by boutiques and coffee shops. I know the owners well, and they've told me that they're still alive because they own the building, they got a

Web site up early, and their product is small enough to ship by UPS. The fabric dealers have put up a better fight, because people still want to put their hands on material before they buy. And bolts of fabric are easy to ship, and a lot of inventory can be placed in a small space. But the dealer that I favored, Brood & Sons, closed up when the two brothers got too old to work and couldn't find a buyer. The fabric business relies on people who know how to sew. Why bother to make your own clothes when they come so cheap from Bangladesh? And why reupholster that sofa you got from Mom when you can spend less for a new one at IKEA?

We arrive at the first stop of the day: a high-end residential furniture dealer. The shop is filled with expensive furniture made by old, established American companies: dark woods, shiny finishes, lots of carving, brass work, overstuffed upholstery, and gilding. Very different from the spare, featureless look that architects love. Fordham and I are greeted by Kipson Jaja, the son of the founder. He serves us tea, and after pleasantries, I give him the spiel. When I finish, he sighs and tells me that I should have been here ten years ago. Back then, his company furnished the many new government buildings in Kuwait. Now that that work has been completed, he is furnishing only private homes. He promises to keep me in mind. More handshakes, promises to keep in touch, and we depart.

The next stop is in a run-down area dominated by auto body shops. Our target's store is filled with office furniture made in China. We are directed to a second-floor office. Inside we find the boss, a very busy man. He's got a lit cigarette in one hand, a cell phone in the other. Something is upsetting him, because he's yelling into the phone in Arabic. Seeing us hesitating at the door, he waves us in and points to a sofa. He ends the call with a curse, I presume, and snaps the phone shut. "I am Kamil," he declares, as if daring us to argue with him. "You. Sit there." He directs me to a low stool in front of his desk. I put my laptop on his desk, screen facing him, so that I have to bend over to advance the slides. I start my pitch, and he says nothing while he watches, furiously puffing on the cigarette. I've been presenting for maybe a minute when his secretary arrives with a thick sheaf of papers. She's stuffed into a tight skirt/ loose blouse combo. And she's no shrinking violet. She pays no attention to me or Fordham, but addresses Mr. K in a stream of Arabic, delivered in an angry tone of voice. She drops the papers onto his desk and starts pointing to places he needs to sign, while keeping up a rapid commentary. She's leaning over his shoulder, and I can see straight down her shirt. I stop my presentation, speechless. Kamil looks up from the papers and glares at me. "Keep going." So I do. He lights another cigarette. This pause brings the secretary's volume up another level. She has at least a hundred pages in her hand, and many need signatures. I decide to simply get through this as fast as possible. Then Kamil's phone rings again, and he holds it with his shoulder, yelling into it, while alternating more signatures with puffs on another cigarette. The secretary never stops talking, nor does she stand up. The view is unavoidable. The only cover she gets are the clouds of smoke that Kamil blows in my face.

When I finally reach my conclusion, Kamil points to the computer. "Go back to start. The World Bank table—how much?" I give him a very large number. It's a very large table. He scowls and says, "I can get that for a quarter of the price in China. Is all your work so high?" Well, no, I tell him, that was an exceptional job. "Go through slides again." He stops at a table we made for a company in Ohio that one might find in any office. "How much?" I give him the number. He scowls again. "You are too expensive for me. I can get any of this in China. I am done."

We head down the stairs in silence. I think to myself, If I can get through that, I can get through anything. Under the worst circumstances, I delivered my message and kept my dignity. I am a real sales professional.

On the way to our third meeting, Fordham tells me, "This gentleman is the top decorator in Kuwait. He has been around for many, many years. Clients are top, top families." We step off the elevator into a small, beautifully decorated office. The walls are covered with architectural renderings, done in pencil and tinted with watercolor. I was taught to do this kind of work in my architecture classes, back in the 1980s. Nobody does these anymore.

We're shown into the inner sanctum of our host, Mr. Akil. He's a short man, oldish, with bronzed skin and a magnificent head of silver hair. A stylish pink silk scarf nestles within his shirt collar. His shirt is open to the waist, revealing an expanse of silver fur to rival his head. A perfectly fitted blue sports jacket, gray slacks, and soft leather slippers completes the ensemble. A decorator, indeed.

I ask him who does his drawings. "Of course it is me who does them!" he says with a smile. "Nobody can draw like this except me!" I ask him whether he is busy. "No, not like ten years ago," he admits with a sigh. I ask whether he would like to see my work. A smile reappears. "Of course! Did you bring me a book?" I tell him no and pull out my computer. He frowns and asks again, "You don't have a book? All my suppliers give me a book." He pulls a beautifully bound volume, with the name of a prominent Italian manufacturer, from a shelf full of similar books. It's as large and thick as a high school yearbook. I open it and see hundreds of pages of exquisite photographs of upholstered furniture. "It is this year's book!" he exclaims, the very thought giving him pleasure. "They make another every year. I am the first in Kuwait to get the books." I apologize for not having a book with me and start showing him the slides. When I finish, he sighs. "You should have been here ten years ago, when they were building the government complex. That work is done now. But I might find some work for you. You must send me your book and I will do what I can." I tell him that I don't have a book. "Then you must make one. All the best companies have a book. You will see. With a book, the clients understand what they will get. Send me your book as soon as you have it done. I would like very much to have it." I make a half-hearted promise to start work on a book as soon as I get back.

In the elevator, I turn to Fordham. "Can you believe that, those books? That's really old-fashioned." Fordham smiles. Mr. Akil has made a good living with his books in Kuwait, and me—nothing so far. So it's something to consider. And reject. I used printed brochures before the Internet came along. And it was an incredible struggle to come up with something convincing. Photography, graphic design, printing: all expensive, all time-consuming. And immediately after printing, it's obsolete. You can't change a brochure. The story it tells is frozen at the moment of its creation. A Web site is so much better for us. Instant additions and subtractions, and we can get away with mediocre photography. We can update the text and prices. Potential clients can see it whenever and wherever they want. And it's been working for us. With limited resources, I don't want to dilute my efforts by returning to paper catalogues.

Driving to the next appointment, with a man I'll call The Sheik, I'm suddenly overcome with exhaustion. I doze until we arrive at a low, windowless building. Inside, there's a surprisingly fancy lobby with displays showing how The Sheik's grandfather launched an empire, bringing American-made lanterns to Kuwait. Seventy years later, the family runs a multi-billion dollar conglomerate, ranging from retail stores to pharmaceuticals to automobiles to building materials—all American.

Fordham decides to wait in the car and answer e-mails. I am

introduced to Kurtis Johnson, assistant to The Sheik. He's an American, ex-military, here since the Gulf War, and very friendly. I give him the show. Kurtis praises my work and then says, "I need to tell you what's going on here. I like your work, and I think the boss should see it, but it's not a good day today. My boss has a kind of difficult situation. He has a large family, many younger brothers and sisters. They don't participate in the company, but they all have shares, and they want to make sure the money keeps coming. Once a year they have a meeting. That's today. I'm not sure he'll be able to see you, but I'll go talk to him now."

Kurtis comes back a few minutes later. "He wants to meet you. Right now. Bring the computer." I follow him into a magnificent conference room, dominated by a gorgeous maple table. I'd be very proud if it came from my own workshop. Kurtis helps me connect my computer to the projector. After a few minutes, people start arriving, all youngish men dressed in robes. I am not introduced to anyone. Eventually the table is filled, except for one seat at the end. And then The Sheik walks in, beaming, hands outstretched to me in welcome. "It's an honor to meet you, come all the way just to see us!" He turns to the others. "This is Paul Downs, and his company makes very fine American furniture. He will show us his work. Pay attention." I launch into my show, pleased at such a respectful welcome from such a wealthy and powerful man.

At the end he exclaims, "Magnificent work! Why have I never heard of your company before?" I tell him that we are small and specialized, and give him a very short version of how Google found us and how we became conference table makers. "That's fascinating. So what do you want from me? How can we work together?" I tell him that I hope he will call me when one of his projects requires a very special table, of unusual size or design. He replies, "There are two difficulties. First, you should have been here ten years ago, when the government was building. We had so many contracts then that we could not keep up. We could have kept you very, very busy. The second problem is that I have my own workshops, and they do all this work for us. This table here. Do you like it?" I tell him that it is superb, the whole room is stunning. "Thank you. Now, I would like to help you. If you could send Kurtis some of your marketing materials—your brochures, your samples, whatever you have—we can see what happens." I promise that I will get some to him. And then I give him one of the little trivets that we made to give to the people I meet. It's nice, but not grand. The Sheik reacts as if I just handed him an enormous diamond. He thanks me profusely and announces to the room that this will be a useful addition to his wife's kitchen. Then he shakes my hand again and sweeps out of the room.

Kurtis and I spend the rest of the afternoon touring some of The Sheik's furniture stores. At each we're greeted by nervous store managers, and my opinion is solicited on all aspects of running a store, even though I know nothing about it.

Back in the car, late in the afternoon, I give Fordham a brief recap of the encounter, and he's very surprised that I met The Sheik. "He is a very important man, very busy. It is an honor for you." Given the amount of time that Kurtis spent with me, I think that they were trying to figure out exactly who I am, and they erred on the side of respect in case I turned out to be a good potential partner.

Back at the hotel, I eat a stunningly expensive meal and contemplate the day's events. Can I be a good partner for any of the companies I have visited? They seem to think I am something that I'm not: a much larger company that can provide all the sales support that comes with size—printed materials, samples, and sustained attention from me. I don't think I can come up with any of those things without making a serious investment in time and money. Which, if the rest of my business disappears, I may have to do. But it's obvious that the boom days in the Middle East are over and that I would be competing with local companies that have plenty of capacity and are a safer bet for a local buyer.

At ten the next morning, Fordham and I head off to our meeting near the airport. I show my slides to the owner, Mr. Jabril, who represents a prominent American furniture manufacturer. He compliments my work and lists the problems he has getting custom work from his current company. They aren't nimble, and their engineering on custom jobs is subpar. On the other hand, their standard products are decent and a good value for his market. He asks about my prices, and I repeat the show, with numbers this time. Jabril tells me the same thing I've heard everywhere: "You really should have been here ten years ago. I would like to use you, but I don't have anything right now. If you can send me your brochures and your catalogue, I can start passing them out when we make sales calls. For now, you should probably go to Saudi Arabia and Oman. There's still a lot of work there."

At the airport I give Fordham a hug in thanks for all he has done. Kuwait has been a whirlwind, and Fordham has been a pleasant and enthusiastic companion. He did his best to put me in front of decent companies. He's a credit to the Commerce Department.

TWENTY-TWO HOURS OF FLYING and airports: utter hell. I don't reach my house until midday Thursday, and instead of collapsing in bed, which I'm dying to do, I get my suit back on and have lunch with my family and my parents. It's graduation day. Peter has completed high school. Naturally, everyone wants to hear about my trip, so I try to describe some of the highlights. But I never did anything very touristy, so I stick with "I met a lot of nice people, and there's some work there, but it will take a lot of commitment from me to get it. I don't know whether it was worth it or not."

It's a proud moment when my son gets his diploma, made bittersweet because his twin brother is not there. Nancy and I debated whether to bring Henry home for the evening, but we decided against it. He'd get nothing out of the experience, and it would be impossible for us to relax and focus our attention on Peter. Next Sunday, he'll fly to San Francisco to begin his job.

We get back to our house in the early evening, and I have to excuse myself and go to bed. It's been a week of very little sleep and I'm collapsing. Friday morning I decide to stay home for the rest of the day. I'm still exhausted, and I can feel a tickle in my throat—a little parting gift from a fellow traveler. One e-mail to work, telling them that I'll see them on Monday, and that's it.

On Saturday, I go out to the shop and find it dark and silent, unchanged while I had my adventure. No, wait. It looks much worse than usual. The trashcans are overflowing, the dust bags on each machine are full, and scrap and dust cover the floor. What happened? I have a worker just to sweep and empty the trash: Jésus Moreno, who comes from—Mexico? I don't actually know. Wherever he hails from, he's an incredibly hard worker, and he's done a good job so far. I'll have to sort this out on Monday.

In my office I contemplate the results of a twenty-thousand-mile quest: a dozen business cards. I enter every contact into our database and send each an e-mail thanking them for their time. After some thought, I decide to tell them that we're working on printed materials and will have them ready by the end of July, and I promise to keep in touch. I write to Shiva, the interior designer for the BigOil project, my point of contact going forward. My message: I'd like to start designing, but I need their final decision as to how many people they want to sit and a measured drawing of the room. I ask her to forward those documents immediately.

ON MONDAY, I steel myself and deliver another dismal sales report. We had only ten calls while I was gone and didn't book many orders, either. Nick sold a job worth $9,742, and Dan sold two: one to a small ad agency for $5,765, and another worth $4,224 to Eurofurn, for some uninteresting painted panels. It's not the tsunami of veneered tabletops that I was hoping for. The total, $19,731, is far behind our target of $50,000 a week. We've missed our numbers again. There's a ripple of dissatisfaction from the production workers. They know that the sales team are the highest paid people in the company, and I can feel the questions in their minds: why do they get away with continuous failure? It's a great question, one that I don't want to answer because I'm not ready for a civil war between sales and the rest of the shop. I try to end on a positive note. I tell them why I have increased the budget for AdWords, and that I'm sure we'll see some results soon. And that I've just signed up the sales team for training. I take them through the logic of it, starting with Sam Saxton's results. I finish by saying that the Middle East visit went well and that I even came back with a live prospect that might produce a sizable order.

After the meeting, I ask Bob Foote about the mess in the shop. "Where's Jésus? I didn't see him at the meeting. Do you know what happened?" Bob was on vacation last week. He says, "He's not in yet, but I don't know why. Should I call Simba?"

Simba is the person who employs Jésus, who isn't actually on our payroll. It's an odd arrangement, driven by the fact it's been much harder for me to hire low-wage workers than high-wage workers. My low-wage jobs are low-skilled, implying that many people should be available. But that pool of workers contains a lot of people with problems—and an even larger group of people who are capable of advancing to better jobs, who leave as soon as they can. Businesses that rely on low-skilled labor must have strong supervision and a rigid system of rules and oversight. And they need to hire and fire constantly. None of my skilled workers needs to be treated this way, so we don't have such a system. In the absence of said system, the hiring and firing lands on me. And I hate it, and don't have time for it. What I need is a low-skilled worker who is content to perform a simple, repetitive job, without much supervision, for years on end.

My previous sweepers have been of the "too smart for the job" variety. Bob Foote, for instance, started with a broom, and now he runs my shipping department. Eduardo was the sweeper for a couple of years, but I could see that he had potential and moved him to the bench. I have, on occasion, hired high school students, and they always end up leaving for an easier job or college, even when I pay them twelve or thirteen dollars an hour.

If we don't have a sweeper, Steve Maturin has the whole crew clean the shop. This takes everyone thirty to forty-five minutes, a loss of at least six hundred dollars in production, three days a week. That's $93,600 each year. A ten-dollar-per-hour worker costs me about $27,500 in wages and taxes each year and will clean every day. It's a no-brainer.

Last fall, I tried a different route to filling the sweeper job. There's a factory downstairs from us with about a hundred employees. A van pulls up to the building every morning and disgorges a load of workers, usually a mix of Asian ladies and Hispanic men. I asked the owner how she found her low-skilled staff, and she directed me to her shop manager, Carl. He introduced me to Simba, the van driver. A young Asian guy, he owns an employment service that leases workers. This is a common way to get temporary employees. Some businesses do this with all their workers, to avoid the complexity of HR and taxes.

Simba provides documentation that all his people are legally eligible to work in the United States, and in return he receives a cut of their wages. He'd be happy to set me up with a good worker, he said. He would charge me thirteen dollars an hour, including all taxes. What was I looking for? I told him that I wanted someone who is physically strong, works hard all day, has good English, and is smart. Simba promised to deliver this paragon the next morning. So that's how we got Jésus. He didn't actually speak English, but he did everything else on my list. He followed directions and was an incredibly hard worker. He seemed very happy to be working indoors for a company that treated him like a human being. I didn't worry about him at all, and Bob Foote liked him a lot. He was perfect. Almost. Jésus has a tendency to disappear now and then, and we can never figure out when this will happen, or what causes it. Simba, when we call him, will say only that Jésus will be back soon and offers another worker if we need one immediately. We tried that once but didn't like the new guy, and we told Simba that we'd rather wait for Jésus to reappear.

I told Bob Foote to call Simba, and he soon returns with the story. "I talked to Simba, and he said that Jésus is hurt or something and that he won't be back for a while. Like, months. He didn't say it happened here, so I guess it's something else." We're both thinking the same thing: good that it's not our fault, but it sucks that we won't have Jésus for a while. "Do you want me to call Simba and ask for a replacement?" I tell Bob I need to think about it. Meanwhile, Steve Maturin should have the whole crew do the cleanup. Just like when I fired Eduardo, I can't help but do some quick math: thirteen dollars an hour, $520 a week, $27,040 a year. And one less person to worry about. I've been thinking about matching our labor supply to our reduced workload for the last month, and now two of my guys just laid themselves off. This gives me a little more cash on hand and delays the day that we run through our whole backlog.

I go back to the office and find a bunch of e-mails from Dubai and Kuwait. Mr. Kipson Jaja eagerly awaits my printed materials so that he can start showing my work to customers. Ditto from Jabril and The Sheik. In response to my request for drawings, Shiva says they haven't finalized anything yet; she'll send them when she has them. This is a little worrisome, given the short schedule. I sign the checks that were written last week and look at what money came in. We received $47,511 and spent $56,548. My bank balance stands at $98,059. Two-and-a-half, maybe three weeks of operating funds. But all the money everyone owes me comes to only $56,136.

ON THURSDAY MORNING, we put together the Eurofurn show-room table for a final inspection. Ron Dedrick has done a nice job:

Bob Foote breaks the table down, wraps each piece in a moving blanket, and heads off to New York. The next morning, I find an e-mail from Nigel in my in-box:

Hi Paul,

Bob installed the VC table today and I would like to bring a few issues to your attention.

1. *The removable base panels have a very large gap on each side.*
2. *The removable base panels are loose at the bottom and rattle easily.*
3. *The solid wood edging has inconsistent color.*
4. *Gaps on the data lids are overlarge.*

I have attached some images of the above-mentioned issues. I would also like to show you this in person and discuss some other areas of concern with the table. When would you be able to make a trip up to the showroom? We have some clients visiting the showroom next week and I would like to resolve this urgently.

I'm furious. His list complains of details required to make the table function properly, except for number three—an inconsistent color is an inherent feature of walnut, the wood they chose. In fact, it's what makes the wood beautiful. It's Friday morning; do they expect me to somehow fix all this over a weekend? Are they really unwilling to show my work to a client? I'm so mad, I turn to other projects to calm down. Then I think, Get over yourself. They're being unreasonable, but you need to work with these people. You need money. Remember Nigel's promise of a million dollars in the first year? Even a quarter of that would be huge. Think of that. When I finally call Nigel, he is very cordial, but insistent: he wants me to come get the table, ASAP. I agree to drive up tomorrow morning.

Saturday, seven a.m. Midtown is quiet. Nigel is on the loading dock with the disassembled table. He hands me a list with twenty-two changes he wants to make. Most are very minor adjustments to something that was described in the shop drawings and approved. Some are changes to the actual dimensions—the top a little rounder, the gaps in the lids reduced to one millimeter. Others are about how we executed the design, in particular the amount of sanding. A freshly machined piece of wood has edges sharp enough to cut flesh, so we round them over to make them smooth and friendly. This is all done by hand. It's not something that you put into the drawings; it's a decision that happens on the shop floor. Nigel wants a sharper look to the edges and corners.

I'm stung by the rejection of a perfectly good table. This has never happened to me before. All the things that we do to make sure a customer knows what he will be receiving—the SketchUp models, the shop drawings, the finish samples, the photographs of similar pieces, the interactions with the salesperson—are designed to prevent what just happened. And they have always worked, including our other jobs for Eurofurn.

I explain our choices to Nigel. He agrees that the decisions we made are sensible, but he doesn't like the look. I tell him that the only way to make all his changes is to start over again. He shrugs. Will Eurofurn pay us for that? No. I should look at it as an investment in our relationship. He's got me. I don't want to walk away. I need customers. So I agree to take the table back and start a new one.

MONDAY. I'm sitting in my office, trying to figure out what to tell the crew. Today is June 18. If we had hit our target, we would have booked $126,000 in new orders. Our total so far: $28,503. The inquiry stream holds no promise, either. Last week we got thirteen calls, but six were garbage. The others are the usual grab bag: three from military units, which have a long procurement process; two from schools, ditto; and two from private companies that might be able to make a decision quickly. A fast order or two would be greatly appreciated. Our backlog is below four weeks.

I fought a gallant battle to limit spending last week. I wrote checks totaling $14,653, but we received only one payment: a deposit check for $4,032. We're down $10,621 for the week, $49,716 for the year. I have $87,438 in the bank, less than three weeks of operating funds, and another $34,000 in my personal accounts. If we don't get some cash soon, we'll run out of money before we run out of work.

I have continued to announce our sales figures and cash position each week. I think I should keep on doing this, even though they are terrible, because a sudden stop would be even more alarming. Nobody benefits when management lets wild rumors circulate. The stress leads to wasted time and sloppy work. I need the guys to continue to produce as fast as they can, without errors. We cannot afford rework. We collect cash when we deliver well-made tables to happy clients. None of our customers knows anything about our troubles. They're looking forward to receiving their tables, admiring our craftsmanship, and paying us. Those payments delay the day that the doors close, and give us time for something good to happen.

But what if something good doesn't happen? The thought won't leave my mind, even as I stand up in front of the crew and go through the numbers. Everyone is sitting quietly, as usual, but paying close attention. I wrap up the summary of cash and sales, then pause. How should I say this?

"I think that everyone can see we are not heading in a good direction. I honestly don't know what is happening. All the things we"—I nod to Dan and Nick—"are doing have worked for years. I haven't changed anything big in AdWords. We just aren't getting good calls. And buyers seem afraid to pull the trigger."

I pause again. I haven't let my Monday speeches take such a negative tone before.

"Last time we were in this kind of trouble, in 2008, my partner kept me from telling everyone what was happening until we actually ran out of work. I swore that I would never do that again. So here's the truth. This is not a good situation. We are running out of work, and we are running short of cash. We're not done yet, but I can't pretend that it couldn't happen. I still can't believe that we'll actually have nothing to do. We haven't had a month with no sales since—I can't even remember. So jobs are going to come in. The question is, how do we slow down our operations? There are two ways to do it: everyone works less, and gets paid less, or a couple of people get laid off and the others keep working full time. Worst case, the full-time workers take a pay cut. That's what we did in 2008, and it sucked for everyone. But we survived, and I raised pay back up within a year. I'll tell you, also, that back then I cut my pay by twice as much as everyone else, and I was the lowest-paid worker in the shop. And this year, I've already stopped paying myself. I haven't had a check since April. But I can't promise that I can get us out of this myself. It doesn't save enough money. We may all have to share the pain."

Total silence. I just gave a speech that could prompt the best workers to start looking for other jobs immediately. I'll be left with only those too fearful to make a move until there is no other choice. Is there anything I can say that will prevent defections? Or maybe I'm being too negative? Can I expect loyalty in return for my honesty? I have little to lose.

"Here's what I need from all of you. I'd understand if some of you start looking for jobs. I can't stop you from doing that. But we're not dead yet. I need everyone to keep working, and I need the work to be good and the jobs to go out on time, and for us to get paid for the work on our books. If we do that, we have another month or so of money coming in. And another month might make all the difference. Dan and Nick and I are going to be getting special sales training starting in July. We always get a bunch of inquiries from the military in July and August; some of that is bound to come through. I have a project from Dubai that they need in a hurry. Eurofurn keeps sending us orders, and they have promised a lot more. Maybe the World Bank will call us again. I just can't believe that nobody will buy anymore. I've been through this so many times over the years. We're heading for disaster, just like a truck speeding toward a brick wall. I've found that the only thing to do is to keep the gas pedal hard to the floor, and every time, just before we hit it, the wall just vanishes. Something will happen. I'm sure of it." I pause again, looking around. No apparent reaction to my rousing conclusion. "OK, that's the meeting. Let's get back to work."

I'm heading back to the sales office when Ron Dedrick stops me. "That was a good speech. Thanks for telling us what's happening. I've been through this in other shops and it sucks when nobody tells you what's going on." I give him a confident smile, thank him, and assure him that we'll get out of our bind. "Yeah, maybe," he replies.

DAN, NICK, AND I settle down in front of our computers. I should be doing—what? Proposals? Revisions? Brochures? I've reached a state of perfect paralysis. No matter what I choose to do, I should probably be doing something else. And no choice is likely to lead to immediate success. And that drains any enthusiasm I have for doing anything. I need a distraction, but not a pure waste of time. I decide to see whether my increased AdWords budget has had any effect.

I've managed to stay away from AdWords for almost a month. Hopefully that's long enough to see a pattern in response to increased spending. Whatever Google's data shows, I know that the number of inquiries was worse than it was a year ago and worse than the beginning of the year. Looking at my spreadsheets, I can see that between January 1 and April 1, we averaged 16.23 inquiries per week. Between April 1 and May 20, when I bumped up the budget, that number had dropped to 12.38 per week. And after shoveling more money at Google? Over the past month it declined again, to 10.8 inquiries per week.

I log in to AdWords and see what Google thinks is happening. Since the beginning of the year, they have shown my ads 978,202 times. That's a huge number. Unfortunately, the viewers of those ads were largely indifferent to my messaging. We got 15,286 clicks— still a very large number of interested parties, but just 1.56 percent of the impressions. I hope that the people who clicked did so because they are eager to buy a table, since each click cost me $3.78, for a total of $57,781. But maybe they were just curious, or clicked by accident. How many of those clickers took the trouble to complete an inquiry through our Web site? Just sixty-five. How many of those sixty-five people actually bought something? I don't know, because some people just call us instead of submitting an inquiry through our site, and we don't know which of our buyers did which. I do know how many of my buyers reported finding us on the Web: forty-seven, whose orders total up to $668,816. That's 80.4 percent of our total sales, $831,777. All my other efforts to drum up work have not amounted to much. I really, really need AdWords to come through for me.

After an hour, I stumble upon a graph that appears to answer my questions. I am looking at the pattern of daily spend and daily clicks from January 1 to June 18. Since I don't buy ads on the weekends, the graph looks like a long line of haystacks in a flat field:

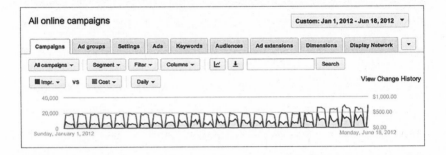

On the day I increased the budget, toward the right side of the graph, the number of impressions jumped up sharply from about six thousand to ten thousand. The highest totals come each Monday, and the highest total of all happened on the Monday after I increased the budget: 18,626 impressions. It's weird that the impressions drop off each week after Monday, with an occasional reversal, but always declining from a peak at the start of the week. That's not what I see in my records of incoming calls, which average 2.58 per day on Mondays, rise to 3.65 on Tuesday and 3.54 on Wednesday, and then drop back to 2.50 on Thursday and 2.55 on Friday. Hmmm. I rejigger the interface to show cost versus clicks:

It's the same pattern: more spend leads to more clicks, but those clicks decline throughout each week. I look at one last combination, costs versus the number of people who e-mail us an inquiry. These are called conversions:

This view corresponds to our reality. The increased spend didn't change the number of conversions, and the total for the past two months has been lower than it was at the beginning of the year. The increased spending hasn't done anything for us, yet. But why not? Google has delivered what it promised to do: more impressions, more clicks. But that isn't translating into calls and sales. What is happening? I'm stumped.

I hear a happy clap of hands from Nick. He has just closed a deal, worth $11,599, to a biotech company in Texas. Maybe this will be the start of a turnaround. At the end of the afternoon, he closes another deal, worth $8,063, to a school in New York City.

On Tuesday morning, Dan starts off with a small deal worth $3,380, for refinishing a table we built before the crash.

My first task is to deal with the Eurofurn prototype. I take Nigel's list of twenty-two changes to Andy Stahl. Leaving out my feelings of anger and humiliation, I tell him what happened on Saturday and ask him to make a revised set of shop drawings with all twenty-two changes. He completes them by mid-afternoon and sends them off.

As soon as Milosz approves the new design, which is almost identical to the old one, I take the drawings out to Ron Dedrick and go over them. He greets me with a wry smile. "Didn't go so smooth?" I sigh. He'll start the new table in the morning.

Later that day, Emma drops a thick envelope on my desk. It's the results from the sales aptitude tests. The package contains two items: a slim folder and a very thick binder, titled "Impact Analysis: Paul Downs Cabinetmakers." Inside the folder are two reports written by an outfit called Objective Management Group. The first is titled "Sales Manager's Self-Assessment for Paul Downs"; the second is called "Extended DiSC Personal Analysis Report: Downs, Paul." Thirty-nine pages devoted to sales management, and thirty-six pages all about me.

I riffle through both. Lots of colorful charts and graphs, a fair amount of text. Then I pick up the binder. It's divided into seven sections, totaling 284 pages. Charts, graphs, text, footnotes. I quickly page through it. My reaction is a mix of skepticism and fascination. Skepticism: this is just boilerplate ginned up to make a bulky pile that looks like it's worth the eight grand I've spent. Fascination: this is about me. Paul Downs. Hopefully, this is all focused on my business and my problems. It will be different from the coaching I've been getting from Ed Curry and my Vistage group, because it's objective, just based on our answers to the tests. My sessions with Ed are conversations, with all the limitations of any dialogue between two people. There's lots of stuff I don't want to talk about with him, and there's probably a lot in his mind that he wouldn't say to my face. This report is supposed to jump over those social boundaries and give me the truth.

I start reading the sales manager booklet. Its opening is in the form of a letter, with a bold-faced heading: "The Dave Kurlan Sales

Force Profile™." "Dear Paul," it begins. "Blah de blah de blah blah blah." I read paragraphs of what purports to be a personal letter to me, complete with Dave's signature. There's a heaviness to the prose, an inclusion of extra words, sentences, and paragraphs that extend the size and length of the document without adding much extra useful actionable information of any worth or impact at this time. And he keeps referring to me as the "sales manager." I'm not the sales manager. I'm the boss.

After finishing this letter, I'm drooping inside. I have to wade through hundreds of pages of this sewage? Did I just shell out all that dough for boilerplate? I answer my own question: you're in no position to reject advice. There's got to be something of value in this report. Now plant your butt in a chair and find it.

This doesn't happen while I'm at work—my day is swallowed by picayune administrative tasks. So I take the reports home. By midnight, I've read it all.

The first section, assessing my prowess as sales manager, bears bad news. I stink at this job. The long list of the things I'm doing wrong falls into two groups. First, we make a large number of tactical errors trying to close deals, beginning with my basic procedure of sending a proposal in response to every inquiry. And second, I don't manage my sales staff the way I should. Here the deficiencies are many and troubling: I am not constantly looking for new sales staff. I don't have a written sales plan. I don't ask my guys to keep records on each prospect. I don't make them document what they do all day, so I don't really know if they are being productive. I accept their excuses when deals disappear. I don't hold them accountable. I let them get away with failure, even though it's slowly killing us. I need to set standards and enforce them, and get rid of the people who can't cut it.

The sales manager assessment does nothing to bolster my confidence. But rather than weep in my beer, I move on. The next section is my personality profile. The premise of the DiSC assessment is that every person's personality is a mix of four different tendencies. "D" is for Dominance, a confident, competitive person who wants to get results and focuses on the bottom line in every situation. "I" is for Influence, a person who is concerned with persuading other people to go along with his plans, who values openness and maintains relationships well. "S" is for steadiness, a person who places emphasis on dependability, sincerity, and cooperation. And "C" is for Conscientiousness, a person who focuses on quality and accuracy, expertise and competence. It might as well be C for "Craftsman." In every person, one tendency will be primary and the others subordinate to a greater or lesser degree.

In each category, the report has given me a positive or negative score, ranging from +100 to -100. As you might expect, my Dominance score is highest, and I have positive Influence and Conscientiousness scores as well. My Steadiness score is negative 100. Yup, they pretty much nailed me. I do like to be in charge, and I don't like to work alone. And look at the work that I have chosen: a woodworker, who cannot be anything but Conscientious. A Craftsman. The test is correct about my weakness as well. I am not Steady. I don't enjoy routines or being part of a system. I am not a rule follower. I'd rather write them myself and get other people to follow my plan. And that is what being a boss is all about.

There are lots of detail about how my personality plays out in my business life. Specifics about things that I will enjoy doing and things that I will find difficult, and warnings about how my interactions might be perceived. I should listen carefully and explain my decisions to people. I can be inspiring if I want to be, but I can also leave others frustrated if they don't understand why I am doing what I am doing. Because I dislike routine, I might avoid creating systems for my business that will allow it to operate without my constant intervention.

The executive summary shows how my company's sales organization ranks compared to the typical company. Again, my sales management skills are non-existent and our selling skills are terrible. But I get a little encouragement—my salesmen have serious problems and it would be reasonable to fire them both, but they might also respond to training and succeed. The thing we do best is gathering leads. Our Internet efforts consistently bring in new inquiries. But the report is based, in part, on Dan's and Nick's perceptions of how our operation works, and I don't think that they understand that our AdWords campaign has stopped functioning.

The next section is stuffed with confusing charts and graphs, and points out Dan's, Nick's, and my failings in detail and at length. It boils down to: none of us knows what he is doing, and I don't hold them accountable when they fail. The next three sections detail those assertions and close with a summary of our strengths and weaknesses. My profile tells me that I am a good decision maker, have a strong self-image, control my emotions, don't give up, want to succeed, and have a realistic attitude toward money and buying. My weaknesses fall under two headings, my failures as a salesman and as a manager. As a manager, I accept mediocrity from my salespeople, I don't know how to hire, I don't replace my worst performers, I don't spend any time managing them, I jump in to salvage a sale instead of letting them learn from their mistakes, I don't have any idea what motivates them, I don't have any regular meetings to track progress, I don't coach them, and I don't do follow-ups to find out what happened when they fail. I'm still spending a lot of my day as a salesman, and here's how I'm screwing up that job: I don't follow any consistent sales process; I don't have any idea who I'm dealing with and whether they have the power to make a decision; I talk too much and listen too little; I'm vulnerable to lies my customers tell me; I don't know why my prospects want to buy; I don't try to get the prospects to agree to make a decision; I don't try to form a relationship with my prospects; I send proposals too soon; and even when I make a sale, I don't follow up or ask for referrals.

Dan and Nick have similar lists, but with a surprising twist. Dan is the most likely to succeed as a salesperson. Apparently Nick lacks motivation and isn't interested in money. I'm not sure I believe that, but I have to admit the report has painted an accurate picture of me; maybe it's uncovered hidden truths about Dan and Nick as well.

When I finish, I feel like I've been punched in the gut. My cavalier dismissal of the report has given way to a recognition that we have big problems and a long, long way to go to fix all of them. So now what? We'll do the training and give it all we've got. But will we survive long enough to complete the training if I don't make changes immediately?

What can I do, what can I do, what can I do? I'm riding my bike into work the next morning, and the question loops in time to my pedal strokes. About halfway through the ride, an answer appears: cut commissions, commissions, commissions. I can send Dan and Nick a strong message by keeping their portion of incoming payments. It's not a huge amount of dough—just 2 percent of the money that we get from sales—and they will still have their salary to live on.

By the time I arrive at the shop, I'm convinced that this is a great plan. But just in case I'm wrong, I review the numbers. I can see on my bank's Web site how much yesterday's payroll will cost: $23,606. We've received three payments this week, totaling just $14,234. I have $78,035 left in the bank. The payment on our credit card, $20,585, goes out tomorrow. After that, I'll have just $57,450. And

I have another pile of bills to send out on Friday, totaling $8,255. Once that's gone, I'll have $49,195. I look back at how much we've been spending per week since April 1: $38,086. So now I have less than two weeks of funds, unless I simply stop paying my bills.

My spreadsheet shows four incoming payments this week, totaling $18,077. Three of those four are final payments from jobs we shipped in May. The other is a deposit from a state university that placed an order in April. We'll probably get the first three, but the deposit payment might be delayed in the university's bureaucratic processes. Theoretically, no deposit should make me put the job on hold, but if I do that, the shop will run out of work sooner. After that, there's very little on the horizon. My total cash-to-come amount is just $50,751. But we won't see any of that until we finish those jobs, and that will take more than two weeks.

I check to see how much I have paid Dan and Nick in commission. Lately, it hasn't been much. In yesterday's paycheck, they each got $2,384 in base pay, pretax. Nick also received commissions totaling $464, again before taxes. Dan's commissions added just $97. These commissions aren't much compared to what they have already received this year. Nick's commissions total $9,145; Dan's sum up to $4,544. I paid myself commissions totaling $4,612 in the first quarter, but I haven't taken base pay or commissions since April. It's time for them to feel some of my pain.

I know from experience that announcing a pay cut is no fun. And this time, the pay reductions are not being shared equally by all workers. I just want to do something to put a little fear into the sales guys. Taking away their commission won't save much money; but every little bit counts when we have only two weeks of operating cash on hand. So I decide to emphasize the financial case for this action.

It's eight-thirty in the morning. Nick and Dan are working on projects. I ask them to stop for a moment and start with a question: "Anything coming in today?" Dan and Nick look at each other and shrug. Nope. I keep going. "OK, that sucks. Because we have a big problem. We're running out of cash. We're going to be down to fifty thousand dollars by the end of the week, and that's just enough to run for two weeks. I need to cut our expenses, right now." Nick is staring at me. Dan is frozen, and he's starting to turn red. He probably thinks I'm going to can him. I see his reaction and think to myself, No, Dan, I'm not going to fire you. When you see me set up a camera, and ask your permission to film the meeting, then you have reason for fear. But not today.

I announce my plan: "I've decided to cut out the commissions. As of right now. I need every penny of the incoming cash, so I'm stopping the two percent payments." Now Nick looks angry, and Dan sags with relief. I continue, "I haven't taken a paycheck or a commission payment since the beginning of April. And I just committed to spend thirty-seven thousand dollars to make us all better salesman. And"—now I tell a big lie—"I'm absolutely sure that the training is going to work, and we're going to come out of this. But I don't know how long it will take. Probably a couple of months. And I need to keep the doors open until then."

Nick asks a sensible question: "You're cutting commissions forever? How long are you going to keep doing this?" I don't know. I haven't really thought about it, because it seems more likely that we'll be out of business before I have to deal with that question. "I can't say. Until things get better. Until we make some sales. Until I can afford it." Dan asks, "What about our salaries? Are you going to cut that, too?" I tell them that I would prefer to avoid this, but if things get worse, it might happen. "So let's not let things get worse. Sell something. And when the training starts, put some effort into it. I'm committed to the program. Remember, it worked for Sam Saxton. I'm sure it's going to work for us." If we have anybody to pitch to. I've put the fear of God into the sales guys. But I haven't figured out where the customers have gone.

WE ALL SIT and start working again. There's an e-mail from Shiva in Dubai. Finally, the drawings from BigOil are here. I can see that the table is big enough to accommodate thirty-eight chairs. But there's no indication of the materials, the base, or even where the wires coming from the floor (or ceiling?) will go. I can't do anything with them. I have one other drawing that I was given at the first meeting. It purports to show the structure of the table. Like many drawings from architects, it shows something unbuildable, and the design doesn't even make sense. The base is far too small to support the top, and it's in the wrong position—nobody would be able to pull up to the table without hitting their knees. So I have two drawings from BigOil, but not what I need to make a proposal. Do they still want this table in Dubai by the end of August? If so, we have to build it by the middle of July. I e-mail Shiva, asking for the missing information. I'd love to get this job—it will be worth at least forty thousand dollars—but I'm stuck.

The next day there's a small reprieve. Hiding in the junk mail I find a check for $1,556. Whoopee! Enough money to run the shop for a couple of hours. Unfortunately, I just sent out bills totaling $8,255. I log in to AdWords again and stare at the same mess of links and data. The Web site won't even allow me to directly compare two time periods in the configuration I want to see them in. Should I stop the campaigns to save money? On the face of it, the $650 I'm chucking at Google every day is a waste. It's not producing anything for me. On the other hand, in all my other years in business, spending money on advertising has been a good investment. My sales have gone up every year except for 2009. I haven't made many changes to the campaign in the past two years, and we've seen steady growth in sales until very recently. But maybe this is the moment to stop spending money on the Internet, and let my organic search results do the heavy lifting. Am I wasting precious cash? The only way to find out would be to pause the campaigns and see what happens. But last July I got a call from a bank in Washington that led to a quarter million dollars in business before the end of 2013. One call. A quarter million. Did they pick up the phone because they saw my ad, or because they clicked the free link? And if I hadn't been running the ad? Would Google still give me good free results? They claim that there's no connection between the ads and the organic links, but that hardly seems credible. They're a business. If I were them, I'd give a boost to the Web sites that pay me money. I'm afraid that if I stop paying, my free links will drift down the page to obscurity, and then I'm out of business. I can't take the risk of losing a single customer right now. Cutting the ad spend will be the last thing I do.

WHILE I'M STARING at my screen, I think of a way to show what might have changed in the campaign over the past two months. With our wide-format printer, I print out screen shots showing the performance of all fifty-five ad groups on one piece of paper. Finally, I've found a way to see all the numbers at once. I print the six-month period from August 1, 2011, to February 29, 2012, when the AdWords campaign worked well, and the report from March 1 to June 20, when it's been failing. I tack them up on the wall outside my office. Each report is two feet wide and more than four feet long, and shows my fifty-five ad groups, each with fourteen associated data points. I start marking up the printouts, dividing one data point into another, and then comparing that to the same calculation from the earlier time period. Nothing jumps out at me. Finally, alone in the office at six p.m., I give up and go home.

Early the next morning, when I look again at the printouts, only two facts seem important: the Boardroom Table ad group, which was producing the most e-mails, has dropped off, and the Modular Tables group has had a big bump in traffic, but produces very few e-mails. Overall, more people see our ads, but the number of people who call has gone down. That fact isn't on these pages, but I have other records that document the decline. Is there something going on that isn't in any of my records?

When Dan and Nick arrive, I give them a brief summary of the numbers and argue that it makes no sense that more views should lead to fewer calls. Have they seen anything happening in the past three months? Dan says, "It seems like a lot of the calls lately have just been crap. A lot of people from schools and local government offices who don't have any money to spend. And I end up with some secretary who doesn't even know what's going on." Nick adds, "And we aren't getting so many calls from bosses, so it's harder to get a quick deal done." I've noticed that, too. Fewer company owners are placing an order after a twenty-minute chat.

We used to get a good number of those calls, generally late in the day. I'd often take them myself, as I'm the only one left in the office after five-thirty. They're the easiest sales we make—boss talking to boss, no nonsense, hammer it out. Where did they go? I've been assuming that the shaky economic news has made them more cautious about spending, but maybe I'm wrong. More calls from schools and governments, fewer calls from bosses with money to spend could explain why sales are falling. And why the inquiries have dropped to such low levels. But when I look at the sales from last summer,

I find that they were decent through April, May, June, and July. We sold to some schools, mostly universities, to some bosses, and to other kinds of buyers. It's hard to identify a common denominator except that they all showed up and spent money. It doesn't look anything like this year's debacle.

I check the mail on my way home. There are three checks, totaling $16,521, bringing my bank balance back up to $67,272. A small reprieve.

ON SATURDAY I pick up Henry from school. He'll be home for two weeks, then return for summer school, which lasts until the end of July. When he sees me, he jumps up with a smile on his face. He's grown another inch since April. Now he's at least 6-foot-4.

He's happy, rocking to the music as I drive home. On arrival, his mood changes. He jumps out of the car, slams the door, and bursts into tears. He's standing on the sidewalk, crying loudly. It's not something you hear very often—an eighteen-year-old boy wailing in despair at the top of his lungs. He approaches the house with an angry flounce to his step and then slams the front door behind him. I can hear his heavy stomping as he runs upstairs. There's another huge thud as he jumps into his bed, which is directly above the front porch. The whole house shakes, and the glass cover on the porch light falls and shatters into a million pieces.

I pick my way through the glass and go inside. I have no idea what set him off. "Henry's home!" is all I can say, as I open the closet to find a broom. Thirty minutes later, it's as if it never happened. He comes down to look for food, all smiles. Where did the raging monster go? Where did it come from? He can't tell us. We'll never know. All we can do is settle into the rhythm of meals, car rides, and listening while he blasts his music.

By Monday morning, I am in full Henry-Care Mode, which means I'm totally exhausted. I've been getting him up in the middle of the night to pee and then tossing and turning for hours thinking about the business. At nine a.m., I stand to address the troops. I simply give them the numbers. Five more days left this month, and so far we've only sold $53,050. We have $67,272 in the bank, about three weeks' worth of funds, and we have four weeks of work on hand. I try to summon up some cheer, but it isn't happening. "We're still alive. Keep working. That's the meeting."

I log in to our bank account and find a surprise—a payment from Eurofurn for $19,837.50. It turns out to cover seven orders—four final payments and three deposits. Thank you, Eurofurn! Later that morning, Milosz sends me an e-mail asking if I got the payment and asks about the rebuilt showroom table—is it complete? Almost, I reply. It's in the finishing room. Oh, that's bad, he writes. We wanted to change the size of the opening in the data port lid from three-quarter inches to eighteen millimeters. What the hell is he thinking? He signed off on a three-quarter-inch opening weeks ago. And the difference between what he approved and what he's asking for now is less than one millimeter. He has another question: what brand of hinges do we intend to use? I refer him to the drawings he approved. That he has a copy of. That he should be looking at, right now, to answer his own stupid question, because it's written right there. A few minutes later, he's back: he needs to consult with headquarters about the three-quarter-inch gap, to make sure it's OK. I don't answer this. He approved it, and we can't change it now.

In the mail I find two checks totaling $5,094, and in the afternoon, a client makes a final payment of $2,519. My cash on hand has risen to $94,722.

The next day I sell a table to a boss, who called in the morning, got my proposal after lunch, and gave me a credit card number at the end of the day for the $4,475 deposit. This is not a huge job, $8,950, but it's the first boss call I've had for a while. This sale brings our monthly total up to exactly $62,000. Four more days left, to sell either $138,000 to make our monthly target, or $334,785 to get back on track for the year.

We work on autopilot for the rest of the week. There isn't that much to do. The phone rings a few times, but the calls aren't promising. We get a few e-mails, ditto. And all that happened at the beginning of the week. Wednesday, just one e-mail. Thursday, silence. It's the same pattern I saw in AdWords last week, a decent number of inquiries on Monday and Tuesday, and then a sharp decline. I keep walking out of my office to study the two printouts, but the pattern of calls doesn't seem to correspond to anything there.

WE'RE ALL LOOKING FORWARD to Friday. Bob Waks is scheduled to spend a morning observing Dan and Nick perform their duties as salesmen. I've taken pains to emphasize the importance of the training. "It worked for Sam Saxton" has become my mantra. To prepare for Bob, Dan has some proposals set aside to send on Friday, and Nick has a conference call with a client that he's been working with since January. He just sent his third proposal to her last week. She has questions about the design and wants to include one of her colleagues in the discussion of the options.

Late Thursday night, I get a text from Nick: his two boys were wrestling after dinner, and one broke the other one's arm. Badly. He's at the emergency room. Nick wants to know whether he can skip work tomorrow. Absolutely not, is my first thought. On the other hand: what would I do if it were me? I wouldn't hesitate to skip work to deal with a family emergency, and Nick isn't the kind of guy to give me stories just to avoid work. It's going to be a long night in the hospital for him. I e-mail Bob, asking whether we can reschedule. It's almost eleven. I send a text to Nick, telling him to do what he has to do.

I'm up at six-thirty and immediately check my in-box. Nothing from Bob, nothing from Nick. I take Henry for a quick walk and get to work at eight-thirty. As I explain to Dan that we might be re-scheduling, Nick walks in. He looks like hell—red-eyed, still wear-ing yesterday's clothes. "I'm here. Surgery went OK, he's excited about his cast. He's already using it to threaten his brother." Dan and I smile. We both have boys, we know the score.

Bob Waks shows up at 8:57. In his crisp business garb, he's a sharp contrast to our shorts and T-shirts. He starts with a little speech. "Here's what I'm thinking is going to happen today. I just want to sit quietly in the background and watch you guys do what you do. I'm not going to make recommendations, I'm just here to observe. Now, Nick has this call at ten-thirty. I'm very interested in hearing that, but I don't want you to do anything different than you would normally do. Just be yourselves." He turns to me. "Is that what you expected, Paul? Did you have anything else you wanted to happen this morning?" I tell him that if that's what he wants, that's what we'll do.

At 10:20, Nick asks whether I will sit in on the call with him. I'm happy to do this. I've noticed that Nick has a hard time getting a conversation going in an organized fashion. He's an excellent listener and good with give-and-take discussions, but he doesn't launch a presentation very well. Hems and haws, doesn't get to the point. So we agree that I will open the call and then hand it over to Nick. Bob asks, "Who are you talking to?" Nick tells him the name of his pri-mary contact. Then he checks the e-mails from her and comes up with a name for the other person on the call. Bob isn't satisfied with that. "Do you know who these people are? Where they fit in the organization?" We don't. The client is the Chamber of Commerce of a mid-size Texas city. Nick's contact is Mary, who called us, but we don't know anything about her. Nick and I pull our chairs up to his phone with the proposal open in front of us: ten pages of images of the proposed table, floor layouts, and photos of wood options. When Mary answers, she says she needs to get her colleague, Kate. We wait. And wait. Those are long minutes. Nick and I sit crouched over the phone, Bob hovering in the background, Dan in the other corner of the room, trying to type quietly. Finally Kate introduces herself. I start our pitch: "Mary, Kate, I'd like to thank you for getting us involved with this project. Nick has sent you his proposal—do you have it with you?" Silence. Then a muffled yes. I keep going. "OK, then Nick would like to review it with you. Here he is." Nick quickly reviews the floor plan, showing how the table will fit in their room, and talks about the folding mechanism he is recommending. Then he goes over the wood samples. During these five minutes, we can hear rustling noises. Nick looks at me, eyebrows raised. I chime in. "Mary, Kate, do you have any questions? What do you think of this design?" More rustling noises, then a loud *bonk*, then an indistinct voice: "How much does this cost?" Nick and I look at each other. The price of the table is in large red numbers at the top corner of each image. "It's on the top of pages two, three, four, five, and seven, and there's a summary of every charge on the last page." More rustling and then murmurs. Then we hear a deeper voice. Is there somebody else in the room? Mary speaks, "OK, I see it now." Long pause. More murmurs. Finally, she says, "I'm going to have to take this to the board. They need to make this decision. We'll get back to you. Nicholas, you've been so helpful with these proposals. Could you just do one more? Can you include the table you showed in the first proposal with these here and maybe some lower cost options?" Nick agrees to do the revisions by Tuesday, thanks them for their time, and hangs up. We look at each other, then at Bob. His face is impassive, but his demeanor suggests he's struggling to find the right words to convey what he's thinking. After a pause, he says, "Well, that was something!" I ask him for a little more feedback, and he says, "I don't want to get into specifics right now, but I'm *sure* I can help all of you. There's a lot of room for improvement here." Bob says he's seen enough; there's not much more he can do with Nick and Dan today.

We retreat to my private office. I ask him, "What did you really think?" His reply is brutal. "You guys are pretty bad. You made just about every mistake in the book. I don't want to waste time today going over that in detail, because we have a lot of other stuff to go over and I have to be back at the office by one-fifteen. The training sessions will cover everything you need to know. So let's talk about the assessments. Did you read the reports?" I tell him that I read every word, and we proceed to have a long discussion about the findings. I haven't seen Dan's and Nick's DiSC profiles, just the as-sessments of their potential as salesmen, so Bob shows me how they scored. High Conscientiousness scores are the one thing all three of us have in common. Nick has a low Dominance score, a very high Influence score, a below-average Steadiness rank, and a high Consci-entiousness score. That makes perfect sense. Like me, his low S score reflects an impatience with routine. He doesn't keep good records and his desk is disorganized (just like mine). But he's an excellent craftsman, hence his elevated C score.

Dan has no Dominance, below-average Influence, above-average Steadiness, and high Conscientiousness. And that matches my experience with him. He never tries to push his opinions and he doesn't try to ingratiate himself with me or with customers. He has a hard time with the quick give-and-take of phone conversation. He deploys his strengths, his organization, and his mastery of his job to come up with very good solutions to clients' problems. But if some further persuasion is required to close the deal, he struggles.

I beg Bob for anything that we can use right now. "Just one tip. There must be something we can do right away. My sales are terrible and we may not survive long enough to put the training to use."

Bob sighs, then says, "Here's one. Never end an interaction with a client without a commitment to meet again. You have their attention; use it to pin down an actual day and time for the follow-up. Don't let them put you off. Put it on your calendar, and then follow up with an e-mail confirming it. It's a way to keep moving on a job. Try that and see what happens."

After Bob leaves, I return to the sales office. I don't want to discuss the assessments with Dan and Nick. Is it my place to criticize the way a person is wired? So I tell them about Bob's tip. We all marvel at the simplicity, the beauty of the concept. Why hadn't we ever thought of that? We let clients get back to us whenever they feel like it. We don't even try to control the pace of the deal. Bob's strategy means that we have an excuse to call our clients back, to make sure that they are moving toward a definite yes or no.

Emma, Dan, and Nick roll out at four-thirty, leaving me alone in the office. It's Friday afternoon, leading up to a holiday week. I don't expect any more calls today and we don't get any. I check with Nancy—Henry is doing OK. So I sit and think. Henry. Money. Sales. AdWords. Dan. Nick. Steve Maturin. My problems are all fighting in my head to see which can bother me the most. A wave of despair washes over me. It's a physical sensation, one that I've felt at intervals over the years. I feel it most when I'm tired, and it's quiet, and

I'm low on cash. I know it will go away because by nature I'm an optimistic person. But while I'm caught in it, I feel very, very bad.

Five-thirty rolls around. Nobody has called. None of my problems have been solved. But I start to feel better. We're not out of work, yet. Henry will go back to school in a week. And that was a hell of a good tip that Bob gave us.

JULY

DATE: SUNDAY, JULY 1, 2012

BANK BALANCE: $91,271

CASH RELATIVE TO START OF YEAR ("NET CASH"): -$45,883

NEW-CONTRACT VALUE, YEAR-TO-DATE: $865,722

Sunday morning. I return from a jog to find Nancy sitting in the kitchen. And no music from Henry's room, which is unusual. She looks upset. "Are you OK? I thought you went shopping?" She starts to say something, then collapses in tears. "I took him to Trader Joe's. You know, he's always been good there? So we were doing OK until we got in line." She collects herself, then tells me what happened. It starts with a small annoyance: the jerk in the checkout line.

The store is crowded and the lines are long. Nancy has a cart full of groceries. Henry is by her side. The woman ahead of her, when she arrives at the cashier, parks her cart, and then does—nothing. Most people will start unloading, to speed up the process, and maybe to be helpful. Not this woman. She gives the cashier a tight smile, and then stands back. *Serve me, now.* The cashier starts unloading the cart for her.

Meanwhile, Nancy is hearing some rumblings from Henry. First, he places her hand on the handle of the cart. He's saying: Mom, push this thing out of here, I want to go. She tells him to be patient. Then he suddenly jumps and gives a short, loud shout when he lands. He's 6-foot-4 now, and weighs 215 pounds. Every person in the store stares, and then quickly turns away. People are very polite about Henry's strange behaviors. They can't help looking. But if we act as if nothing unusual is happening, or announce that this child has special needs, they stop. Oh, one of *those* kids. We know better than to judge, so we'll just ignore whatever is happening.

The woman is still watching as the cashier bags her groceries. Suddenly, she points at the item in his hand. "I don't want that tea." The cashier sets it aside. "I want a different one. Wait for me." She leaves the line and heads up the aisles to find a better box of tea. While she's gone, the cashier does nothing. Nancy holds Henry's hand, speaking to him quietly, telling him he has to be patient for a minute, then they will be able to go for a car ride and have a treat.

The woman returns with her tea. Checkout resumes, again without any help from her. Then she does it again. "I forgot to get eggs. It will just take a second." She gives a fake smile to Nancy as she heads back to the dairy section. The cashier pauses again. She comes back with eggs. Checkout continues. Finally, the last item is bagged. Now she digs through her purse, then pulls out a check book.

Henry jumps and shouts again, this time a wail of despair that lasts a couple of seconds. Again, every eye in the store turns toward him and Nancy, who is still holding his hand. She puts her brave face on—a weak smile, a quick shrug, intended to convey her apology to the public, sorry about the fuss. She turns to him again. "Shhhh, honey, just another minute, then we'll be done, be patient, be a good boy."

The woman asks the cashier for a pen. A sigh of despair passes through the whole line—Nancy has four or five people behind her at this point. He has to look for a few seconds, but finds one in the back of his drawer. She slowly writes the check. Signs it. Fills out the register. Then hands the check to the cashier, who gives her the receipt. She looks at it closely. Then she proffers it to the cashier and points to one of the numbers. "This was supposed to be on sale. I want my discount."

Henry is finished waiting. With a full-throated roar, he attacks. He wraps an arm around Nancy's neck and pulls her backward off her feet. She lands on her side, sprawled on the floor. Then Henry bursts into tears and starts repeatedly slapping his own head with both hands, hard, while he jumps up and down.

Nancy tells me this story as tears stream down her face. "And the worst thing—I'm lying there on the ground while Henry is screaming—and nobody does anything. They just stand there. And that, that"—a lifelong feminist, she can barely bring herself to say it—"*bitch* just walks away, with her stupid groceries, and the check-out guy—nobody does anything at all to help me." Gulp. I have some sympathy for the bystanders. I've been in her place, except for the being-knocked-to-the-floor part, and it all happens pretty fast, although it seems like every second is an eternity. Henry's worst behavior is so outlandish that people's brains can't process the situation—they literally freeze in their tracks while they try to figure out what is going on. And who's going to jump in and try to calm Henry down? He's big, and when he goes off, it's very scary.

"Are you hurt? So what did you do?"

"I left the groceries. I got him in the car, and he calmed down. When we got home he was smiling at me, but I was so"—long pause—"I was just so furious, I sent him up to his room." I express sympathy, as there's nothing more to say. Nancy stops crying and sits with a very sad look on her face. "I can't take him anymore. I just can't take this. What are we going to do with this kid?" I don't know. In the short term, we have another week until he goes back to school. At the end of July, he'll be home again, for five weeks. Nancy continues, "I can't take him out by myself anymore. I just can't do it. I never know when he's going to attack me."

There are four people that Henry pays attention to: Annie, the woman in charge of him at his school; Janice, his longtime babysitter; Nancy; and myself. Annie and Janice are in our lives because of government spending—they're both funded by our local school board, because of its legal obligation to provide local kids with a meaningful education. Even giant autistic kids. But this week, Annie is on her own break, and Janice is available only now and then. Nancy has decided, sensibly, that she can't go out in public with Henry anymore.

The rest of the day passes as usual: loud music, snacks, and car rides. But now every excursion is done by me. Nancy is afraid to be alone in a car with Henry, even if he's in the backseat.

I have a lot of responsibilities. I try to stay strong, but sometimes it feels as if a heavy weight is squashing me flat. The disappearing sales, the vanishing cash, the non-existent income, the non-performing employees, and now this. I'll keep trying to solve the problems I understand. And the others, like Henry? There's nothing to do but ride them out. They'll either get better or worse.

THE NEXT MORNING, I take Henry with me to the Monday meeting. He is usually good for an hour, sitting in my office and listening to music. If I get distracted, he'll head to the refrigerator and start eating whichever lunch looks most delicious. Fortunately, we hold the meeting next to the fridge—I can talk to the crew and defend the lunches at the same time.

Finally, I have a snippet of good news. "We have more cash than we did last week." I point to the number I've written on the board:

$91,272. "We're still down relative to the year, but it's better than two weeks ago. Unfortunately, sales last month weren't so great." I point to that number: $62,000. "I won't sugarcoat this. That's the lowest since July 2008. Our backlog is three and a half weeks. That's bad, too. But we're trying to fix sales. We just had our evaluation from our trainer. We got one good tip from him already, and we start the classes next week. I'm sure this is going to work. We just have to keep going. Something will happen." They're all looking at me, as usual, with little emotion. "OK, that's the meeting." They head to work. I'm pretty sure that some of them are looking for jobs, but nobody will tell me that unless they find one. Henry has been good, so I give him a donut and we leave. Four hours to kill; then Janice can take him until dinnertime. After she arrives, I head back to the shop.

Bookmark: AdWords. Log in. Stare at the screen. It's 94 degrees in my office. I'm keeping the air conditioning off to save money. We've had two inquiries this morning, then silence.

AdWords reports steady clicks for the past month, even as calls and sales are disappearing. Where did the boss callers go? What happened to them? Are they just not shopping anymore? On vacation? Worried about money? Do my headlines no longer appeal? Are the ads even running? What if Google is lying about showing my ads? Now, there's something I can check.

I start running searches to see whether my ads show up. I start with our highest traffic keywords: "Modular Tables." Yup, there's the ad, but I don't see a free link to our site below it, just our competitors. Now the keyword that drives our best organic results: "Custom Conference Tables." There's our ad, with free links right below it. Now "Boardroom Tables." That's the string that generates the most e-mails, and I think it's the one that brings in the boss shoppers. Hmmm. No ad, and our link is in the third free position.

No ad? I recheck in AdWords and see that, yes, I'm offering to pay $7.50 for a single click from that group. This is more per click than any of my other ads, by a long shot. So why aren't they showing it? Is it just a fluke? I know they show different results to different shoppers. Maybe Google knows that it's me doing this particular search, by checking my IP address. So I go out and search "Boardroom Tables" from my bookkeeper's computer. No ad, weak organic result. I recheck "Custom Conference Tables." No ad. Then "Modular Tables." Ad is there. Back at my computer, I use Google to find proxy sites. I can pretend to be searching from anywhere in the country. I spend the next forty-five minutes channeling searches through cities where we have done a lot of business: Houston, Pensacola, San Francisco, New York, and Chicago. Everywhere, it's the same pattern. The "Modular Table" ad is running, the "Boardroom Table" ad isn't.

The next morning I repeat my test. In every trial, both "Modular" and "Boardroom" ads are running. When I do proxy searches again in the middle of the afternoon, the "Boardroom Table" ad is gone. At the end of the afternoon, only the "Modular" ad is still showing.

Why does the "Boardroom" ad stop showing in the afternoon? Why is that ad so important? My old theory, back in April when inquiries started to drop, was that the economy was going down the toilet again. Then my Vistage group told me that they didn't see this, and that I had screwed up my marketing. I believed this for a while, but then decided we were experiencing a seasonal dip—more calls from schools, less from bosses, because of the end of the school year and the start of vacations. But what if the ad that bosses like best isn't even showing late in the day, when bosses shop for tables? I don't know for sure that the "Boardroom Table" ad is the one that brings the bosses to us, but it used to generate the most e-mails, and "Boardroom" conjures up an image of big, expensive tables used by powerful leaders. And what are we showing instead? "Modular Tables." The inquiries for those tables usually come from institutions that need flexibility because they can't afford a dedicated boardroom. Cheapskates. These are not the shoppers we want.

So why does Google show the "Modular Table" ad instead of "Boardroom Table"? I think it's because of the huge search volume related to the "Modular" concept. The click-through rates are really low, but that ad generates more revenue for Google. As my money starts to run low, they turn off the other ads and keep the "Modular" ads going until I've used up my daily budget. By the end of the day, when the bosses have time to shop, the ad aimed at them has disappeared.

I don't know how long this has been going on, but the inquiries started to dry up in April, shortly after I introduced our new modular table ads. And increasing the spend didn't help, probably because the additional money was wasted showing the "Modular" ad to more people. Google's algorithm thinks that every click is a good click. It doesn't care whether it helps me or not.

It looks like the "Modular" ad is sucking the life out of the rest of the campaign. It's a theory. I can't prove it. I don't have enough information about which ad drives which kind of customer to call. So I could be wrong, but there's no doubt that the "Boardroom" ad is disappearing by mid-afternoon. Is there some way I can tell Google to put priority on the "Boardroom Table" ad? That's a great question, and I spend the rest of the afternoon trying to figure out the answer, without success. Frustrated, I head home.

The next day is July fourth. In the morning, we take Henry to the local parade, which he enjoys. I persuade Nancy to watch him at home for a few hours, and I go in to work. I'm obsessed with finding a way to keep my "Boardroom" ad going without turning off the

"Modular" ad. But I can't find an answer. It's incredibly frustrating. Google's help features are almost useless, and AdWords doesn't have a help desk. Like so many tasks I must do, there's no way to figure out the best approach. And I don't have the time or money to hire a consultant.

In the back of my mind, I've been wondering what happened to the BigOil project. I haven't heard anything since my e-mail on June 21. When we crossed into July, I abandoned hope. There's no way we could make a late August delivery. Imagine my surprise, on the fourth, to see an e-mail from Shiva. Her direction: use the drawings that we provided. Fantastic. Those are almost useless. Should I sink a day into designing something that I think will work? Instead, I reply, asking whether the drawings show the location of the boxes, or whether it is schematic, and they might be somewhere else in the room. Further surprise: Shiva's boss sends a drawing, shown to scale, with the boxes located. But it's a very odd design, clearly done by someone who knows nothing about building tables. The dimensions are non-standard, and it will be very difficult to assemble. On the other hand: forty thousand dollars. I reply that I will have a design ready to send tomorrow. The following morning I decide that crazy won't do. Four hours later, I send them a complete proposal, showing a practical design. Total cost: $47,884. At this point, I have little faith that I'm going to get this job. But I've done my best.

At home, whenever I find a few minutes, I continue to search for a way to prioritize my "Boardroom" ad. I finally find the answer, deep in the Web site of an AdWords consultant. It involves reorganizing the entire account so that the ads I want to emphasize are in a separate campaign, with their own budget. If structured this way, I can ensure that the ads run over the whole time I specify. I'll make separate campaigns for "Boardroom Tables," "Custom Conference Tables," and "Modular Tables," and leave the rest together. Four campaigns, four buckets of money.

The reorganization should be easy—the equivalent of dragging files from one folder to another—but it isn't. Google provides no mechanism for moving an ad from one campaign to a different one. Instead, I will have to manually re-enter all the information from the old campaign in order to make a new one. Each line of text needs to be correct. Each bid needs to make sense. That's a lot of work—there are dozens of ads, and hundreds of keywords, each with their own bid amount. This is not work that I could pass to an intern, even if I had an intern. It's both boring and important at the same time, like so many of my duties. At least it can be performed on a laptop, at home. So I get started on Friday and work whenever I can. I do most of the work late at night, after Henry is asleep.

Sunday morning: I return Henry to his school, then head straight to the shop to finish up the AdWords project. After a couple of hours, I'm one click away from activating the new campaign architecture. Will it be effective? Will it bring back the bosses? I don't know. The theory I came up with a few days ago still seems plausible, but I've devoted most of my time to figuring out a way to put it into effect, not to coming up with another alternative. But things can hardly be worse, so I press the Save button and the changes go into effect.

MONDAY, JULY 9. I deliver the numbers. Cash in: $17,510. Cash out: $30,317. I started last week with $98,009, ended with $85,202. New orders? Just one, worth $9,636: a billionaire's girlfriend has decided to enter the fashion business and needs a large table to lay out dress patterns. He called and asked for a beautiful Mission-style table, ten feet by four feet, to be delivered as soon as possible. I tried Bob's trick and scheduled a call to review my proposal for later that afternoon. The proposal didn't take long to make, and the second call yielded a credit card number. Just that simple—this time.

The other nugget of good news: fourteen inquiries, a surprising amount for a holiday week. I explain my adjustment to the AdWords campaign and posit that the jump in calls is the result. And I tell everyone that the sales team is having its first training session today. All in all, this meeting has been more positive than those of the past few weeks.

At ten-thirty, the sales team drives four miles to Bob's office. This will be the first of our monthly company consultations. We'll also be going through eight group-training sessions, once a week. Bob starts the meeting with a preview of today's session: an introduction to sales, considered as a profession. He's clearly given this talk a million times. My bullshit detector is on high alert. As he continues, though, I relax. Somehow he manages to draw us all in, with interesting questions about our goals in life. His responses indicate real concern for each of us. This is a different Bob. He's less sales-y, more interested in the challenge of turning a bunch of woodworkers into closers. An hour and a half goes quickly. On the way back, I ask the others what they thought. Everyone is surprised at how well it went—Dan and Nick, in particular, had not been impressed when they first met Bob three weeks ago. He seemed to be arrogant and unsympathetic back then. He was much nicer today.

When we get back to the shop, Nick finds an order for a huge table, forty-two feet long, worth $31,362. His client is a smaller woodworking shop in Ohio that had built a lot of cabinets for a local college. When asked to build a new boardroom table, they realized that they didn't know how and turned to Google to find a source. Bob, the owner, has been very worried that the college will try to buy from us directly. He's kept us from any direct interaction with the client. We'll sell to him, he'll sell to them. The deal is structured in four payments. Bob gives us his credit card for the first: $8,000.

On Wednesday, Nick calls me over to his computer. "Remember when Sam Saxton talked about using a screen-sharing program to review proposals with customers?" I dimly recall the discussion. Sam had been emphatic about the value of doing this, and I had done nothing about it. "I think I found the program—it was called 'Glance,' right?" That sounds right to me. Nick continues, "I think this would be really great. We could show people our SketchUp models while we talk to them, instead of just static images." We give it a try—he's in his office, I'm in my private office. The proposals we send are nice, but seeing the model zooming in and out, looking inside, and coming up from underneath, it's an entirely different experience. Nick asks whether it would be OK to try this with a client. He sent them a proposal and scheduled a call this afternoon to review it. When the hour arrives, Dan and I are sitting behind him. We're curious to see how this works.

Nick calls the client. We wait while he rounds up a few colleagues. Nick starts by asking if there are any questions. There are: how many people will the table seat, how will it fit in the room, what about the woods, where will the data ports go? All this is clearly presented in the proposal. At least we think it's clear, but maybe it isn't. Eventually Nick tells the client, "Hey, I can help you guys understand the design better. I can show you the models we used to make the proposal, live, in real time." He tells them what to do to log in. When they're connected, we'll hear a tone. We hear typing, then, "OK, we did it." Nothing happens. Nick speaks to the client, "This can take a little while." I'm counting seconds. Ten. Twenty. Thirty. Finally, at forty-two seconds, we hear the tone.

With the connection made, Nick brings up different views of the table, zooming in and out, and pulling back to show how the table fits in the room. The questions change immediately—everyone is much more interested in what we have to say, and their confusion has vanished. Nick wraps up the call by scheduling his next contact, just like Bob told us to do. "Wow, that really was great," I tell him. "I'm going to try that with my next call." Dan says he'd like to use it, too.

Later that afternoon, I walk around the shop floor. The mess is getting out of hand. Having the whole crew do the cleaning isn't working. On my way back, I stop to see Will Krieger. He's been working for me for twenty-three months. In August 2010, a week after I had hired a new bench worker, Will called. He'd just been laid off and had seen the want ad I forgot to discontinue. I had nothing to lose, so I agreed to see him. When he arrived the next day, he didn't look like much: T-shirt and jeans, long ponytail, scraggy beard and mustache, and carrying a lot of weight. But his résumé was impressive. He'd graduated from a good trade school, worked in three different shops, and represented the United States in cabinet-making in the 2009 WorldSkills Competition—the trade equivalent of an Olympic competition.

I gave him my standard shop test, a four-page document with fifty questions, covering mathematics and geometry, plan reading, machine identification, wood species, and safety procedures. I wrote it in 2007, when I was doing a lot of hiring, having realized that interviews told me little about an applicant's skills. It's proven to be a good way to weed out the bad applicants without much effort on my part. I let applicants take as long as they want, ask me any questions they wish, and tell them to double-check their work. Most of them take an hour, and some more than three. When I handed it to Will, he glanced through the pages, raised his eyebrows, and got started. He completed it in nineteen minutes—a new record—with a perfect score. I hired him on the spot.

Will has the rare combination of superb technical skills, an inquiring mind, and a winning personality. And he has helped me solve problems from the day he arrived. I started him in the finishing room. That job was being done by a guy I'll call Old Crusty. He was high-strung, expensive, and lazy, but very highly skilled. He knew that if I fired him, work would stop going out the door, and clients would stop paying me for completed projects, and I'd be in trouble. So he did just enough to keep me from canning him, but not one bit more. It's very difficult to find good finishers and I couldn't be sure that a new hire would work out before I ran out of cash, so I had let the problem fester for years. While accepting my job offer, Will casually mentioned that he knew how to finish. So that's where I started him. His skills were evident from the start, and Old Crusty knew that his power over me had vanished. He quit a week later.

Alone in the finishing room, Will set to work. By pulling huge overtime, he cleared out the logjam of unfinished tables that Old Crusty had left behind. A month later, with the situation under control, he came to me. "You know, we're mixing our finishes by hand, in small batches. It's screwing up my work flow. Either I run out of finish in the middle of spraying a big table, or I have to mix up too much for a small job and end up throwing a bunch away. We could get a mixing pump that automatically mixes the finish as we spray it. That would save lots of time, and I wouldn't be throwing away buckets of unused finish."

Wait. Did I just hear an employee identify a production problem and propose a solution? I never get that from Steve Maturin, even though he's in charge of shop operations. Will's idea sounded promising. I started with the obvious question: "What's a mixing pump?"

He explained, "You know how we have to mix the catalyst into the finish to get it to harden? I'm doing this by hand. I can only do a quart at a time, as the finish starts to harden as soon as the catalyst is mixed, and I only have fifteen minutes before it goes bad. A mixing pump has two chambers, one for the finish, one for the catalyst, and two lines that meet at the tip of the gun and get mixed at the exact moment of spraying. So we only catalyze the finish we are putting on the piece. I never have to hand mix, and we don't have to throw any extra away. And the gun is smaller and lighter, since it doesn't have a reservoir. Much easier to spray." Sounds great. "How much does it cost?" He looks down. "I don't know." I told him to find out.

He returned the next day. "I talked to the rep from the pump company. Each one goes for about ten grand, and we need two, one for sealer and one for topcoat. Twenty thousand dollars. So I guess that's that." He started to walk away. I told him to stop. "How much time do you spend hand mixing every day?" He estimated two to three hours. "And how much finish are we mixing, and how much does it cost?" Two to five gallons, at $135 a gallon. "And how much do you throw away?" Half of that. "Two gallons a day of waste, that's $270. Three, no, let's be conservative, two hours of your time that I could charge out at $85 an hour. That's $170. We're wasting $440 every day, and there's 220 working days in the year. That's $96,800. Those pumps will pay for themselves in three months." He asked the obvious question: "Do you have twenty thousand dollars?" I didn't. But I could lease the equipment and pay it off over three years. Payments for twenty grand would be about six hundred dollars a month. I told him to go ahead and get a formal quote. He left with a spring in his step.

A couple months later, I watched him spray a large tabletop. He's dressed in a protective suit and respirator, holding the gun out at arm's length and slowly moving back and forth as he sprays. He finished and came over to see what I wanted. Nothing at all, I told him. "I'm just watching you. You do a hell of a good job."

He took the compliment with a smile and gave one back. "You know, I couldn't believe it when you told me to go ahead with that pump. I never worked for a guy who would spend five dollars on new equipment, and twenty grand would be out of the question." I thought about that for a second: "I don't think I've ever had an employee ask me to spend twenty grand on a piece of equipment before." It's true. I constantly catch woodworkers fiddling with half-broken tools, even stuff that costs less than a hundred dollars. "Just ask me for a new one," I plead. "I'm happy to pay for it. You're wasting more time messing around with that thing than a new one will cost. And you aren't getting any work done."

Will smiled. "Yeah, my last boss was just like that." I pointed out that the last shop he worked at had suddenly gone broke. He laughed. "Well, this place is different." I sure hope so.

Will did the finishing job by himself for a year, working fifteen to twenty hours of overtime a week. Then he told me that a friend of his, a finisher, was looking for a better job. Could he tell him to call me? I thought, Why not? Will has good judgment and knows what kind of worker I want. And that's how I hired Dave Violi, who has been just as good as Will.

After Dave Violi settled in, Will asked me whether he could move out to the shop floor, to get back to actual woodworking. I said sure, as long as Steve Maturin could find work for him. That wasn't a problem. Steve immediately put him to work on our toughest construction problems. After I fired Eduardo, I was a little surprised that Steve assigned Will Krieger to build table bases. They're easier to construct than tabletops, so it seemed like a misuse of a highly skilled worker. On the other hand, Eduardo's bench was on the opposite side of the shop from Steve's, and Eduardo had regularly made errors that caused problems in the finishing room. Maybe Steve was thinking that putting his best guy on that task would solve the error problem and release him from the obligation of walking across the shop. A win for the shop floor manager, if a bit of an insult for Will. But Will didn't complain. He moved his tools to Eduardo's bench and got to work. Within a week, perfectly built bases were flying together in half the time that Eduardo took. Shortly after, Will designed and built a hydraulic clamping jig to speed up part of the process even more.

Chatting with Will has cheered me up a bit. He's always thinking about doing his job better and likes to bounce his ideas off me. He's made me remember that my guys really want to keep working here, or they'd have left already.

I'm up early the next morning for the first of our sales classes. Dan, Nick, Emma, and I will have eight sessions, each devoted to an aspect of the Sandler method of selling. We're not alone. There's a group of very beefy guys to our left, all in green, from a gym. A cluster of red shirts to our right, from a plumbing company. And a dozen others in a variety of outfits, from business attire to wife-beater T-shirts and shorts. A quarter of the attendees are female. I'm the oldest person in the room by at least twenty years. The only boss? Hard to say, but I think so.

At seven-thirty, we meet our teacher. I was expecting Bob Waks again. Nope. This is a short guy, balding, fireplug type. He introduces himself: Robert Sinton. Like Bob Waks, he crackles with energy. Rob gives us a little background on how he got into sales: poor kid, from a tough neighborhood, fought his way to the top.

Sinton has everyone's attention from the get-go. He has each of us introduce ourselves and say why we are here. It's a mixed bag of sales situations. Some, like the gym guys, want to respond to walk-in customers. The plumbers need to persuade a client to commit to the fixes or maintenance they need. A number of people make cold calls, spending their day on the phone—the toughest way to sell. And there's us—craftsmen who don't have to prospect for clients, but must guide buyers through a complex sales process and close the deal. It's striking how, after saying a few words about themselves, some of the students come off as pleasant and interesting, while others sound so dull you'd do anything to get away from them. And most are in the middle—not repulsive, but with no obvious charisma.

Introductions done, Sinton launches into the first lesson. He asks us, "What do all prospects have in common?" Silence. Then, from one of the gym guys, "They need something?" Sinton shakes his head. "Anyone else?" Sinton turns to the whiteboard and in large block letters writes: P. A. I. N. "*Pain!* They have a problem. It's bothering them. And the problem might be that they need something, but often it's completely different. After all, sometimes you can sell something to someone who had no idea that your offering existed when you started the conversation. What made them change their mind? They didn't even know they needed anything. But they had pain. You"—he starts pointing at people around the room—"and you, and you, and even you there in the back, you found it. You found their pain. You took the time to get to know them, you dug a little, and you identified the issue." He launches into a good half-hour expansion on this theme, keeping us riveted. He's constantly moving, gesturing, writing on the whiteboard, asking questions, and telling jokes and stories, usually about his own mistakes.

He emphasizes one point over and over: you need to know with whom you are dealing. You need to understand where they stand in the decision-making hierarchy, because that will determine what kind of pain they have. A boss's pain is getting the deal done. But his executive assistant, tasked with doing the groundwork, has a different pain: the boss. She's going to be working closely with the boss for years, and we need to find a way for her to look good to him. A mid-level corporate buyer's problem is reputation. She needs to choose a reputable firm so she can demonstrate that other companies have come to the same conclusion she did. And she needs the stuff she buys to work really, really well, so that nobody points a finger at her if things go wrong. As I drive back to the office, I think about everything Sinton said. Pain. It seems so obvious. Why didn't we ever think of it that way?

When Dan and Nick get back, we talk about pain. It makes sense to them as well. Nick tells me about a client, Ginny, from a company called Brand Advantage, who seems to have lots of it. She has asked us to design a large U-shaped table, ten feet wide and ten feet long, that can be folded up and wheeled away when not in use. She needs thirty of them, with a strict budget of fifteen hundred dollars per table. And she absolutely has to have them on September 1.

But Nick is having trouble getting answers to his follow-up questions. She's made several references to "branding" on the table, but she hasn't explained what it is. There's also the problem of the budget. Our folding-leg sets would be perfect for this job, but her target size is too big to do with a single tabletop. It should really be three tables, each with a set of legs, that clip together to form the big U. But then the price of the leg sets and the cost of fabricating three tops drives the price to $2,100 for each set. He's stuck. I tell him to try reducing the size to a 9-by-9 square. Then we can make the U in two pieces, each of which can be cut from a single 5-by-10 sheet. We can use two leg sets—they each cost about $275—and still have enough money, barely, to pay for the labor. We won't be able to fit the whole freight cost into the budget, but what else can we do?

Nick starts working on a 3-D model. He has a call with Ginny at four p.m. and wants to show her a model using Glance. I ask him what he thinks her pain is. His reply: "She's a pain in the ass. Her e-mails don't make sense. I keep asking her to explain the branding and I get nothing. The budget is a problem, and the time is a problem. We need to get started if we're going to ship by September." That's a lot of pain. "Is she a decision maker?" Nick isn't sure. It seems unlikely, because she's so bad at explaining what she wants. In our experience, people with power are usually very clear about what they need.

"What about other calls we got for this?" We've received three inquiries from furniture dealers asking whether we could price a 10-by-10 U table that folds and rolls, but they provided fewer details than Ginny. We can tell that they're asking about Brand Advantage because the design they want is so unusual. Ginny must have called them, too, and when they didn't have any idea how to do this job, they found us.

She's in a box. She's running out of time to place an order, and the other people she's called can't do it. I tell Nick, "I think we can press her hard to go forward. Can we get her boss involved? How about you call her right now and see if she can get that to happen?" He reaches Ginny and tells her that he's confirming this afternoon's phone appointment and, since time is short, asks whether she'll be the decision maker on this job. She tells him that she'll need approval from her boss. Nick asks whether that person can sit in on the call. He listens, then reports to me, "She said she'd do her best. She didn't sound happy."

But when we call Ginny, her boss, Monica, is on the line. With Glance, we show them the model of the U table, in two pieces, and how it folds and rolls. Each set will be $1,377, excluding freight. A month ago, I would have sent her a proposal confirming all this, and then we'd wait to see what happened. But there's no time for that, so I ask a bold question: "Are you ready to commit to this, right now? If we don't get an order by Friday, we won't be able to do the work." Monica ignores my question, asking instead whether we would make a set and ship it to her for examination. I suppose we could. On whose dime? I ask, and she says that she could pay the quoted price, $1,377. I'm not happy about that. On a job like this, a significant chunk of our cost goes into the design and programming. It's the same whether we make one or a million. The $1,377 presumes that we are making thirty pairs, and I'm folding the design costs into all of them. Even so, everything will have to go perfectly on the shop floor for us to make money. I make a counteroffer: "How about you order the first one with the design charges included, and if you like it and order the rest of the tables, we'll give you a credit to cover that cost?"

She says she'd like to think about it. I keep trying. "You don't really have time to think about it. It's the middle of July, and you need these by September first. We'd like to do this job, but we need time to get it done." She asks how much for the first one plus the design charges. Nick and I review our costs: $5,466. She has to run it by her boss. Nick and I look at each other: she has a boss? We thought she was the boss. She continues: send a formal quote at $5,466 and she'll make a decision as soon as she can.

The next day, I try my first Glance session. I'm pitching to two buyers for a Houston accounting firm. They're opening new offices in multiple cities and the owner wants them all to have identical boardroom tables. This could be a nice stream of orders.

Using Glance, we review various aspects of my design. They're very interested. They are getting much more information than they would from a static document. But it feels weird to me. I can't see anyone's face, so it's harder to tell when to jump in with a comment or to anticipate a question. And it's inherently nerve-racking: a live performance, with plenty of opportunity to make an error—to have no answer for a reasonable question, to misstate a number, or simply to cough or burp at the wrong time. Do I sound pleasant, or does my voice grate? Am I interesting, or boring? Is humor appropriate? This is an entirely different experience from sending written proposals.

And much of what is being conveyed is purely visual, but it feels wrong to leave dead air while I manipulate the model. We're so used to a constant stream of talk accompanying any moving image that silence sounds amateurish. I really need some lessons from a baseball announcer, or any expert on running one's mouth while nothing is going on. Or do I? Maybe, in this context, silence is OK. We haven't done enough Glance sessions to get a feel for it yet.

The call concludes with no promises, but they thank me for my effort. I do get them to commit to a follow-up call in a month. I think I did OK, but it wasn't an immediate sale.

ON SUNDAY, I get a call from my son Peter, who's been in San Francisco for a month. His job is going well. He's written the code that allows his company to accept PayPal payments. His bosses are delighted with his work. "Are you cooking anything? Are you eating?" No worries—his company provides all meals. There's a well-stocked fridge, tons of snack foods, and they treat him to dinner every night. "You're still there at dinner?" Apparently the San Francisco dot-com workday starts at about ten a.m. and lasts well into the evening, sometimes all night. Everyone's on salary, so management encourages the workers to stay at work all the time. It sounds awful to me, but to Peter it's simply the way things are. We talk for about forty-five minutes. He closes with more assurance that everything is going well. But it's sad to hang up. I miss him.

On Monday, I have nothing positive to report. Sales for the first two weeks of July: $42,648. Inquiries have been slightly better than last month. Inquiries up slightly from June, but no boss callers, no easy sales. Cash: dwindling. We took in $17,086, and spent $26,188, leaving $76,101 on hand. The cash-to-come number is $67,707. That's up a bit, thanks to the order for the huge table. But next week's payroll and credit card bills will take almost $65,000 out of my reserves. I'll have only a couple of days of funds left. Our backlog is as close to zero as it's ever been: two and a half weeks of work. I don't mention layoffs, but everyone knows that we are very close.

I go back to my private office. I have no sales jobs to work on. There are a few e-mails from customers, but they don't take long to dispose of. What can I do now? I've heard nothing from Dubai about the BigOil job. What about Eurofurn? When will I see the flood of production work they promised me? Maybe I should press them a bit, get them down here, give them some lunch, maybe a beer or two, and see what comes next. I send an e-mail to Nigel and Milosz, and within an hour they respond: sure, happy to stop by. I call Nigel and we make a date for the twenty-third.

Then things get a little better. Monica at Brand Advantage receives the go-ahead for the prototype table. She gives us a credit card for the whole amount: $5,466. The mail, for once, is loaded with goodies: three final payments, totaling $7,275. And at three p.m., Dan hears from a law firm that's ready to proceed, having reviewed the proposal he sent in May. That's worth $13,884, with a $6,942 deposit. Dan is elated. This is the first sale he's made in more than a month. I'm happy, too. Our monthly sales are still way behind target, but it's more cash. I end the day with $95,784.

On Tuesday morning, I gather a pile of pay sheets, each filled out and signed by an employee who expects a check tomorrow. I've been making a payroll since 1988. This will be my 601st iteration of this ritual. There are lots of ways a business owner can tamper with this process to save a little money. Paychex's involvement takes away some of the obvious tricks, like not paying the payroll taxes, but I could still modify the amounts withheld for health insurance and pick up about a thousand bucks. But I would never do that, no matter how desperate I am.

I process the sheets for twelve people. They spent, in total, 847 hours working for me over the last two weeks, about thirty-six hours per person, eight of which were a paid holiday. Some of the shop floor guys are taking unpaid days off—they know we're running out of work and they're staying home in order to delay the day when there's nothing to do. In the short term, that saves me a little money, but if we don't get the work done and out the door, we won't get paid for it. I need that cash. My last payroll cost me $23,014. This one should be similar. Pam, my longtime bookkeeper, tells me that the bills for today total $14,130. Half of that is payments to our materials suppliers—wood and hardware companies. A big piece of it, $7,595, is from Independence Blue Cross. I hate them—they've been jacking my rates up 10 to 20 percent every year since the turn of the century. Theirs is one bill that I routinely pay late, but after three weeks, they always send me a cancellation notice. This month I'm out of time. We'll have to pay it.

Bills and payroll will eat at least $35,000 of my cash. I'll have $60,000 left, but I need to pay my credit cards. I have two. The first is dedicated to AdWords. Earlier in the year, the monthly bill was around $10,000. This month, it's $14,000, the consequence of increasing my daily spend. The payment is due on the eighteenth, two days from now. My credit limit on that card is $27,000. If I roll it all over, I'll probably max out the card next month. Hmmm.

The other card payment is $30,330, higher than normal because of the $8,500 deposit to Bob Waks. This card has a $60,000 credit limit. The minimum payment for the AdWords card is $280; for the other, it's $303. If I pay the minimums and roll the rest, my short-term cash position will be $43,747 better than if I pay the whole balance. That's almost two weeks of additional life for the business. Both cards give me a point, worth a penny, for each dollar I spend. I currently have 45,751 points on the Google card and 387,017 points on the other card. The total, 432,768 points, gives me an extra $4,327.68 to factor into my calculations.

I'm fundamentally leery of borrowing money, but I will make an exception if the purchase makes me money and I'm sure that I will be able to pay it back. I didn't mind leasing the mixing pump—the payback was almost immediate, and the loan was secured by the pumps themselves. But rolling over credit card balances just delays the day of reckoning. It's not an investment. It's desperation. Next month I'll be in even worse shape, with an even bigger balance, and then what?

You may be thinking, Why don't you call a bank? Don't they loan money to businesses all the time? Yes, they do. But not after they've heard a story like mine, in which a long-established but barely profitable company enters a downward spiral. Banks want one thing: their money back, with interest. They only want to do business with a company that has a good plan to pay them back, and plenty of collateral available if that plan doesn't work out. They aren't interested in propping up a company that's in trouble. And clearly I'm in trouble. Everything is wrong here—the fact that I've survived for many years without building up a healthy cash reserve indicates bad management, and our disappearing sales indicate incompetent marketing. Showing up, hat in hand, at a bank, when I may be out of business in a few weeks, would show a serious lack of judgment on my part.

Back in 2003, after The Partner bought into the company, we established a line of credit, at his insistence. He called the bankers who had funded his previous businesses, and we got a hundred-thousand-dollar line within a week. All we had to do was personally guarantee it. He had lots of assets, I had my house. But we maxed out that line within a year and didn't manage to pay it down until the fall of 2008. Then my partner took all our operating cash, without my permission, and closed out that account—he was afraid we were about to default and he didn't want the hit on his credit rating. Nothing about that experience, and my subsequent history, has made me want to borrow money from a bank. Even if one was willing to lend to me, they would require my personal assets as collateral. If we close our doors, I don't want to lose my house.

I decide to pay off all $14,000 due on the AdWords card and make a partial payment on the other one. I'll turn in 400,000 points and give them an additional $2,500 from my operating funds. I'll be borrowing $23,830. The interest won't cost much—at 12.99 percent, the charge for the first month is just $258. I'm much more worried about returning the principal. But if I run out of cash, I won't be able to pay anything at all. Better to keep the doors open as long as I can.

On Thursday morning, the sales team is back in the classroom. Bob is lecturing about Self-Management. As he explains it, a particular set of personal habits leads to success in sales. First and foremost: persistence. Every salesperson fails a lot. It might be a significant percentage—we make a deal with 25 percent of our prospects—or it might be almost always, like those poor kids sitting across from us who make cold calls and close one or two of every hundred calls. You can't take rejection personally, Bob tells us. It's going to happen. Get over it. Then he gives us a number of techniques. The first one: visualize success in very concrete terms. Think of that car you want to buy, that vacation you want to take. He suggests that we buy a blank diary and fill it with pictures of the things we desire, cut from magazines. We should leaf through it every day and tell ourselves that making that next phone call, writing that next e-mail, sending that next proposal, is moving us closer to our goals.

I'm gagging. I don't see myself as someone who needs to drive a Mercedes or go on vacation in Africa to believe that I have succeeded. But Bob's scheme gets me thinking about success. What does it mean for *me*? What do I really want? First on the list: a cure for Henry. But that's not possible. Other than that? I'm happy with my family. My business is not a financial success, but I've kept the doors open for twenty-six years and done a lot of good work. I have almost everything I want.

What would really make me happy would be to stop worrying about money. I'm sick of the tension. My shoulder is always tied in a knot, and my stomach seems to be permanently clenched. I toss and turn all night, then fight to stay awake after lunch. I know how good it feels to have a big pile of cash. That's how the year started. I thought that I had finally figured it all out, but now my confidence has vanished. I'm back where I spent the previous five years—in a state of constant anxiety. How much would it take? What's my number? What should I put into my success diary? Maybe a hundred and fifty thousand in the bank and plenty of sales coming in? A business that's growing instead of dying. An upward trajectory.

Do I deserve success? Does anyone? I don't think so. There are so many people who have been less fortunate than me. I'm not starving to death in Somalia. My neighbors haven't decided to murder me, like in Rwanda. Nazis haven't shown up in my town and shipped me and my family to the gas chambers. I'm a very long way from the worst that life has to offer. I have no right to complain about anything.

I glance at one of the gym guys, sitting on my left. He's written

"Camaro" in his notebook and underlined it twice. That brings me back to earth. Just because I'm not heading to Auschwitz doesn't mean that I have to accept failure. My workers and their families are relying on me. It's OK to want to make payroll, to bring home some dough for myself, and to get my company back on track. I need to listen to Bob.

WE PICK UP three small sales on Friday the twentieth, bringing us to $73,468 for the month. Still bad, but at least we've tallied more than we did in all of June, with seven business days to go. Inquiries were also better: sixteen calls and e-mails, but nobody hot to place an order.

Payroll has gone out. The credit card payments have been made. The health insurance payment has gone. The vendors have all been paid. Total outflow for the week: $54,307. Fortunately, on Wednesday and Thursday I received seven more payments, totaling $21,944. In all, during the past five days I've taken in $41,627. So I have a net cash loss of $12,680. I have $63,420 left. Two weeks, give or take.

MONDAY MORNING: relief, of a sort. I've been worrying all weekend, a loop of dark thoughts that keeps repeating in my head. Cash. Layoffs. Failure. Now that the weekend is over, at least I have work to do. And the Eurofurn guys are coming down for lunch today. That will keep me busy for a few hours.

I walk into the shop at seven-thirty. It's a mess, as it's been lately. I tell Steve Maturin that we're going to be having visitors mid-morning and that we need to clean up. He says nothing in return, as usual, but as I head back to the office, I see him gathering the shop floor guys together, with a broom in his hand. At the meeting,

I announce the sales from last week. I also go over our cash position but don't explain that we only have money because I rolled over the credit card.

The Eurofurn crew arrives at eleven-thirty. I watch from my window as Nigel, Milosz, and Jeff emerge from a black BMW. They last visited more than a year ago. I hope they don't notice that there are fewer people around than last time. I need this to go well. Their stream of repeat orders would be mighty handy right now.

When we spoke last week, Nigel mentioned that Eurofurn is considering whether to open a separate facility in the States to assemble tables and chairs. We have plenty of room to spare, and if we're making tops, it would be simpler to assemble the tables here as well. That would be more work and more revenue for me, but I'm not sure I can do it as cheaply as the German factory, since we don't have the assembly jigs they use. But I'll deal with that when I need to. I turn on the charm. "Let's take a quick walk through the shop. I want to show you what's going on."

First we stop at the huge table we're building for the college. It's an impressive sight. The base has been assembled, and the guys are fitting the top panels. There's an intricate logo in the center, consisting of laser-cut letters and pictures. The Eurofurn crew *ooh* and *aah* politely. Then I walk them to a spot near our freight elevator. It's a 5,000-square-foot space that could easily become an assembly area. But when I get there, I realize that this area doesn't look good. It's crowded with excess stuff, it's dark, and the lights are either missing or have flickering bulbs. I try to get them to look past the debris, but this is nothing like the Eurofurn factory.

Tour completed, I take them to lunch at Chick's Bar and Grill, down the street from the shop. The Eurofurn crew loves it—so authentic, so charming. No pretense, especially compared to the Midtown eateries they frequent. We have a few beers with lunch, and conversation is easy. Then I ask Nigel about the status of the tabletop orders and whether he thinks we could take on the assembly as well. Instant mood change. His expression switches from Ordinary Human to Corporate Neutral. He starts unrolling one of his circuitous non-answers. The decision will be made at headquarters, and they will evaluate all options, taking into account multiple factors and making sure that every consideration has been entertained fully but judiciously, blah de blah blah blah.

I'm not willing to be put off. "Come on, Nigel. Can't you put in a good word for me? We have plenty of room, and we're close to all your markets. Can't you help me here?" Now his face shifts to Corporate Near Panic. He wants to say no, but something in his personality prevents him from being straightforward. He emits another cloud of words. It's like interviewing a politician.

We walk back from the restaurant. Nobody speaks. The Eurofurn guys are poking at their cell phones, and I'm just pissed off. We arrive at their car and exchange polite goodbyes. I'm mulling over the encounter as I go up the stairs. I don't think these guys are ready to give us anything beyond the dribs and drabs we've had so far.

When I enter the sales office, Nick has a broad smile. "Got one!" It's an order from a law firm in Washington, D.C., worth $12,221. And even better, the next day I have a call with a hedge fund in San Francisco. I cue up the model we've prepared, fire up Glance, and talk my way to a credit card payment. Another $8,134 in the pot. We're now at $93,823 for the month.

Our sales training on Thursday is about Unpaid Consulting. Bob Waks is teaching. A buyer, he explains, has a problem. Something in their life, or company, is not optimal, and they need to improve their situation by making a purchase. To that end, they approach sellers. "I have this problem," they say. "How would you solve it for me?" This sounds familiar. It's how we do business. We wait for inquiries, ask the potential customer some questions, and then come up with a solution.

Bob continues with what happens next. It varies, depending on who is doing the buying. If it's a boss, give a comprehensive proposal. The boss buyer will make a quick decision using the information you provide. Again, this sounds like my life, both in sales and when I shop. Sending a proposal directly to a boss isn't a bad idea, Bob continues, but it's a disaster if you are dealing with mid-level buyers who work for a large organization, whose sole job is to evaluate vendors and make purchases. They're not in a hurry and their criteria for a successful purchase are very different from the boss buyer.

The boss buyer doesn't care so much about nickels and dimes. The mid-level buyer does. The boss buyer wants to get the purchase over with. The mid-level buyer wants to delay a decision for as long as possible. He needs something to do all day to impress his superiors with his diligence and prudence. Mid-level buyers love working with multiple sellers who give them rich, detailed proposals full of useful information and pricing. Armed with many proposals, they play the sellers against one another. When a seller has been responsive in the first go-round, the mid-level buyer asks for revisions. And more revisions. Why not? The hapless seller, eager to please, keeps them coming, and each time he does so, the buyer has another option to consider, another chance to show his bosses how hard he's working when they ask how the project is coming along.

The canny mid-level buyer tells each vendor how great their proposals are, that a purchase is coming soon, and that just a little more help will make a big difference. He may leak the best ideas from one vendor to another that he prefers, or make no decision at all. The job may never have been that important, or the bosses, after seeing a bunch of options, may simply cancel the project. Suddenly, the mid-level buyer disappears. She stops answering phone calls or e-mails, or she sends a short note: "We've decided to go another direction, thanks for your efforts. Buh-bye!"

Nick gives me the raised eyebrows: we've been down this road too many times. Dan slides me a note: "Cali Heavy Industries." Yes, and Nick's Air Force job. And that jerk from the Kaiser Family Foundation who took Nick through twenty-three proposals and then disappeared forever.

Having described the problem, Bob starts to talk about solutions. First: make sure you know with whom you are dealing. The tactics in this situation are determined by where your customer stands in the organization. Are you dealing directly with a decision maker? A pure "D" on the DiSC profile? If so, give her the information she asks for. If you are dealing with a person in the middle of a large organization, you have a much tougher task. The trick is to tease him, showing just enough to demonstrate that you are the best company for the job without giving away valuable information. You can say anything to a client, you can show all kinds of examples of how you have solved your other clients' problems, and you can demonstrate your sterling reputation by trotting out a list of the important companies that have been your customers—but you must never, ever hand over a written proposal full of specific solutions to their problems. Never give the mid-level buyer anything he can pass on to others. Once he has that, you're toast.

Bob tells us that we should provide specific solutions only after a commitment. A real, solid, irrevocable decision to proceed. A purchase order or a deposit. Get them hooked, and then give them everything they ask for and more. Over-deliver. Bathe them with your love. Show them that choosing your company was the best decision they ever made, and make sure that this is true. Then you can ask for a letter of recommendation and referrals. These are what will get you past the next mid-level buyer.

The next day, Dan and Nick and I ruefully review all the times we've been chumps in this situation; then we start to plan our next moves. Dan has sent a proposal to a large computer company in Maryland, and now his contact is asking for a revision. He's about to send it off, but we decide that, instead of giving her the package, we're going to show only her highlights, using Glance. We'll tell her anything she wants to know, but not give her anything in hand until she tells us that we're the preferred vendor. This client has a deadline coming up—construction on the new buildings has started, and a move-in date is scheduled. She's told us she likes our work and intends to go with us. Now we'll see if she has been blowing smoke, or not.

Friday brings one more order, for around $10,000. This is Dan's job. The buyer called us in March and asked for a twelve-foot table. Dan sent a proposal, priced at $10,940. And heard nothing. Now the guy is back with a counteroffer: ten grand and he'll place the order today. Dan asks if this is acceptable, and I say, "Absolutely! We need every job we can get." Never mind that we're giving up the profit margin. Total sales this month: $103,823. Terrible. We're three weeks in, and just passed half of my monthly target. The only consolation is that it's better than last month. Inquiries were OK this week. Sixteen calls and e-mails, just like last week. And seventeen in the first week of July. We're matching January's average and doing a lot better than the second quarter. From April 1 to July 1, we averaged fewer than twelve inquiries a week. Did restructuring the AdWords campaigns make a difference? Maybe. Probably. No, just maybe. A lot of those inquiries were referrals and repeats, not from AdWords. It's likely that the increase is just random variation.

There's no payroll this week and all the other big bills for the

month have been paid. I spent only $4,148. Shop operations contin-
ued to rack up costs, nearly $7,000 a day, but the bills will be due
later. And even though incoming cash was weak, just $19,748, I
ended up ahead. I'll have $79,021 in my account on Monday, enough
for more than two weeks.

The weekend passes quickly. It's the last one before Henry returns, next Wednesday. He'll be with us for all of August and the
first two days of September. He'll be in a day camp for the first three
weeks, then nothing. My mind keeps returning to the Middle East.
It's almost two months since I promised to send printed catalogues.
I've done nothing. Every time I think about it, my will to invest in
those relationships vanishes. My confidence that I can manage a
long-term, expensive project has disappeared. And if I devote a lot
of hours to designing and printing a catalogue, I'll be ignoring other,
more promising work. I don't want to waste money on brochures
that won't produce income until some point far in the future. And
with what I've learned from Bob Waks, I have even more reason to
give up. I can't see how we could interact with Middle Eastern clients in the manner that Bob suggests. It's going to be very difficult
to avoid sending complete proposals, and it will be almost impossible to do Glance sessions. The time difference is too much.

I decide to drop the whole thing. I talk myself into this by arguing that I don't think anyone in Kuwait or Dubai will be terribly
upset. They weren't pining for my presence, and they won't miss
me. In the back of my mind, though, I have nagging doubts. It's
hard for me to walk away from the potential for business, no matter
how unpromising.

On Monday, I report that our position is slightly better than it
has been. More cash. Stronger inquiries. Some sales. Backlog at three
weeks. Nobody has quit. Then, for the rest of the day, the phone
rings and e-mails appear. Suddenly, customers. By four p.m., I've

spoken to four potential buyers and assigned them to Dan and Nick. And we hear from three clients who are ready to place orders. The first owns an electronics store in Queens, and I've subjected him to the new sales methods for a couple of weeks. He places an order worth $11,650, for a keystone table. The second client, Nick's, is an interior designer from Mississippi, trying to get a large university to commit to a table. He sent her a detailed proposal back in March. Since then, she's made multiple requests: samples, drawings, more samples, better drawings. All spring, we meekly complied. Last week, she asked for a complete set of engineering drawings, assuring us that the client had started construction and would place the order soon. But they needed to know where to drill holes in the floor. No more Unpaid Consulting! Nick politely told her that we couldn't provide those drawings without an order. We were nervous about doing this. It's so provocative. But here's the purchase order, for a twenty-eight-foot-long table. Another $27,620 on our books. Then we take three more promising calls from mid-level buyers in a hurry to get a table delivered. We deploy the new sales methods. No one resists. They have no idea that we've completely changed the way we respond to potential buyers.

After lunch, a drop-in visit from the headmaster of a local private school, looking for a table for his office. He'd like a six-foot round, but we don't have one on hand. Except, it occurs to me, for the Eurofurn prototype. I pull it out and assemble it. He's fascinated by the way it goes together. He's got only eighteen hundred dollars to spend, but keeping the table in storage produces zero dollars for me. I tell him how much it cost me, and that it's his for the money he's got. He's delighted. All the supposed flaws that sent Eurofurn into a tizzy? He didn't see them. I'm vindicated. There is nothing wrong with that table.

I meet with Bob at seven-thirty the next morning, the last day of

July. His office is neat and organized: lots of sales books, pictures of his family, awards for being top salesman, inspirational posters on the walls. I'm in a good mood. Yesterday's orders brought our monthly total to $144,893. Two of those came with deposits and we also got a couple of final payments, increasing my cash supply by $28,062. I've now got $107,083 in the bank, enough to make payroll today and run for a couple more weeks. Inquiries have been steady since the beginning of the month, and we've transformed our methods for dealing with them, thanks to Glance and the training. "Thanks, Bob," I conclude. "You've really helped us."

He says, "Yeah, that's all fine. I'm glad that things are turning around. Not that I expected anything else. But there's a lot more work to do. We're just getting started." And then he asks me a series of questions. How many potential clients are we working with right now? If we sold every one of those jobs, how much money would that bring in? Who are those clients? Can I quantify how many are bosses, or assistants, or low-level people? Have I scored each one for quality, so that we know which ones to concentrate on? Have I started regular sales meetings with Dan and Nick? Am I listening in on all their phone conversations? And what about after the call is done? Are they happy? Are they excited by the new methods, or just following orders?

I answer most of these with a simple no, but the last ones make me think. Nick seems happier because the new methods seem to come easier to him. He tried Glance first and he's good on the phone. Dan seems flustered by the loss of a scripted procedure for dealing with customers. We used to treat every caller the same way, but now the situation is fluid. We have to make decisions throughout the process about what to show, what not to show, what to give them, and what to hold back. I tell this to Bob and mention that I stopped paying them commissions at the end of June.

"Hold it right there," he says. "Why did you do that?" I explain my cash situation and that the evaluation reports emphasized that I don't hold my salespeople accountable for their failures. Holding back commissions seemed like a way to put some pressure on them. "Did it work?" Not really, at least not right away. They sold very little in the weeks after the cut. But now it seems to be working, along with everything else. "How much money did you save?" At least a couple thousand dollars. "And what did it cost you in sales?" I don't have a number. We missed our quota by a hundred and forty thousand in June and we're still sixty thousand short for July. I confess that I'm not sure that the slump is their fault, that it might have been a problem with AdWords.

"Then why did you do it if it's not their fault and they didn't instantly start selling like crazy?" I tell him that I cut my own pay months ago and I was sick of being the only one to suffer. He's not impressed with this reasoning. "You're not making sense. It sounds to me like they're being punished even though they've just followed your methods. That's not going to help us over the next few months. You think that everything has been fixed and that success is assured. Wrong. Those guys are still a long way from being effective. They're going to be challenged by what comes next. You need them to buy in and reward them when they do. The money you save is nothing compared to what you'd have if they start selling. If they are using the new methods, and it's working, give them back the commissions."

I'm embarrassed by my stupidity, but Bob isn't done. The fact that I know very little about our prospects is unacceptable. It will lead to chaos if we get busier, and I won't be able to manage the sales process without more information. He tells me that I need to implement some kind of customer relationship management system, and the sooner the better. Our hour is up. I have a lot to think about.

My first task at the office is payroll. Should I put Bob's advice into effect immediately and reinstate the commissions? We've taken in $100,862 since the last payroll. At 2 percent, the commission on that is $2,017, almost enough to pay for a month of Bob's services. It's my decision—I can pay it, or not. I decide to wait two weeks. Things could be better by then, in which case it's obvious what to do, but if they're worse, I'll need that money.

IN THE SHOP, the prototype Brand Advantage table is complete. It's not complicated—we just had to cut the top out of a sheet of prelaminated flakeboard and put an edge on it. This is not fine woodworking. The client's budget doesn't allow for it. I stand in front of the two tables—a left and a right, each shaped like a J that together form a large U shape:

I placed the legs so that the top is balanced on the axis of rotation. This keeps it from crashing from horizontal to vertical when the latch is released. I try the mechanism and it works very well. But I'm a little uneasy. Each top is much heavier than the recommended maximum for this leg. It doesn't seem like a problem when the top is flat, but when it's in the vertical, folded position, the whole weight of the top is hanging on eight small bolts. It seems a little weak.

Well, this is why we make a prototype. The best solution would be to make each U out of three pieces, but that would blow the budget. I tell Bob Foote to ship the set to Brand Advantage and let them decide whether it's acceptable or not. I also say that he should ship the table assembled, and build supports under the folded tables to support the weight of the tops during transit.

It being the last day of July, I have our final build-and-ship numbers for the month. Jobs worth $115,337 have been built, a very low number that reflects the lack of incoming orders for the past three months. We shipped a little more than that: $141,659. My accountant says that I'm making a profit when I ship more than I spend each month. I achieved this goal in July, mostly by being very, very careful with cash flow. I've spent only $141,557. Theoretically, I've made a profit of $102. Woohoo! But my cash position continues to deteriorate. In July, I took in $126,489 and spent $141,557. I'm down $15,068 for the month. If I hadn't rolled over the credit card, I would be in worse shape. As it is, I'll have $82,942 in my accounts when August starts tomorrow.

AUGUST

DATE: WEDNESDAY, AUGUST 1, 2012

BANK BALANCE: $82,941.70

CASH RELATIVE TO START OF YEAR ("NET CASH"): -$54,212.61

NEW-CONTRACT VALUE, YEAR-TO-DATE: $1,010,615

Goodbye, July, good riddance. Hello, August, please be better. I start the month by distributing the pay stubs to everyone, except me. That task completed, I go out to Henry's school. The summer session is complete, and he's going to be home until September 1. As usual, when I pick him up, he's happy to see me. He really loves the car ride home, bopping to the loud music. I leave him with Nancy and return to work. She still won't leave the house with him. But starting tomorrow, he's got three weeks at a day camp for special needs kids.

It's been a good week for inquiries, fifteen so far. We also get a nice order, for $13,834, from a defense company in the D.C. suburbs. They've been sitting on our proposal since November and today they sent a purchase order, out of the blue.

Thursday I'm up early with Henry. He's awake at dawn, insisting on hearing his favorite Beatles album with the volume all the way up. Nancy and Hugh sleep through the din. I make his breakfast while he carefully listens to each song, loudly inhaling and exhaling in rhythm with the tune. And at track 14, which he doesn't like, he hurls the boom box across his room, then thumps down the stairs. I have his breakfast ready. Eating calms him down. A few minutes later, a van shows up at our door to take him to camp. Whew! Seven hours of peace. He'll be dropped off at home at four p.m.

I zoom over to sales training. Today's session leaves me cold. Bob Sinton is talking about prospecting, the techniques for finding people who might need your product. We don't do this; we wait for potential buyers to come to us. We don't have the resources for any kind of sustained outreach. We're stuck with Google. After I get back to the office, I start thinking about a CRM (customer relationship management) system. Bob's questions last week highlighted a big problem: we have good ways to administer jobs after they're sold, but nothing to track inquiries before we write a quote. I need to come up with one, or we might lose track of a potential buyer. And I want to be able to see what Dan and Nick are doing without having to ask them. I don't want to spend a lot of dough, and I don't want it to be complicated. No new software packages. It needs to be part of our FileMaker database. To save money and to minimize the learning curve, I'll do the programming myself.

This isn't the first time I've done this. In a tiny company like mine, it's up to the owner to invent the way the company operates and to design the systems that keep track of what is happening. Fortunately, I find this to be an interesting challenge. If I had wanted to build only furniture, I could have kept myself very busy, but the company would not have grown. Without a rational way to handle information, we would have descended into permanent chaos.

Thinking about information is different from ordinary work. The challenge is to find good ways, using data, to describe what's happening in the real world. It's aligning the description of the company with the activities of the company. My job as boss is to monitor both of these and to continually modify the description to fit the reality. My employees can't do it—they each work on their piece of the process. I'm the only one who sees everything. I decide what to keep track of, and how to do it.

I have two information systems. First, there's my subjective impressions of the state of the shop, the mood of the workers, the eagerness of the customers, drawn from my observations and conversations. The second is objective, actual data that lives in separate fiefdoms: the accounting system, in QuickBooks; the contract and productions system, in FileMaker; e-mails and customer folders sit on our server; AdWords data lives in the cloud. So do our shared Google Docs spreadsheets, which act as supplementary databases. There are also a bunch of Excel sheets, dating back to 1997, when I first computerized (twelve years after starting the company). None of these subsystems talk to one another. Information passes between them via the people who use it. I'm the only person in the company who knows how it all fits together.

This system is neither optimized nor rational. I have tacked it together over the years, and it has grown as my ability to handle the software has evolved and the computing environment has changed. Back in the mid-1980s, the most sophisticated instrument I had was a calculator. For more than ten years, I kept track of all my jobs with some 3-by-5 cards and a corkboard. Now we're using more than a dozen different software packages. It's been my responsibility to evaluate these, figure out how we will use them, and introduce them to my people. We're too small and poor to have someone below me do this.

I never abandon a program if it's useful. I'm constantly layering new capabilities on top of old ones. Most of the older programs do one or two things very well. There's no urgent need to replace them, so I don't. I just start using newer stuff that does different things. I don't know whether this is a good idea or bad, or whether someone has invented a single program that does everything a small custom woodshop would want (I suspect not). It's just how things have developed. And if it satisfies me, and seems to be working, then we'll continue. There's nobody over me to say otherwise.

I've mastered some programs and know just enough to do simple work in others. FileMaker, where I want to put my new sales tracking system, is a mystery. Our database was written by The Partner's daughter, Sasha, who worked for me from 2003 to 2009. It's a brilliant achievement and vital to our operations. I've been using it for years, but I don't really know how it works. I'm nervous about tinkering with it. What if I inadvertently cripple it while trying to add a feature? Disaster. So I start small. It takes some hours of Googling to even figure out where to begin, how to switch from just using the program to modifying it. Fortunately, FileMaker is designed to be easy to revise. After the first day, I've made some simple changes, like the color of fonts and the location of text boxes. Even after I've done these, the program is still functioning, on my own computer anyway. I check on Dan's and Emma's machines and see that my changes have propagated throughout the network. Cool. I'm in control. Now I can start work on a CRM system.

Later, I'm driving Henry, making a double circumnavigation of Philadelphia, when Peter calls from San Francisco. He's upset. "Something weird happened at work today. My boss called everyone together and told us that the investors don't think that the company is going to succeed." That's strange. They publish e-books, and unlike many dot-coms, there's an actual revenue model. I ask Peter: "What, aren't they selling anything?" He replies that their only successful book is the one that inspired the founder to create his start-up, ironically titled *Making Money with Your First Start-up*.

Revenue growth has leveled off and the investors have lost interest. They're going to lay off everyone and just let the site run on autopilot, taking in whatever money it can. Half the workers got canned this morning. The rest will take an immediate 30 percent pay cut and lose their health insurance. They'd like Peter to stay on for a couple of months to make sure the site is operational. He's already got $2,200 saved from his first six weeks working, so he can hang on for a while.

Then the question: "They chose me to stay out of all the others. Should I stay on and finish the job?" Or, I'm thinking, maybe you should come home. He has a month-to-month lease, so he can walk away when he wants. I tell him, "First of all, you don't owe your boss anything. He hasn't been loyal to you, don't waste your loyalty on him. I think they want you to stay because you're the cheapest guy who can do the work. If I was them, that's what I'd do. But forget those assholes. Do you want to come home?" Ummm, no. He's enjoying doing real work and he likes the city. He doesn't say it, but I think that he doesn't want to give up on his new adult life and be a kid again. My advice: "So how did you find this job in the first place? Whatever you did, do it again. Right now. Don't hesitate. You need to look out for yourself first. Keep your head up. If it doesn't work out, come home. You've learned a lot about the work world already. You've got your first shady boss story. But remember, I've got your back. If you need anything, just ask me."

MONDAY, AUGUST 6. During my pre-meeting shop stroll, I find Steve Maturin standing in front of a table that's ready to go into the finishing room. It's got sparkling flame cherry veneer on top, surrounded by a solid cherry edge. The base is mahogany. Wait. We never sell a table with this wood combination. There's no point—

they look similar at first glance but have a different texture, so they end up looking a little strange when used together.

I ask Steve what happened. He turns and stares at me, then says, "That's what's on the plans." Really? I take a look. There's a mock-up image of the table, taken from the initial proposal, with the woods clearly labeled: both top and base are cherry. But the cut list and notes, on the next page, call for mahogany.

I'm pretty sure I know what happened. Andy Stahl, the engineer, makes all our plan sets. He reuses portions of plans from previous projects. He regularly does this—it makes perfect sense—but he's supposed to update all the text with the correct species. This time, he didn't do it. I presume he was in a rush to get a plan sent out to the floor so that the shop guys wouldn't be held up.

When Andy started drawing, back in 1998, we did fifty projects a year. Since then, we've quadrupled that number and added the CNC machine, resulting in even more engineering work. Andy does all this. He's also in charge of ordering all the wood that the shop uses. Is it fair to have one guy try to keep up with that much work? Maybe not. But Andy seems to be keeping pace with the shop, especially since sales have been so slow. I know that errors like this happen, and I haven't seen his workload as a crisis. So I haven't tried to find help for him.

I ask Steve why he didn't catch the discrepancy. He shrugs. I try to control my anger. "You need to be on top of this stuff. It's your job to double-check those plans and make sure that everything makes sense. Andy has a lot on his plate, and there are going to be errors now and then. That's why *you* need to review the plans, to catch those problems and fix them before they get downstream. Is that clear?" He gives a tiny nod. I tell him to make another base. Out of cherry. Even though that's not on the plans.

I return to the office, still furious. That mistake cost at least a thousand dollars. I collect myself and start the meeting. Last week's numbers, for once, were all good. Three new jobs came in, totaling $48,812, from the defense contractor, my dot-com company, and a bank. The last two received our new sales treatment, and it didn't take months to close the deals. We've also had strong inquiries: twenty-three calls and e-mails, a mix of bosses and corporate buyers, the best so far this year. And we received more cash than we spent, despite payroll. Starting balance: $79,021. Income: $39,940. Outflow: $32,040. We're up $7,900 for the week, and I have $86,921 on hand. I'm still down more than $50,000 since January, but for once, all indicators are positive.

To close, I recap the error at Steve's bench and make a plea to stay alert for inconsistencies in the plans. "I think that we're going to get busier soon," I say hopefully. "Everyone has to pay attention to what they're doing. Look at the plans and check that the woods match what's on the first page. If something seems odd, speak up. Tell Steve, or tell me, if he's not around. Errors are going to kill us, so let's sniff them out before we build the wrong thing. OK, does anybody have anything to add?" To my surprise, Steve speaks up.

"We wouldn't be having these problems if Andy didn't send out so many fucked-up plans."

Stunned silence from everyone. Steve never addresses the group meetings unless I ask him a question. We all wait for Steve to clarify this statement, but he says nothing more. He's completed what he considers to be a useful contribution.

Andy's face is turning red. Uh-oh. Andy is a very calm, courteous guy, until the very rare occasion when he gets angry. Then it's an instant transformation into a volcano of rage. And there he goes. He's up and shouting at Steve, who gives it right back. The rest of the crew is watching this exchange with interest. This is even better than the donuts. I am appalled. I hate shouting, and I try to never do it myself. And I've never seen two of my people fighting, ever.

I intercede. "Hold it, hold it, hold it! This is not the way to solve this. Andy, clearly you made a mistake. Apologize. Steve, you should have caught the error. Next time, check with Andy to find out what is correct. The rest of you, this is not the way we interact with one another. When we have problems, I want to concentrate on fixing them, not blaming one another." I look at Steve and Andy. They've both calmed down and look embarrassed. Should I make them apologize and shake hands? Can I turn this into an uplifting moment of renewed brotherhood? Probably not. "OK, time to get back to work. That's the meeting."

I watch Steve walk away, then stop to see Andy, since his office is next to mine. "Are you OK?" He nods, then apologizes. "I shouldn't have done that. I don't know what comes over me. OK, I missed the mahogany notes when I pasted the cut list. He should have seen it." I ask him if his workload is too much, but he says he can handle it. Now what? I can take him at his word or initiate a giant effort to increase our engineering capacity. Hire a trainee? Except Andy is the only one who knows how to do the drawings and program the CNC machine, and he's already overloaded, or close to it. Will the workload get back to normal, or shrink even more? Then what will I do? I can't see how instant action would make my life better, so I decide to trust Andy's judgment and do nothing.

AT THE END of the afternoon, Will Krieger asks to see me in private. My mind races to the worst possible outcome: he's quitting. I don't know what I'll do without him. It's been an unpleasant day; now it will end with me losing my best guy. I steel myself and lead him to my office. "So what's up?" I ask. He hesitates a second.

"Ummm, I've been thinking." He pauses. "I want a raise. I've been here two years now, and I'm still getting paid the same as when you hired me." I sag with relief. This is easy. "How much do you want?" I'm willing to bump his pay, but in a negotiation like this, the first person to say a number loses. He might ask for what, to me, would be a trivial increase, like a dollar bump to the twenty-five dollars per hour he's earning.

No such luck. "I was thinking thirty dollars an hour." Given the amount of overtime he's working, that's close to fifteen thousand dollars a year. Hmmm. In his favor: he's an intelligent, innovative worker with multiple skills. He gets along very well with everyone and has recruited an equally valuable friend. He is very professional: he keeps a clear separation between his personal life and work without being mysterious and aloof. He's a credit to both himself and the company. I want to keep him happy.

Arguments against? I can't think of anything. However, thirty dollars an hour is the top pay rate on the shop floor. That's what I'm paying Steve Maturin. If I give Will a raise and word gets out (and it always does), Steve is going to ask for more money. And I don't want to reward him. The shop is always a mess, and he's impossible to talk to. He's still on my shit list for ignoring Eduardo's theft. And that display this morning was unacceptable. But I've had bigger problems all spring and summer, and I've avoided taking action.

As I think these points through, a strategy forms. I can solve two problems at once. I tell Will: "OK. I can do thirty. Honestly, you deserve that and more, but I can't afford to give you a bigger bump. But there's something else I want you to do. Thirty bucks is foreman's pay. And you aren't doing the foreman's job. You're a great bench hand, but you don't have the foreman's responsibility. There's a whole world of planning and worrying that you haven't done. Steve Maturin has been taking all that on, and I don't think you have any idea what's involved." I'm certain of this. Will is twenty-six years old. He has worked at three jobs since he graduated from technical college, and none of them had any management responsibilities. "If I'm going to pay you more, I want more from you. I'd like to put you in charge of all shop operations. Everything. You're the only one out there who knows both the finishing and the shop floor. You're smart enough to learn what Bob Foote does in a day. I want one person to be in charge of running the whole shooting match. And I think you can do it. The most important thing, to me, is that everyone likes you and respects you. Hell, I like you and respect you. But it's going to be a shock to some of those guys, who are older than you and have been here longer. I'll back you up, though. So what do you think?"

He's surprised and hesitates before he says anything. "What about Steve Maturin? I've got a lot of respect for that guy." Sure, as a craftsman, Steve is superb. But Will doesn't know about all my issues with him. "I'll take care of Steve. If you want, you can even keep him doing exactly what he's doing, running the bench guys and the CNC. I want to put you in charge of everything. That's a new position for us. We've never had one person doing that." Well, except for me. But it's been impossible for me to really do it. I've been stuck in the office, and the shop operations have become too complex.

Will takes all this in and then he repeats my argument back to me, saying it himself in order to own it. And his tone becomes more energetic, more enthusiastic. "I want to do this. I can do this." He gives me a firm handshake.

On the drive home, I review the logic of promoting Will. My gut says I made the right move. I hadn't planned on it, but my beef with Steve Maturin has been bothering me for months. If I keep things as they are, someday Will is going to realize that he could be working someplace better, or start his own shop. Will's request for more money has broken through my unwillingness, on any given day, to confront one of my workers. I've let Steve Maturin's subpar performance continue because I don't have the guts to address it. The Zen of a very small business: When the Boss Is Ready, the Solution Will Appear (Sometimes). But it's going to be an unpleasant conversation with Steve Maturin tomorrow.

All night, I'm caught in a mental loop, rehashing the pros and cons of my decision. It's a relief to wake up and prepare Henry for day camp. Then off to the shop. First task: talk to Steve. He's at his bench, enjoying a morning cigarette. I sit and greet him with a good morning. His reply—a nod. I start right in. "I've decided to make a change in the shop management. I'm creating a new position, operations manager, one person who will be in charge of everything that happens outside the office—bench guys, finishing, and shipping." He looks at me warily but says nothing, so I continue. "I'm going to put Will Krieger into that position." No reaction. "That means that from now on, you will be taking orders from him. I expect you two to work closely together, and I expect you to cooperate with him in every way." Silence. "Do you have any questions?"

He exhales a cloud of smoke, though not in my face, and flicks his butt into a bucket of water. "Are you demoting me?"

"No. The exact scope of your duties is going to be worked out by you and Will. He may take over some of the things you do, or all of them, or none of them. That's up to him." We both know that I just dissembled. Of course it's a demotion. He's lost power. I continue, "Since you've been here so long, I'm not going to cut your pay. I'll keep you on at thirty, but you'll have less to worry about. You might even like it more. Less work." Steve flinched when I mentioned a pay cut. I don't think it occurred to him that it would be reasonable to do that when reducing someone's responsibilities. "Do you have any questions?" He has none. "I'm going to announce this at the meeting on Monday. In the meanwhile, I'm going to let Will figure out how to make the transition. And as I said, I expect your full support and cooperation with whatever changes Will decides to make." He says nothing, doesn't even move. I get up and go back to the office.

WE'RE DEALING WITH the surge of calls from last week, and with our new methods, working through a backlog of inquiries is a lot more complicated than it used to be. More phone calls, more time doing screen shares with Glance, and more discussion among the three of us as we figure out who is on the other end of each inquiry and work out tactics for different types of buyers.

As usual at this time of year, we get a lot of inquiries from the military. Their fiscal year ends on September 30, and senior officers with money left in their budgets are finding ways to spend it. Upgrading their conference rooms always seems to be a popular choice, so they put some junior officer to work finding a table. Here's an example:

> *Sir,*
>
> *We are looking at having a conference table custom-made to fit our needs. I would like to send you a design plan on what we are looking for. Are you on the GSA schedule; and how long does it normally take you to make a customized table?*

Federal contracting and invoicing rules are very complex. What's our relationship with the General Services Administration? Will the government allow this buyer to buy from us, even if they want to? And even if they will, end-of-fiscal-year military clients aren't as

committed as a private-sector client. I've been told that unit com-
manders like to ask for a wide array of proposals and revisions and
then choose the ones they like best. I like to do business with the
military, because the shop floor guys like to make their very cool
logos, and the federal government is a reliable payer. Unfortunately,
most military projects end like this one:

Sir,

*I am sorry that we were unable to make this purchase due to
funding issues and will have to re-address in the future.*

We can't deploy our new methods on military inquiries, because
we almost never have access to the decision makers. So we decide to
continue sending written proposals. All our other clients are now
getting the full treatment, and Dan and Nick feel as if they are guid-
ing them to a commitment instead of just firing off proposals and
crossing their fingers.

Thursday's sales training session is a good one. Bob Waks takes
us through a technique called the Up-Front Contract. It's simple:
before you launch into your spiel with a client, give them a brief
summary of what you plan to talk about and ask whether that's OK,
or whether they had a different agenda in mind. There are two reasons for this: to force us to understand our pitch well enough to
describe it in a single sentence, and to make sure that the client is
ready to hear everything we have to say and not be distracted by
some other issue. If they are, you can address the mismatch directly.

I marvel at the beauty of the concept. Most of what Bob teaches
is plain common sense, but each lesson works with the others to
create a coherent approach to sales. Why didn't I think of any of
this? How many jobs have I lost over the years because of my rigid
tactics? I'm also amused by how Bob used all these techniques on

me in our first meeting. I sensed that I was being managed and didn't like it. But I bought anyway. My pain was disappearing sales. I needed his help, and I'm glad I got it.

ON WEDNESDAY, Nick closes a sale to a Pittsburgh architect. Using our new game plan, he got a commitment from her before making a design. He gave her a price quote and told her that she didn't have time to do it any other way. She sent us her signed contract and promised that a check was on the way. The deal is worth $17,206. Dan and I, like disappointed fishermen who watch another angler reel in a trophy bass, keep working on our projects. By Friday we've had twenty-one calls and e-mails, and again, they're a mix of bosses, mid-level buyers, military, and worthless. Heavy on the first two, lighter on the last.

On Friday, I take stock. Our monthly tally is $66,209. At this pace we won't top $150,000 for the month. A small consolation: my cash position hardly changed. I took in $27,169 and spent $27,860. The net outflow isn't enough to worry about. I'll start next week with $86,230 on hand.

AT MONDAY'S MEETING, after the numbers, it's time to announce the regime change: "I have one more thing. I've decided to change the way that we run the shop. I want to have one person, not me, in charge of all operations: build, finish, and shipping: an operations manager, responsible for making sure that everyone is working together and that work flows smoothly. I'm putting Will Krieger in this position. I think you all know by now that he's the right guy for this job. He's been coming to me with great ideas for how to make the shop work better, and I want to get those projects going as soon as we can afford to do them." Pause. What next? Should I go through all my other reasons for picking him? Talk about Steve Maturin? I don't want to say anything negative here. Most of the guys look happy and nod toward Will. With two exceptions: Steve is gloomy, as expected. Ron Dedrick looks a little sour as well. He's older than Will, has worked for me longer, and was in charge of the shop at his last job. He's brought me ideas in the past, and I like him. But the other guys don't—he has a tendency to point out their mistakes in a very grating manner, and he leaves a mess everywhere he works. And he has never asked me for more responsibility. I make a mental note to talk to him later.

After the meeting, I ask Will if I can see him before he heads to the shop floor. We retreat to my private office. I start with a question: "What do you plan to do first?" Will says, "I'd really like to start cleaning this place up. I wish we had Jésus back." Me, too. We've heard nothing from him for two months. I have another question: "What are you going to do with Steve?" Will has already addressed the issue. "I spoke to him about that last week. I'm going to keep him doing what he's doing, running the CNC. I want to learn how to run it myself, but that will take a while. And I'll start getting the plans from Andy and reviewing them myself. I guess I'll keep assigning work the way Steve does it. And I've got the jobs I'm working on, I'll keep building as much as I can."

That sounds sensible, but I have some other thoughts as well. "I think that's a good place to start, but there's a lot more to this job than you might realize. What I really want you to do, first, is to spend more time looking at how the other guys are doing their work. I believe Steve likes to just stay at his bench and work, right?" Will agrees—Steve is hardly a micromanager. I continue, "So right now, everyone is doing their job a slightly different way. And they can't all be the best way. I don't know which guy has the best approach to any particular task, but I suspect that it's usually you or Steve." They are the best craftsmen in the shop. "But it might be anyone. Ron Dedrick knows a lot, too. He's worked in a bunch of different shops, more than anyone else here. So he might know some method that nobody else has heard of." Will doesn't look too enthusiastic about this. Ron can be arrogant. I keep talking. "Aside from just the basics of running the shop, you have two big problems: Steve and Ron. Those two are very productive workers. They both have good reason to be pissed off: Steve because you just took his power, and Ron because he didn't get this promotion. So I'm challenging you to show them that I've made the right decision, and the best way you can do this is by treating them with respect and using some of their suggestions. Show that they're valued for their ideas as well as their hands."

Will nods, and I give him my last piece of advice. "When you're out there, I want you to do it like I do it. I may not be a rich man, but I've kept the doors open for twenty-six years, so I know something about running a shop. And people don't quit, so I can't be all that bad. Here are my rules: take everyone seriously. Don't discount someone because of how they look, or where they came from, or because you don't like the way they talk. I've had a lot of employees, and they all usually have some flaws along with their strengths. Try to get past the weaknesses and bring out their strengths. Always stay calm. Never shout, never even raise your voice. If someone does something good, tell them, right there and in public. If somebody screws up, take them to a private area to discuss it. I don't like to spend time blaming people for mistakes. Move right to figuring out what happened and how to keep it from happening again. And don't forget to listen. Let your people have a chance to contribute their ideas, or their excuses. Then you get the final word. That's being a boss. Does all that make sense to you?" Will thinks for a minute and then starts to talk. As on Friday, he repeats my advice back to me, in his own words. I'm relieved—it looks as though he's got it down. "So you're ready for this?" is my last question. He says that he is, and heads out to the shop floor. I hope I've made the right decision.

WHEN I GET HOME, Nancy has bad news. "They've kicked Henry off the bus. They said he attacked the driver. They wanted to kick him out of camp, but I spent all day on the phone begging them to reconsider, and got them to agree that he could come tomorrow. But we have to drive him both ways." The driver swore that Henry grabbed him from behind and started shaking him. "While they were driving?" It seems unbelievable. He likes to look out the window and rock back and forth to his music. We agree that I'll make the morning drive, and she'll pick him up.

The next morning, after driving an hour, I pull up to the camp. I'm fifteen minutes early. A woman with a clipboard tells me that I need to wait in my car until camp opens at nine. While we're waiting, buses and vans carrying more campers are showing up. The clipboard woman directs them to a circular drive, where they line up and wait. Nobody gets out. All these vehicles are packed with special needs kids, simply sitting.

At a few minutes to nine, I can see the camp staff come out of the cabins and line up near the vans. There are lots of them, mostly young women. Everyone waits, but the counselors are smiling and waving at the vans and buses. And then at nine, Clipboard Woman blows a whistle, and the first van opens its doors and disgorges about a dozen campers. This first group is greeted by about a half-dozen counselors and heads off to the cabins. The counselors are very cheerful, and most of the campers seem happy as well. The same procedure is repeated for each bus and van. There are fourteen vehicles. This is going to take a while.

I walk in with Henry, and one of the counselors, a young man in his late twenties, comes up and introduces himself. "I'm Robert. I take care of Henry. And how's he doing today?" He takes Henry by the hand and leads him to one of the buildings. I ask Clipboard Woman what happened yesterday with the bus driver. She seems very happy to meet me. "Oh, I heard about that. It was right here, while the bus was waiting to unload." Now it makes sense. Henry, packed in a van with a dozen other kids, waiting for some indeterminate period. A recipe for disaster. I ask her whether he is still welcome if my wife and I do the driving, and she says, "Sure, we love Henry. We didn't have a problem with him. Just that driver." Whew. Driving him out every morning will eat two hours of my day, but it will give my wife some relief.

WEDNESDAY AFTERNOON. It's a payroll week, and my Ad-Words credit card payment is up as well. And the other credit card, which now carries a balance of $36,644, is due next week. And one of the orders we got, from the huge bank in Washington, has net-30 terms (meaning they have thirty calendar days to pay). I won't be getting any money from them until a month after we deliver. My cash position is not secure. I'm trying to feel confident that all my fixes are going to work, that the clump of sales that started the month wasn't a fluke. Are all those inquiries as good as they seem?

Thursday morning finds us back at sales training. In last week's session, Rob Sinton gave us an hour on bonding and rapport. Schmoozing the client to establish a human connection is critical when there's repeated interaction between the buyer and the seller. That's us. Sinton gives us techniques, but he doesn't address something that intrigues me: charisma. Some people are just fun to talk to and be with, and others, you can't get away from fast enough. I don't think that I have an unusual amount of charisma. I'm not a good schmoozer, which probably comes across very clearly. It's why our old selling process was so hands-off. Our proposals demonstrated our expertise without a lot of personal interaction. Sinton reminds me that getting caught up in some friendly chat with buyers is less important than making the effort to do it. It's like the hymn that starts a church service—a way to separate buyer and seller from the dramas of their day and get them to focus on each other. It's a prelude to the real action. "You're in a great position to close the deal, or to work the situation in other ways. To see your competitor's proposals. To get a chance to revise your bid. To get referrals."

Later on Thursday, a couple of big jobs come in. Dan's client in Maryland follows through. It's a $33,180 order for three tables. And two weeks after we shipped their prototype, Brand Advantage at last is ready to go ahead with the whole order. No complaints about the prototype. They still need us to ship by the beginning of September. For $40,266, we'll make it happen.

On Friday, Nick closes with a trucking company in Virginia, an eighteen-foot table that we can make in our sleep. Another $16,042 goes onto the week's tally. We finish the week with a total of $89,488. It's our best since February. Even better, Dan's computer client and Brand Advantage sent us checks to seal their deals. We've picked up $62,795 in cash. I send out $45,903 for payroll, the AdWords card, and to pay my vendors. My bank balance is $16,892 bigger than it was on Monday.

ON MONDAY, I report that sales this month have been good so far. The total stands at $157,128, with two full weeks remaining. We have work through the end of August and the beginning of September—almost a month of backlog. I'd really like to see the shop speed up production. July's total was terrible. The guys completed projects worth $115,337, way below our target of $200,000. I'm hoping that Will Krieger will help turn this around. Is there anything I can do to help him? It's odd that I should even ask this question. But I'm used to a very different relationship with my shop foreman, and I'm not sure what to do differently.

A way to help Will falls out of the blue. After lunch, Bob Foote comes to my office. "There's someone here to see you." A very tall, strongly built young man gives me a big smile and holds out his hand. Grip like iron. "I'm Nathan Johnson, sir, and I'm looking for work. Any work. I'm strong, and smart, and I work hard. Are you by any chance hiring today?" I hadn't considered it, but now that this fellow is here, and some work has come in, maybe it's time to hire a helper.

"We could use someone to keep the place clean and take the trash downstairs. Would you be interested in something like that?" He gives another huge smile. "Absolutely, sir, you bet I'd consider it. When can I start?" Hold it, pal. "I haven't decided to hire you yet. Put together a résumé. Make sure it has three references. You can fax or e-mail it to me. I'll call your references, and if I like what I hear, I'll call you for an interview. Make sure you have a phone number on the résumé." Nathan promises to have a résumé to me first thing in the morning. We'll see.

Tuesday, seven-thirty a.m. I've persuaded Nancy to drive Henry to camp so that I can attend my Vistage meeting. I've invited Will to join me. A guest speaker starts with the steps he took to transform his business, an ordinary accounting firm, into a place where people enjoy their work while taking care of customers, too. And everyone makes money. I wish I had that kind of business. The second half of the talk is about how we can transform our own culture. His people have to follow thirty-six rules, and he's instituted a ritual to make sure they live up to them. Each week, one of the rules is the focus of their team meeting, and employees are asked to contribute examples of how they implemented it. And after thirty-six weeks, when they've gone through the whole list? They start again at number one.

I'm looking at the rules, printed out on a business card. I try to imagine how this would play out with my crew. Would any of them contribute a sparkling anecdote for tip number 3: "Practice A-Plus-Ness as a Way of Life"? Would Steve Maturin follow tip number 10: "Keep Things Fun! The world has much larger problems than our own. Keep perspective! Be lighthearted, and smile, smile, smile!"?

When the meeting adjourns for a few minutes, I ask Will what he thinks. "It's a different way of doing things, that's for sure. And a lot of it makes sense. We should try some of this stuff." I'm a little surprised to hear this, as I had dismissed it as fast as I was hearing it. Will continues, "We're already doing a lot of it. Some you tell us all the time: 'Do What's Best for the Client.' Or 'Practice Blameless Problem Solving.' And 'Maintain a Solution Orientation Rather Than a Problem Orientation.' That's exactly what you told me to do last week. And you remember when he was talking about how they treat new hires, how they give them all these rules and make sure they know what to expect and what to do? We should do that." He's got a point. Will heads back to the shop, and I stay and report to the group that there's been a small improvement in my situation. Trying to revamp our sales process has been very interesting, but it's too soon to tell whether I've really fixed the problem. And I just replaced my shop manager with a new guy who has a lot of ideas and energy. My peers seem glad to hear that I've done something.

After lunch, I'm surprised to find Nathan Johnson's résumé on my desk. Three jobs listed, no typos or grammatical mistakes. Nathan has been working at a local moving company for almost a year. Before that, six months with a temporary agency, then a four-year gap, preceded by a year at McDonald's. And he's got three references: a fellow worker at the moving company, his mother, and a minister.

I call the minister, who tells me he's the pastor of a Baptist church. I tell him he's been listed as a reference. Does he know Nathan? "Nathaniel Johnson? Sure, I know him. Nathaniel is doing pretty well these days. I'd say that of all of the younger men I have, he's a pretty good bet. He's been coming to church since . . . for a couple of years now. A very energetic young man." Would he hire Nathan for the kind of job I have open? He would; Nathaniel would make a good fit. I arrange for Nathan to come in at eleven-thirty tomorrow and then I tell Emma to do a background check on him.

WHEN I PICK UP HENRY, Robert the counselor tells me that Henry is sweet, and no trouble, especially compared to some of the other kids. He laughs. "One of them came after me with scissors yesterday. And I got bit last week." He shows me a crescent-shaped scab on his arm. Robert has been working at this camp for seven years. During the school year, he's an aide in an autism support classroom. That's a hard job—I've been in those classrooms. So what does Robert do during his summer break? The same thing. Robert is a good example of the kind of person who works with kids like Henry. They genuinely love children and do their best to work with the most challenging ones. It makes me wonder. Why is one person devoted to helping kids while another spends his day at a workbench, making furniture? How does our internal circuitry determine the jobs we do? Was it inevitable that I become a boss, no matter where I worked? Or am I better suited to be a worker and am in charge only by accident?

THE NEXT MORNING, I contemplate my $36,644 Chase credit card balance. I have more cash on hand than I've had in months. Just three days into this week, I've added $31,018 to Monday's balance, $95,835. I sent out a bunch of bills yesterday, to lumber vendors and for the health insurance. I have $113,898 left. Sales are not bad. I closed a deal yesterday, to the accounting firm on the receiving end of my first Glance session. Total for this month: $172,490. I could pay off the whole thing. Is this prudent? I'd have $77,254 left, with another bunch of bills due on Friday. And next Tuesday, another payroll. And at the end of the month, rent. All that will add up to another $50,000 or so due before Labor Day, when everything slows down. I decide to send Chase just enough to cover my new purchases and a bit more. That's $15,000. I'll roll the rest to next month and see what happens after Labor Day.

Financial decisions complete, I find Will Krieger. Does he want to interview a potential helper? He'll be in charge of Nathan Johnson if I hire him. He's happy with the idea. "We're wasting so much time moving trash. These guys should be busting out tables, not hauling garbage. If you like this guy, come get me and I'll talk to him."

Nathan Johnson appears at 11:25. I take him into our little conference room. I'm struck by how large and strong he is. He could be an NFL linebacker. "I see that you've been working at the movers and temping for the last two years. Before that there's a four-year gap, and then the McDonald's job. What were you doing during those four years?" I suspected that he might have been in prison, but Emma's background check turned up nothing. Was he in the military? Traveling in foreign lands? Or just hanging out?

Suddenly, he's sweating, but he keeps smiling and delivers his answer with surprising confidence. "Oh, you know how it is when you're young, you can make mistakes and fall in with the wrong people."

"So you were in jail?" He hesitates, then admits that he was. "What for?" I'm not sure I'm legally allowed to ask this question, but I don't want to hire someone with a conviction for a violent crime. "Listen, I just want you to tell me the truth. I suspected that you might have done some time. If I weren't interested in giving you a chance, I wouldn't have called you for the interview. Your minister had nice things to say about you. So tell me what happened." He relaxes a bit. He and some friends robbed a local drug dealer. Nobody got hurt, but they got caught. He's been trying to stay straight for the past two years. If I give him a chance, he'll make sure I'm glad I did. I do want to hire him. He showed up on time and he's made a great impression with his confident demeanor. Will meets with him and confirms my impressions. "I'm OK with it if you want to give him a try." I offer Nathan twelve dollars an hour, full time, benefits. He's delighted. He'll start on Monday. I watch him go through the door, walking tall, a man with a new job. A good day for everyone. It's one of the best things I get to do.

WE BOOKED ONE MORE SALE on Thursday for $15,419. Total for the month: $187,909 with a week to go. On Monday, I rush through the good numbers: $30,781 in sales last week, for a monthly total of $187,909. We took in $7,880 more cash than we spent. And we received twenty-three inquiries, tying our best inquiry week, also this month. Then I introduce Nathan. "I'd like to introduce our new helper, Nathan Johnson. He'll be doing what Jésus was doing, keeping the place clean and helping bring in materials."

I've been thinking about something the Vistage speaker said about on-boarding a new employee: you want to tell them how the company works and explain how they fit in. Fill their mind with your message before they come to their own conclusions. I ask Bob Foote to give me a minute. We go into my private office.

"So you are going to be in charge of Nathan Johnson minute-by-minute. Will spoke to him last week at the interview and he thinks that he's OK. But he's going to let you take charge of him. Here's what I want you to do. Don't just hand him a broom and walk away. I want you to tell him why it's important that we have a helper. That keeping the shop clean makes the other guys more efficient; that they rely on him to do a good job; that his trips to the loading dock for materials are essential for feeding the factory; that everyone will respect what he does if he does it well. And that he can ask you any questions about how it's going, and that he's free to ask me questions as well. Can you do that?" Bob says he certainly can; he'll have that chat right away. Terrific.

Out on the shop floor, Will Krieger is heaving a 5-by-10-foot sheet of melamine onto the CNC machine. It weighs about a hundred and forty pounds, but he manages to shift it onto the machine bed. "Is this Brand Advantage?" He confirms that it is. "How long to cut all of them?" He tells me that they will be done by midday tomorrow. "When will the legs be here?" They are shipping today, if I sent them a check last week. I did. We sold the Brand Advantage job for $40,266, but the leg sets are costing me $15,574. Subtract as well the sheets, crating, and shipping, and the balance is not adding nearly as much to the bottom line as I would like.

WEDNESDAY MORNING is our second monthly company meeting at Bob Waks's office. We report that we've been having a decent month using his new methods and spend the rest of the time going over the Sandler way of addressing our problems with customers.

Sometimes that advice makes sense, and sometimes it doesn't seem to fit very well. We discuss some instances where we think the method won't work. To my surprise, Bob accepts our judgment. He tells us, "Every company lives in a different world, and I want to understand it. We need to be flexible to be effective. It's OK to adapt the training to what's happening at the moment." That's a reassuring message.

After an hour, Bob and I have our private counseling session. His first question: "What did you do about the commissions?" I tell him that at the beginning of the month I was worried about cash and did nothing. But since things are going a lot better, I paid them out in yesterday's payroll. "You gave them everything you owed them?" Uh, no. Just what they racked up since the last payroll. "And how did they react?" Happy, as you might expect. They've both been more cheerful over the past couple weeks. I think that just making sales has been the most important factor. They don't feel like they're failing at their job anymore, and we're getting close to making our target for the first time in six months. Maybe they can see that I'm feeling better, too, although we're still behind on cash. Sure, I've changed our advertising and our sales methods, but what if I'm doing something else that's causing another problem? I blundered into the AdWords situation without realizing what would happen. How can I know that whatever I do next won't cause bigger problems?

"You can never know, unless you never change anything. And then a competitor will show up and eat your lunch." Bob's right. I can't avoid taking risks, even if they don't always work out.

ON THURSDAY, Nancy and I try something daring: we take Henry to New York City. Our plan is to take him to Times Square and, if that goes well, have lunch. On arrival he starts crying, but as we maneuver him through the crowds, he starts grooving on the energy of the city. We have a quick meal at a diner, and on the way back, Nancy and I marvel that we all had fun. It was a joy to see him in Times Square, dancing around as he looked at all the lights. It's easy to focus on his bad moments, harder to remember that most of the time he's good.

I'm back at the shop on Friday morning, Henry in tow. I can see Bob Foote and Nathan Johnson working on the crates for Brand Advantage. The tables are complete. Bob tells me that they'll be on the dock by four p.m. He hopes they get picked up today. Good. Monica has been asking us every day to confirm the ship date. In the sales office, Nick says the phone's been ringing off the hook and he closed a deal yesterday worth $12,698. That gets us to $200,607 for the month. We've hit our target for the first time since February. He's done a great job implementing the new methods and his monthly sales total shows it—six sales, totaling $115,465, more than half of our total for August. I sold three jobs, worth $50,340. Dan was even worse. He closed just two, worth $34,802.

Should I put up with his performance anymore? I'm supposed to be holding my salespeople accountable. On the other hand, we've hit our target and I wasn't such a hot performer, either. I can't claim that the new methods are an inevitable path to success if I didn't match Nick's results. I decide to give Dan more time.

SEPTEMBER

DATE: SUNDAY, SEPTEMBER 2, 2012

BANK BALANCE: $76,626.16

CASH RELATIVE TO START OF YEAR ("NET CASH"): -$60,528.16

NEW-CONTRACT VALUE, YEAR-TO-DATE: $1,211,222

On Sunday, I drive Henry back to his school. When we get there, I talk with Annie, his housemaster, who asks me whether I'm looking for a helper. "We haff a verker here," she says in her Finnish accent, "who is fferrry interested in finding a chob." She sings the praises of this young man, Kristian Scheld. I listen politely. "He sounds good, but I hired someone last week. Tell Kristian to send me a résumé, but I don't promise anything." Let's see if he can follow this instruction. It would be good to have a possible backup for Nathan Johnson.

I head back home and collapse. Briefly. Tomorrow I'll be driving to see a potential client in Newport News, Virginia. I've subjected him to all my new tricks, and he's very enthusiastic about moving forward. But he's crystal clear about what he wants next: for me to show up in his office, so he can see whether I'm for real. This could be a hundred thousand dollars' worth of work, so I agree. Six hundred and twenty-four miles of horrendous traffic, and a night in a cheap motel. That's my Labor Day break.

When I arrive at work on Wednesday, the crates for Brand Advantage are on the loading dock. I promised that they'd ship last Friday. I track down Bob Foote and demand an explanation. He's apologetic. "They didn't get them on Friday, and the truck they sent yesterday was too small, so the driver left a note saying he'd be back tomorrow." Fortunately for him, the crates go out by day's end. Brand Advantage owes me $22,448 on the fifth day after delivery. I really need that money. I have $76,626 in the bank. It's not a payroll week, but I need to pay my rent, the electric bill, and some vendor charges, more than $28,000. And payroll next Tuesday will be about $25,000. My working capital could drop below $30,000—that's the edge of failure.

Dan and Nick are working through the inquiries from August. We got more calls last month than we've ever received before—an average of twenty-one a week, up from 16.8 in July and 11.8 in June. Some were from repeat customers, some from Eurofurn. Did my AdWords adjustment work? Maybe. I need more time before I'm sure.

Other August numbers aren't so hot. We had a very mediocre build total, just $144,926. The ship total was worse: $102,881. That's not surprising, considering the terrible sales in June. There just wasn't enough work for the shop crew. They all showed up, though, and I paid them. I also spent a lot of money on materials for the orders that we'll build in September. My cash outlays for August total $197,926. By accounting rules, subtracting my ship total from my spending, I've lost $95,045. My cash flow isn't quite that bad. I went into August with $82,941 and exited with $76,626: a net outflow of $6,315.

There's nothing to do but keep going. Dan, Nick, and I put our heads down and work our prospects. Yesterday, the day after the holiday weekend, was quiet—just one call—but five potential customers call on Wednesday. And we make our first sale of the month.

A returning customer orders a custom countertop to go with his table, for $3,422.

The next morning, the three of us complete our sales training. The final lesson: what to do when an active client suddenly stops answering our calls. We used to just give up and move on, but Bob has a better idea.

"Give them the '*No.*' Make them say they are done with you. It's easy to do: just give them an ultimatum. Send an e-mail, or leave a message, saying that it appears that you, the salesperson, have been unable to come up with a way to move forward. You apologize for this, and then say that you intend to close the file and move on. Just say that, nothing more. If the client wasn't finished, if they were just toying with you, then they'll get right back to you. Believe me, this will happen. And if they are truly done and you hear nothing, then you can strike them off your list and move on to greener pastures."

Bob suggests another useful tactic. "Suppose you're afraid that your client is thinking about going to a competitor, or you're worried they are going to take your ideas and give them to someone else. Or anything, really, that you think might go wrong. Here's how you deal with it in a non-threatening way. The technique is called 'My Biggest Fear.' You ask the question like this: 'You know, Mr. Client, my biggest fear is that you are going to . . .'" Bob asks us for a list of ways that a deal can go wrong and starts listing our answers. So many fears: the client might give this job to someone else; might not be able to find enough money for the job; might recommend someone else to the decision makers; and on and on. Bob continues, "Whatever your fear is, that's what you confess to the client. In a humble way. You aren't trying to bully them into anything. You are going the other way, making yourself look pathetic. If they are human beings, they're going to feel some sympathy for you, and you'll get the difficult issue out in the open so that you can address it." Brilliant. I can't wait to give it a try.

After class, I shake Bob's hand. "You've been great. All this has been very, very useful." Bob smiles. He's heard this before. But I know, from my own encounters with my many satisfied customers, that it never gets old.

The lectures are over, but we'll continue to work with Bob until June of next year. I'll see him twice a month: a one-on-one session, to analyze my performance as sales manager; and a group session with Dan, Nick, and Emma. We'll all review how the sales process is going and get Bob's advice. Each session will cost me more than twelve hundred dollars, but I'm confident that I will get my money's worth. That good feeling is reinforced the following day. I close a deal worth $14,326. Dan tops me with one worth $21,039. Nick hasn't sold anything, but he assures me he's got some good ones coming in. We've booked $38,787 in a week shortened by a holiday, and there's still half a day left. Not bad.

My happy mood is erased by a phone call from Monica at Brand Advantage. She's very upset. The shipment has arrived. Five of the thirty tables are damaged, the tops ripped off in transit. I'd love to slam down the phone and cry, but that won't help anyone. So I ask her to send photos and assure her that we will do everything we can to fix them as soon as we can. "I'll have someone at your facility on Monday. We're going to take care of this."

Monica doesn't sound reassured. The tables are supposed to get their branding—I still don't know what this means—on Monday, in time for the first event next Friday. I tell Will Krieger and Bob Foote what happened. Bob looks especially down. I ask him: "Didn't you make supports for the tops like we did the first time?" He confesses that they did for two of the crates, but not the last one, because they were rushing to get them onto the loading dock. I'd like to kill him, but that won't do any good.

He offers to be the one to go to Atlanta. Damn straight, I'm thinking. The trip is going to be awful: early-morning flight, then hard work all day, a cheap motel, and another dawn flight. The three of us consider how we can make the tops stronger. We decide to screw threaded metal inserts into the existing bolt holes to reinforce them, and to also glue the tops to the bases with auto-body adhesive. I book the flights for Bob, then head home for the weekend.

On Sunday morning—surprise!—a message from Shiva in Dubai:

> *We would like to have your revised proposal on the executive meeting table as we have not yet finalized this issue. Please find attached CAD drawing for the sixth floor showing meeting table for 38 people.*

Having heard nothing from her since I sent my last proposal in July, I've assumed they chose someone else. Apparently not. Now what should I do? If this job comes back to life, I should see whether our new sales tricks work on a foreign customer.

The new design she has sent is strange: the top of the table, an open square, will have a continuous strip running around the inside edge for the power/data hatches. Eighteen of those will be positioned at even intervals, with longer pieces, the same width as the hatches, filling in the spaces between them. They want both the hatches and the filler strips to be removable, and they want two sets, one in ebonized oak to match the rest of the table and the other wrapped in gray leather.

This makes no sense. Why not choose one or the other and be done with it? And important information is still missing. I don't have a target budget, or a time frame. Shiva hasn't even said when she wants us to submit our proposal. I could just e-mail her these questions, but that would go counter to our new sales methods. So I reply by asking her for a phone conversation to discuss the project.

The Monday meeting on the tenth is short. We received $8,484 more than we spent and now have $85,110 on hand. The rent bill didn't arrive until Friday, so we'll be paying that tomorrow along with payroll and the AdWords credit card. And a bunch of other vendor bills. We'll be sending out more than $60,000. Brand Advantage owes me $22,448, so it's critical that we get the tables fixed today.

Bob calls before lunch. "It's pretty bad," he reports. The bolts on the five tops in the skimpy crate have ripped right out. "I'm going to put in the inserts and glue them like we discussed. I think it would be smart to do it to all the tables while I'm at it." I tell him to go ahead.

I spend the rest of the day perfecting my home-brewed CRM system. We've been using it since August, and it's starting to look good. Dan and Nick helped me decide what information we should be recording for each client and the best way to organize all that in FileMaker. Now I can see the promising inquiries and who is in charge of them, and which salesman has a better close rate.

But only if they use it. As I've been working on FileMaker, we've debated whether gathering more information is worth the additional work to record it. Keep in mind that a lot of the inquiries do not end up as sales. It's discouraging to do a lot of clerical work to track inquiries that go nowhere. I wish data could be recorded without any effort on our part, but that's simply not possible. In the end, I make decisions that the two of them can accept about what we will record and what we won't. I'm glad they aren't fighting it. It should help them process more inquiries. And it's the information I need to hold them accountable.

Bob returns from Atlanta on Wednesday. He worked until three a.m. on Tuesday to complete the fixes. And he can finally tell me what the branding is all about. It turns out it's the kind of logo decal that you see on trucks and buses, applied to the tops of the tables. They'll change the branding for each event.

I don't know why Monica and Ginny couldn't convey any of this to us. We could have put the bolts all the way through the tabletops if we'd known they would be covered by the branding. That would have been very strong. I need to know whether they'll pay me, so I ask Bob, "Were they happy when you left?" He doesn't know. All the Brand Advantage people went home hours before he finished.

I thank him for his efforts. He's done a great job in a difficult situation. What motivated him? Did he do it for himself, or for the good of the company? His future is tied to the company's success, but not as closely as mine. He can walk away if we go broke. I'll be wrapped in tentacles of debt.

On Thursday, I finally hear back from Shiva. She won't commit to a phone call, so I send her my questions: When do they need the table, is there a target budget, and when do they need the proposal? Again, I've missed her working day and won't hear from her until tomorrow at the earliest.

EACH MORNING THIS WEEK, I've walked through the shop. Even with our new helper, it looks like it always has: dust on every surface, random offcuts around each machine. Surrounding the workbenches, too many pieces of interesting wood that the guys can't bear to throw away. Woodworkers are packrats, and the shop looks like a giant nest.

Is it too early to see the effect of replacing Steve Maturin? Certainly the August build total was not impressive, but there's a good reason for that—not enough jobs to work on. But now we've had a solid month of sales, and the first week of September has been pretty good, too. When can I expect Will Krieger to transform the shop into something much better? I'm trying to damp my rising impatience.

On Thursday afternoon, the question suddenly rearranges itself into a much better one: what am *I* going to do to help Will change things? I realize I've fallen into the same pattern of behavior that was such a failure with Steve Maturin: letting the shop manager run the place however he wants, without any input from me. I have great faith in Will's abilities. But he's never managed anyone. And this issue is much more complex. He'll need my help.

It's really a problem of culture. The shop has become a mirror of Steve Maturin's personality: all work, no communication. Every bench hand is left to his own devices and doesn't have much to do with the other guys. And they receive minimal guidance on the best way to do things. The result: errors and inconsistent results. We always deliver a well-crafted piece to our clients, but it's often after considerable rework. And when the problems are the result of correctible mistakes from the office, nobody on the shop floor takes the time to tell Andy Stahl what needs to be fixed, so his errors reappear over and over.

Our shop culture has its origins in the way I managed my first employees. Back then, I knew nothing about being a boss, but I found myself in that position anyway. How should I act? What kind of employee behavior should I encourage? Never having worked in another woodshop, and knowing nobody who did, my ideas came from books and magazines. They all agreed: the ideal woodworker is a Heroic Solitary Craftsman, who solves every puzzle with some kind of technical magic. A hard worker who uses modern machines when they are convenient, but who reserves his respect for traditional hand skills. My sources said nothing about teamwork. Nothing about managing a group of workers. Nothing about coordinating the efforts of the sales staff with the engineering department with the shop floor, or making shop operations efficient by incorporating technology.

Steve Maturin was one of my first hires, in 1994. By 1996, I had put him in charge of the other shop workers while I continued to do all the sales, engineering, administration, and delivery. Steve is the archetype of the Heroic Solitary Craftsman. I didn't know back then that he was the wrong guy for a larger, busier shop that must adapt to changing technology. He was stuck in the past. He led by example and didn't care how closely his subordinates followed him. He worked very hard and fast, and expected the other guys to learn his methods through observation alone. He didn't want to spend time working with Andy Stahl to refine our designs. And he never made the slightest effort to keep me informed about what was happening in the shop, or to ask my opinion on how things should proceed. I let him get away with this for fifteen years. He was never quite my biggest problem, until the day came when he was. It was only the combination of his intolerable attitude and Will Krieger's initiative that led me to replace him. So now I have a new guy in charge, and I'm doing the same thing again—focusing on sales and letting the shop manager drift into failure. I need to change, and right away.

Inspired by the coaching I'm getting from Ed Curry and Bob Waks, I decide to schedule regular meetings with Will. I'm picturing extended sessions away from the distractions of the shop floor. I want to discuss—what? Whatever comes up. I hope that a free and frank exchange of ideas will help us work out a game plan for change.

I find Will at his bench on Thursday morning. He stops working when I approach. I tell him, "I've been thinking about how we can implement changes to the shop floor. I haven't been focusing on this because of the work I've been doing with the sales training and writing software. That's all finished. I want to take some time tomorrow afternoon to sit down with you and go over what your plans are, so that you and I can be on the same page. And I mean more than just a couple of minutes—I think that this is going to take at least an hour. Does that sound OK?" He thinks it's a great idea.

EARLY FRIDAY MORNING, there's a message from Shiva's assistant. They want a final design and pricing by Sunday, the sixteenth. And it needs to be delivered in mid-November. Just like last time, the delivery date is the biggest problem. Eight weeks is tight even if the table were going to New York. Subtract the shipping time, and it's almost impossible. But I'll make one last attempt to land this job. If I can talk to her, maybe I can buy more time. I send an e-mail to schedule a conference call for Sunday morning, six a.m. If she doesn't agree to talk, I'll let the project slide.

I've just hit Send when Monica calls. I sent Brand Advantage an e-mail yesterday, the fifth day after delivery, asking for permission to charge their credit card for the $22,448 they owe us. I give her a cheerful greeting. "Hi, Monica. Can I go ahead and charge the card?"

She's grumpy. "No, you can't. You've got a big problem. The tables won't fit in the truck." I'm flabbergasted. "What truck?" She tells me that they have leased two trucks to carry the thirty tables to each event, and they can't get them all in. "And why is this my problem?" She sputters that they don't fit and that she won't pay. I think fast. Telling her to deal with it herself won't get me my money, so I stay calm and tell her that we'll do everything we can to help. If she can get me the dimensions of the truck interior, I'll see if I can find a way to pack them. Oh, and can I talk to her boss? "He's very busy right now. I don't think he can come to the phone." Grrrr. I keep my voice buttery smooth. "Really? He's got more important things than this? I'm pretty sure I can solve the problem, but I need to speak to him first. If you want all this to go away, I need to talk to him." The idea of her problems disappearing seems to calm her down, so she tells me she'll ask him to call me.

Now I'm anxiously waiting for the call. After thirty minutes, Monica sends the truck's interior dimensions, and in less than ten minutes, after modeling the truck with my software, I solve the problem. Should I make a quick plan and send it to them? I decide to wait and see if the boss calls.

An hour later, Mark Jones, president of Brand Advantage, is on the phone. I thank him for choosing us to do this work and commiserate about the difficulties we've had. He's gracious. "Yeah, this whole project has been, um, mishandled from the beginning." Is he saying that everything has been our fault? OK, we didn't make that one crate correctly, but I fixed it right away. I point this out and tell him that this latest problem really isn't our responsibility. We had no control over what size truck he leased, and it's not our problem to figure out how to pack the tables. Monica should have planned that when she got the prototype. Mark agrees. I throw him a bone. "Monica sent me the truck dimensions, and I've worked out a solution for you. You'll be able to fit fifteen tables into each truck with room to spare. But I'd like you to pay me the money you owe me before I send it down."

Long pause. "How much do we owe you?" I tell him: $22,448. Another long pause, then: "Paul, I'll be honest with you, I don't have it. This whole thing is going to hell, and I won't get paid until we do the first event." Is he trying to stiff me? I can let him solve his own problems and hope I'll collect the money—when? If they continue to screw up, they'll never get paid. Maybe he just wants to see if I'll go away, or if I'll threaten to call lawyers, or if I'll settle for less now and hope for the rest later. I have an idea. I ask, "How about a partial payment?" He comes back with, "I can do fifteen right now." I have little confidence, based on their performance so far, that they're going to emerge from the mess they're in. And I need money right now. "Can I charge the credit card?" Mark tells me it's maxed out, but that he'll cut a check in the next fifteen minutes and e-mail me an image of it. I'll have it Monday. Trust him or not? I'm going to have to. And if it bounces next week? I'll deal with it then. Fifteen minutes later, his bookkeeper e-mails the picture of the signed check.

Nick says, "I've been listening to you deal with this shit storm all morning. I just want to tell you that I've picked up three orders." Nice work! Another $27,401 coming in. He continues, "The first one, Bright Jupiter Inc.—you won't believe it—I asked for a deposit, they told me to charge the entire amount. They want to pay for it all this quarter." That's $18,871 to go along with the fifteen grand I'll get on Monday. Whew!

All this has happened before lunchtime. I've got my first session with Will Krieger in an hour. What am I going to talk about? First thing: I want to make sure he knows that he's one of the bosses now, not just another worker. I want him to see things from my perspective, so that he doesn't waste time with plans that, while they might make sense from the shop floor, I can't approve because of factors that he knows nothing about. What's the best way to bring him into my world? I decide to start with a question that I've been pondering for a while: am I paying the right wages?

I suspect that I'm paying more than I should for some of the guys. Others could probably earn more elsewhere, but don't realize it. When they do, I could lose a valuable worker. I don't know what any of them would make in another shop, only that, when layoffs loomed in June and July, nobody jumped ship. Why not? I'd like Will's thoughts on the situation.

I make a quick spreadsheet. The first column is a list of every shop floor worker—the people he is directly in charge of—starting with Will himself. Alongside each name, I put the current pay rate in dollars per hour. These numbers range from twelve to thirty dollars an hour and add up to a total of $186 an hour. (This is just gross hourly pay, excluding vacation time, health insurance costs, and taxes.) I label the next column "Other Shop Pay" and the column after that "What We Should Pay."

Will arrives, and we retreat to my private office. I shut the door. My first question is a warm-up. "How's it going out there?" Will shrugs. "It's going." "Are any machines broken? Do we need any new tools?" He says that one of the veneer sanders could use a tune-up, and the veneer splicer is way out of adjustment. "And how is Nathan Johnson working out?" Will's brow furrows, but he says that he's doing all right.

I could have had this conversation on the shop floor. I'm not learning much from Will, and he's not learning anything from me. Time to change tack.

"One of my goals for these meetings is that you and I talk about what's happening in the shop with complete candor. Nothing held back. I'm going to be relying on you to tell me how you see things out there, but you won't have the same viewpoint as me unless you know what I know." He nods. "I'm going to be asking you to make decisions about all the guys, and that's going to involve making judgments about their performance. And you can't judge somebody's performance unless you know how much money they're making. I've been wondering for a long time whether I'm paying the right amount to each person. And I want to discuss that with you today."

He thinks for a second and then asks, "Wait, you want me to

know how much all the guys get paid?" He looks uncomfortable. "Yes, I do. You need to know this if you are in charge. Otherwise, you have no context for thinking about them. Payroll is our biggest expense, by a long shot. I want to turn this into a profitable business, so that we can all work hard knowing that it's producing enough money to secure our futures. I couldn't find a way to make that happen with Steve, so we stumbled along for years. I don't want that to happen with you. I want you on my side, and I want to be on your side. This is where we start." I open up my laptop and show him the spreadsheet. "Take a look at this."

He looks at it, and then, when it sinks in that he's seeing everyone's pay rates, he pushes the laptop away. "Um, I'm not sure I should be seeing this." I turn it back in front of him. "You need to see this. It's another reality. You're used to thinking of the shop as tools and woodwork, with people doing stuff. I see it that way, but I also see the numbers behind all of it. The whole business is like that. The numbers are just as important as the rest of it, maybe more important. If they don't work, we won't be here."

While I'm talking, he's looking carefully at the spreadsheet. His first comment: "You're paying Tyler Powell wa-a-ay too much." We spend another forty-five minutes filling out all the cells. He says that he doesn't know what the guys would be worth in other shops, but I tell him to make his best guess, because that's what I do when I don't have hard facts. So he gives me what he thinks each person would make in the real world, and what they should be making here. The totals for both columns aren't far from where we are now: real-world wages would come to $182 an hour, as opposed to the $186 we're spending. But that's in aggregate. We go back and discuss each worker. When I ask for a summary of each worker's performance, he offers thoughtful evaluations of their strengths and weaknesses. He's clearly been paying attention to their work.

We both agree that Steve Maturin is getting foreman money without the responsibility: overpaid. And Dave Violi puts in a tremendous effort in the finishing room, and his skills are top-notch: underpaid. Tyler Powell is making the same twenty-five dollars an hour I paid him when I brought him on in 2007. Will thinks that he's worth eighteen dollars an hour, tops. He works very fast, but he makes a lot of mistakes. He doesn't do things the same way every time, which to my mind means he's trying to find better methods, a good thing. Will sees it differently. Tyler's experiments usually end up with rework. But even with the backtracking, he still completes his jobs much faster than our targets. Will is judging the quality of his output; I'm focusing on the fact that he consistently beats his targets. By that measure, he does much better than everyone except Steve and Will, but we give him only very easy things to do, because he messes up more complex work. There's no obvious solution.

We review the rest of the crew. Will has abandoned whatever qualms he had about judging his former peers. We have a productive discussion. I wrap up with this thought: "We have these mismatches between what the guys are getting paid and what they should be getting paid. I can't afford to give the underpaid guys a raise right now, and I hate to just go out and cut someone's pay. It's cruel. People build their lives, and particularly their debts, around their income. If I just cut pay because I feel like it, it can cause real trouble. So your challenge is to find a way to make the overpaid guys worth the money we're paying, and to make the shop profitable so that I can give the underpaid guys a bump. You seem to know how these guys work. Now it's time to define a standard method of work for each thing we do. You're going to be spending more time teaching and less time doing your own work. That's OK. Just do it, and let's see what happens." He leaves with a thoughtful expression on his face. I'm very happy about the way this has gone.

SUNDAY MORNING, six a.m. Shiva sent an e-mail yesterday agreeing to talk at this time. After she logs on to Glance, I give her a tour of the table I've designed, which does everything she asks for. She can see how it fits in the room, how the wiring works, and how we will switch the accent stripe from leather to wood. She's very impressed, but would like me to send her images and pricing.

I don't want to send either without some commitment, or a conversation with the actual decision makers, but she says that it will be impossible. "I need images and pricing today. And the sample. We will need the sample to make our decision."

The sample. It's going to be a pain to make—and a bigger pain to ship. "It will take some time for us to finish it. We're very busy in the shop right now. And it will take time to ship it. Are you sure you need it?" She is. The job is worth $47,884. And it might open up a new market for us. I send her pictures and the quote.

MONDAY MORNING, I deliver the sales and cash reports. We've received $65,998 in orders in the first two weeks of the month— better than nothing, but not fantastic. At least inquiries have been strong. We got twenty-two calls and e-mails last week.

I tell the crew that sales will probably be OK, but I can't think of a way to sugarcoat our cash position. Last week, I sent out $29,719 more than I took in. The full payment from Bright Jupiter helped, but I ended the week with $55,391 on hand. Eight days of working funds. I'm not quite as scared as I was in June and July, when customers weren't calling. But it's still a precarious situation.

After the meeting, Bob and Will ask to see me in private. Now what? Bob tells me that he doesn't like Nathan Johnson, the helper.

Why not? "Well, he seems kind of lazy. Moves slow. And he doesn't do a good job of cleaning." I have to agree—the shop is cleaner than when we had no helper, but it's nowhere near as nice as Jésus kept it. Bob continues, "And he asked me whether I wanted to hang out with him on the loading dock. Like he just wanted us to sit there and do nothing. I didn't even know what to say. I just don't think he's going to work here." I ask Will, "Do you agree that he's not a good fit?" Will says that he does. "And you don't want to talk to him, try to get him to start doing what he should?" He doesn't. "OK, have him come in at ten-thirty. I'll talk to him." Should I tell Nathan the truth? That we're canning him because he's lazy? How will he react? This is an enormous guy who's done some prison time. He's probably got a hundred pounds on me. If he gets upset, I'm in trouble.

This problem distracts me for the next hour, as my mind spins up one horrible scenario after another. I don't think of myself as a coward, but I'm scared because anything could happen. I decide that my best strategy is to tell a shameless lie.

Will brings Nathan into the small conference room, and we all sit down. I start: "Nathan, you heard what I said about sales being slow so far this month and that we're short on cash. I'm very sorry to say this, but I just don't have enough money to keep a helper right now. You've been a good worker, but I have to make cuts. I'll give you a week's pay to tide you over, but you can finish up your work this morning and leave after lunch."

Nathan gives me his big smile, stands up, and holds out his hand. He tells me that he's very sorry it's come to this, but that he understands. He thanks me for the extra pay and tells me to please call him if things pick up. I'm relieved that it went so well. After lunch I ask Will, "How did it work out with Nathan? Did he leave quietly?"

Will tells me that he went without a peep. And then he gives me a little smirk. Does he think I'm a coward?

I have to say something. "Look, I could have told him the truth, but what good would that have done? Telling him we're out of money isn't far from true, and it let him keep his dignity. So I'm sorry if you think that was the wrong thing to do." Will says he understands perfectly why I did it. "Just don't do it to me. Don't ever give me bullshit. I can take the truth."

I head back to the office to try to get some work done. There's a thin FedEx envelope on my keyboard, from Brand Advantage. My fifteen thousand dollars has arrived. This cheers me up a bit.

Will Krieger sticks his head in the sales office on his way home. I ask him, "What do you want to do about a helper? I've got this kid, he works at Henry's school. He's supposed to be good. He sent a résumé just like I asked." Will says that he sounds OK, he would like to have a decent helper.

On Tuesday, Dan sells a ten-foot boat-shaped table for $7,376. We collect a deposit for half of that. We've been able to collect pre-ships and finals for four jobs, totaling $30,234. The following day, Nick closes a deal worth $13,670 to a very large defense contractor, and Dan closes one for $15,325 to a multi-national environmental consultancy. That takes our sales total to $102,369—still a little behind target, but getting better.

On Thursday, Nick starts with a $13,581 job from the Broward County sheriff. Dan strikes back with $7,471 from the U.S. Army. Nick closes the day with $18,345 from an industrial laser manufacturer. And on Friday, Nick finishes our week with another army sale worth $20,835. It's been a great week—seven jobs totaling $96,603. Our monthly tally stands at $162,601.

Not bad, but all the jobs we took in from government clients were awarded on net-30 terms. I won't see any money until thirty days after we deliver. But even without those deposits, I've taken in $68,954 and only spent $19,943. I'm up almost $50,000 from Monday, and end the week with $104,401 on hand. If we'd been able to get our preferred terms from the government buyers, I'd have another $20,000 in my hands, but at least I'll have enough to make payroll and put something toward the credit card.

It's a relief to stand up on Monday and report a really solid week of sales and an improvement in our cash position. And a healthy backlog—we've got seven weeks of work queued up. I take some pains to explain the problem of the government jobs to the crew—we've just committed to do a lot of work that must be delivered on time, and we don't have nearly enough money on hand to complete it. We must continue to ship work at a good clip and hope that sales continue to come in, or we could run out of cash. But it's not hopeless. I can delay outgoing payments for a while if I need to.

On Monday afternoon, I try to log in to my bank accounts and get a short message: "Accounts unavailable at this time." What the—? I try again. Same result. And again. Ditto. I can't believe that PNC Bank would turn off its Web site in the middle of a workday. I try the home page. It loads as normal. I head back to my account login. I still can't get through. I turn to other tasks, and an hour later, I try again, but still no access. What's going on?

Even during the panic in the fall of 2008, I knew that the government would backstop my bank if it failed. Until this afternoon, I've never been kept from my own money. Fortunately, at the end of the day, the accounts come back online. It's all in the *Times* that night: Iranian hackers took down the five biggest banks. I briefly consider whether to take my business to a smaller bank, but then abandon the idea. Way too much trouble. I'm sure it will never happen again.

As it turns out, I'm wrong. I'm locked out four more times in the next two days, but only for a couple hours at a time. It's worrisome, but I continue to do nothing. Funny how fast I can get used to something that had me so upset when it first happened. Especially when it would be a ton of work to fix.

Dan owns the last week of September. He gets his first order—another military job, with no deposit—on Tuesday: $30,045 for a big U-shaped table for an army base in Arizona. On Wednesday, he scores a smaller job for folding modular tables worth $9,660. And he caps his week with a twenty-four-footer for a general contractor in California, worth $18,055. After that one, I give him a handshake. He's brought in $108,971 in orders, and for the first time has passed his monthly target. Nick is close behind at $93,832. I'm in the dust with just $17,558. I'm hugely relieved. For once, I can stop worrying that Dan can't do his job.

We've booked $220,361 in new orders in September, $1,431,583 so far this year. If we'd consistently made our monthly target, we'd have sold $1,800,000, and I would have collected at least another $250,000 in cash.

I can dream about what might have happened, but eventually I'll wake up and see reality: payroll, another $20,000 to the credit card, and vendors. Last week, I spent $28,382 more than I took in. That puts my ending balance, on the last day of September, very close to where I was at the beginning of the month. I started with $76,626 and ended with $76,019.

In my second Friday meeting with Will Krieger, we review the build-and-ship totals for the month. They're good: $195,262 build; $221,612 ship. I managed to hold my spending to just $154,674 for the whole month, so we have a book profit of $66,938. It's a good demonstration of the disconnect between standard accounting and what really matters—cash. Will knows nothing about accounting, but he's very interested in this new way of looking at the business. "If we ship more than we spend, we're making money?" Pretty much, although there are some things, like equipment depreciation, which have to be taken into account. I explain that in the short term, cash flow isn't directly connected to profit and loss. But if we continually ship more than we spend, eventually we'll start to see our cash reserves grow. It might take a while, but it should happen. I'm going on faith. I've never been able to consistently perform this feat, and I've always struggled with cash.

OCTOBER

Date: Monday, October 1, 2012

Bank balance: $76,019.18

Cash relative to start of year ("Net Cash"): -$61,135.14

New-contract value, year-to-date: $1,431,583

At the meeting, I'm positive when I talk about sales, cautious when I explain our cash situation. I explain the payment terms for the military work: if these had been our usual buyers, we'd have another thirty-two thousand dollars on hand. I emphasize that we now have eight weeks of work. We need to get it all done quickly, without errors. Do I detect a lift in mood? From most of them, yes. Steve sits, as usual, hunched over and grim. I wish he would forget the past and cheer up when there's good news.

The week proceeds with plenty more to celebrate. On Monday afternoon, Nick gets an order from a defense contractor. Two weeks ago he sold them a pair of credenzas worth $13,670. Now they commit to the rest of the room, an additional $77,690. We'll get a credit card for 50 percent of that today.

On Tuesday, Nick writes a much smaller order: $7,460. On Wednesday, he completes the trifecta: an order from a company that supports large retailers, worth $19,684. Dan gets a whopper of his own. It's the boardroom table for a local pharmaceutical company, worth $66,932. He's been chasing this job since February.

In three days, a total of $171,766! We've collected deposits on all Nick's orders, and some pre-ships and finals as well. We've added $100,056 in cash this week, and only spent $34,706. For the first time since March, I end a week with more cash on hand than I had at the start of the year.

My Friday meeting with Will focuses on how to do all this work. I tell him that we have a potential helper ready to go. Kristian Scheld sent me his résumé as I requested. I interviewed him last week. He made a good impression by mumbling his way through the interview, sweating profusely, barely able to meet my eye or answer a question. Typical woodworker. Will agrees that he's worth a try. I call him after Will leaves. He'll start next week.

The following Monday, it's all good news: whopper sales, cash to match. Our backlog is up to ten weeks. I conclude by introducing Kristian Scheld. He waves to everyone but says nothing.

In the office, we agree that there are jobs that might land soon, but a down week seems more likely. We're mistaken. By Friday, we've closed another $75,625. I win salesman of the week, with one large order for $47,816. And I get another small one the next day, $561 for data ports. Dan brings in $11,365 on Thursday, and Nick wraps up the week with a nice $15,883 order on Friday morning. Two weeks into the month we've sold $247,391.

I'm basking in this success on Friday when Bob Foote knocks on the door. "Uh, do you have a minute? My credit card just got refused." Bob was ordering the cardboard we use to wrap all our tables. We usually buy a thousand sheets at a time.

I log in to my accounts and see that I've used $67,097 of my $70,000 limit. I consider whether to pay the whole balance. I've got $124,087 on hand. We're still waiting for deposits to arrive from the non-military deals we've closed in the past two weeks. Taking out what I owe on the credit card leaves me with just $56,989. I decide to send in $25,000 and hope that more cash comes in soon. I end the week with $97,042. I'm back to negative relative to my January 1 balance. Oh, well. It was nice while it lasted.

On Friday afternoon, I tell Will that we need more overtime work from everyone out there. "And not just you and Dave," I emphasize. Dave has been working an additional fifteen to twenty hours a week, and Will is not far behind. "You two can't carry the whole shop on your back. Tell the other guys to step it up. I want at least five hours a week out of everyone."

I rarely ask for overtime from the guys, even when we're very busy. I know from my own shop floor experience how tired one can get after a long day, and how that leads to trouble: you're hurrying to finish a cut. A little voice in your head is saying that something might go wrong. You ignore it. And then—I never removed one of my fingers, but I came very close. And I spent a lot more time in the emergency room than I saved by trying to cut corners.

I learned my lesson. I've always told my workers that if they hear a little voice, stop what they are doing immediately. That seems to have worked. We've had no amputations in the twenty-six years we've been open. Now I'm telling Will to get the guys to hurry up, but I don't want him to give them the impression that they should cut corners, either in quality or safety.

"So how are you going to tell the guys they need to work OT?" Will shrugs and says that he'll just tell them to work some overtime. "Will you get them all together and tell them? Or one at a time? What exactly are you going to say? And what if someone says he can't do it?" Will clearly hasn't considered how to deliver this message. I continue, "When you're in charge, you need to know what you are going to say before you start. Otherwise you might find yourself tongue-tied in front of a bunch of guys. That makes you look stupid. It's OK to write down notes with the things you have to go over. And you have a choice here—discuss this at the Monday meeting, or call the shop guys together afterward and have a smaller meeting, maybe out on the shop floor. Which do you think would be more effective?"

He considers. "I don't know. In the meeting, the whole company gets to hear the announcement. If I do it afterward, then it's just the shop guys, but it might not seem like criticism. They already work hard. But then again, it might be more special because it's not just the meeting."

"Good points. Now make a decision." Will suggests that we do both—I'll announce it at the meeting and then he'll repeat it in a huddle on the shop floor, to make sure everyone understands that it's mandatory. I like that—it's better than what I came up with.

Next Monday, my speech focuses on sales and why we don't have the cash balance to match: missing deposits and military orders. And then I tell them about overtime. No visible reaction, as usual. The guys drift out the door to the shop, where Will is waiting. I watch. They pay more attention to him than they did to me.

The rest of the day I design a table for the CEO of the same defense company that placed the big order two weeks ago. They must be doing well. They've already run up a $91,360 tab, and now their boss is going to tack on another $35,000 or so. While I'm doing that, three checks arrive, totaling $27,213.

The next morning, I take a quick lap around the shop. Double take: it's Jésus, missing since May, here sweeping sawdust. I find Bob Foote and ask where Jésus came from. He stares at me, then asks back, "Didn't you set this up?" I wave Will over and say, "Jésus is here." He gives me a "No shit, Sherlock" look. I fill him in: "I didn't call Simba. He just showed up by himself. Do you want to keep him?" Will thinks, then says that with Jésus back, Kristian Scheld will be able to concentrate on learning to make bases.

I call Simba. "Jésus just showed up this morning. Did you send him out here?" He didn't, but he's happy to resume our previous deal. I go out to see Jésus. He gives me a big smile and holds out his hand for a shake. I take it—it's like shaking a brick. "Where have you been, Jésus?" He keeps smiling—no answer. No English. Just work. I drop his hand and head back to the office. This is a nice piece of luck. I'm back to the same number of workers that I had at the beginning of the year.

On Tuesday, I look to see who owes me money. Number one: Brand Advantage. We've heard nothing since their check arrived last month. I send another invoice. I've had a nagging feeling all morning that I've forgotten something, and suddenly it pops into my head. The sample for Dubai. I've had no response to the proposal I sent to Shiva in September. But I was supposed to send her the sample weeks ago. We must have lost the job. If we were in the running, she would have pressed me for the sample, right? I send her an e-mail, asking whether she still wants it. No answer the next day. Or, as it turns out, ever again.

In our Friday meeting, Will says that he plans to spend significant time training Kristian Scheld, who's showing great potential. I'm very pleased. Will is exactly what I've been missing all these years: a shop foreman with energy and imagination, who likes working with others and wants us to be a profitable business. My other workers are all excellent craftsmen, but none has Will's extra spark. Where did it come from? His family is of modest means—his father works in a warehouse. But the Kriegers have a deep streak of mechanical genius. His father and grandfather can build or fix anything: welding, carpentry, electrical work, plumbing, auto repair. Will grew up helping them with all this.

Will got his first paying job at the age of fourteen in a local cabinet shop. His shop teacher knew talent when he saw it and encouraged Will to enroll in a local technical college, Stevens Tech. When he graduated, Will started working at a local sawmill, then moved on to another cabinet shop. One day it ran out of money, and Will was back on the job market. That's when he saw my want ad.

Will's background—modest education, modest college, bouncing from one crappy job to the next—is typical of the guys who work for me. I even have a couple who never went to college at all, and I suspect that Dave Violi didn't finish high school. That doesn't bother me. I'm not interested in credentials. I care only about performance. These guys are smart, and capable of doing excellent work.

When I look at Will, I'm looking across a class divide. He's a very intelligent, capable man. His rural upbringing, and his choice of woodworking as a career, put him in a sector of the economy where very few people get rich, and most barely stay afloat. What would his future be if he had been raised in a family like mine and went to a decent school? He'd be on his way to the C-suite somewhere, by way of an excellent university. He'd be like my son Peter, who is also a self-starter. Peter, left to his own devices, taught himself to write code rather than work with his hands. Our local schools provided him with a solid education in math and writing to supplement his self-taught skills. And he's gone directly to a well-paying, professional job, even before getting a college education. What if Peter was more interested in auto repair than software? If he worked in a succession of small repair shops, for workman's wages? Would his classmates call him a success, or would he be a cautionary tale of brains and talent wasted?

That's probably how my peers see me. I'm the guy who jumped off the professional track after college and ended up working with his hands. Struggled all my life to keep the business afloat. Never made real money. Never got advanced degrees. I get no recognition from my professional peers—woodworkers don't have professional organizations. I'm buffeted by an economy that encourages manufacturing to go to countries with the cheapest labor.

I attribute my survival, in part, to my intellectual abilities, not my manual skills. I've taken my Ivy League education, and my design and marketing talents, and built a business that, despite many problems, has grown and produced decent jobs. If my sales issue is really fixed, my next challenge is figuring out how to move beyond survival. I need to improve as a businessman. In order to make a more secure future for myself and my workers, I have to get out of selling, step away from minute-by-minute operations. Otherwise, I won't have the time or energy to take the next steps toward success.

For that to happen, Dan and Nick need to succeed. And if they do, we're going to need to change how the shop operates. Will looks like the guy who can drive that transformation. Today I saw something that I haven't seen in eighteen years: a shop foreman eager to spend time training a new worker.

At the Monday meeting, I report our sales for the month: $261,371. And cash is strong. Incoming deposits have reversed last week's slump: $78,372 in; $24,310 out. Our balance is now $151,104.

The following morning, I check the overtime numbers on the pay sheets. My guys get paid time and a half for every overtime hour, which I see as a bargain. If I assume that I cover all my fixed costs in the first forty hours they work, OT hours are almost 25 percent cheaper, due to the lack of overhead. If the guys can keep working productively during the extra hours, the more they work, the better. But our call for overtime has yielded mixed results. Will Krieger and Dave Violi, as usual, are doing plenty. The problem is the other guys. Kristian did fourteen extra hours—a good effort. Ron did nine and a half hours. Bob did three and a half hours in the first week, but didn't even make forty hours the second week. Sean worked just one extra hour. Steve Maturin did none. I'm baffled. Who doesn't want to make more money?

On Friday, Will and I discuss the situation. He's talked to the slackers and has listened to a variety of excuses. It seems that some of the guys just don't want to be here any more than what's required to cover their bills. What should we do? We've already told the guys that it's mandatory, but we don't have a policy in place that addresses what happens when they don't comply. I could write one, but what would it be? Should it be a termination offense? Firing someone would teach a lesson to the remaining employees, but dismissing a highly skilled, difficult-to-replace worker would not help raise short-term production. It's one of those situations with no clear best choice. We decide to do nothing.

Friday afternoon, after everyone has gone, I stare at my cash spreadsheet. We sold another $98,157 last week. Much of that came with deposits, and we're still getting pre-ship and finals from work we've completed. Our haul this week: $81,852. It was tempting, as I wrote payroll on Tuesday, to give myself a paycheck. I'm just surviving on the $3,225 monthly interest payment that the company is paying me for the money I've loaned it. That takes care of my mortgage, but Nancy and I are in recession mode for all other expenditures: no new clothes, no travel, lots of macaroni and cheese. Peter will be starting school next fall, and I don't have enough money to pay for it. Maybe he'll be able to save some of his salary, and maybe I'll get some financial aid, but I don't want to assume anything.

Before I'll pay myself a penny, I want to clear up the credit card debt. The balance—$42,097— is due on Saturday. And I've just sent out a heavy payroll and a bunch of vendor bills: goodbye to $81,274, more spending than any other week this year. I end up $578 ahead of where I started. Paying off that credit card, though, is a huge relief.

On the last day of the month, we get three more orders, bringing us to $396,697. It's been a good October.

NOVEMBER

DATE: THURSDAY, NOVEMBER 1, 2012

BANK BALANCE: $150,716.50

CASH RELATIVE TO START OF YEAR ("NET CASH"): +$13,562.18

NEW-CONTRACT VALUE, YEAR-TO-DATE: $1,828,279

Will November bring another flood of orders? For the past three years, October's sales have been higher than September's, and November's have been much lower. But I've made drastic changes to my sales process. I hope to see a very different result this year.

Despite our huge sales last month, my cash position isn't nearly as strong as I want it to be. October's credit card payments subtracted $67,097 from my working capital. My yearly net cash is currently positive, but next week brings payroll, rent, and a long list of vendor charges. I'll be back into negative territory. The good news is that if we finish all the work we have on the books, we should collect $249,349. That's way up from the low point in June, when it was $50,751.

The main reason that the cash-to-come total has grown is that we took six jobs worth $117,644 on net-30 terms. Four are either military or large banks, one is the Houston accounting firm, and the last is a small electronics firm in Arizona. I know that the military and the bank, a repeat client, will pay on time if we deliver a good product. The others might not, but that risk is better than having no work to do.

I've been watching the October sales as they were booked and thinking about which ones we should build first. It would be easiest to always build them in the order they came in, but each buyer has different requirements for turnaround. Some want their order as fast as possible. Some of them demand quick turnaround but then aren't ready when we complete our work. A lot of clients who order a table are either renovating an old space or building a new one. If we deliver a table into an uncompleted room, it inevitably gets used as a work surface or scaffold and gets damaged. We can easily hold a completed table in our shop, but a lot of clients won't make their final payments until they receive their table.

Clients who aren't doing construction can take their table as soon as we complete it. It would be sensible to push these jobs to the front of the queue, and sometimes we can. But the shop floor guys hate being yanked off one job to start another. It interrupts their planned build sequence and seems to lead to more mistakes.

For the past decade, Andy Stahl and Steve Maturin managed the day-to-day workflow. They both arrived at the shop very early, between five-thirty and six a.m. I presume that they started their day by reviewing the schedule, but I actually don't know how they did it. It's yet another problem that I've let slide for years and been too busy to address. I decide to bring it up with Will in our meeting. "How are you deciding what jobs to work on each day?"

He says he goes to Andy's office every morning to see what drawings are ready, then reviews them with Andy before taking them out to the shop floor. He checks whether the required materials are on hand. Frequently, they aren't. Either Andy hasn't ordered them, or they're still in transit, or they were used to fix errors in a previous job. If something is missing, he goes back to Andy to try to figure out what happened and to get Andy to order more. If all the materials are on hand, he cuts the required parts on the CNC and stacks them on the carts. Those go to whomever he tells to build that table. I ask Will why he's running the CNC, a job Steve Maturin has always done.

"I haven't run a CNC before and I want to make sure I know how it works. And I need to be there if it crashes. Andy leaves a lot of mistakes in the code." Those are good reasons. And they point to a capacity problem in engineering. I really need a second person doing that job, but I don't have anyone on staff suitable. It's very different from bench work. Even if I did, Andy would have to devote significant time to training them. We'd fall further behind. I tell Will, "Let's assume there's no short-term fix. Andy's already tapped out. If we pile on more work, he may break down completely. I did his job for eleven years before I hired him, and it drove me crazy. So what can you do to compensate?"

I'm hoping that he'll move Steve back onto the CNC so he can devote more time to pre-checking the plans and managing the materials. From my seat in the office, that's what I think would be best. But what do I know? I'm starting to realize that my daily walk-through isn't enough to understand a very complex environment. Will considers my question. "I'm not sure what I can do right now. I'm still figuring out the CNC, so I don't want to stop doing that. I suppose I could be keeping better track of the materials, but I'd need to watch that all day, and I wouldn't be able to keep track of anything else. Guys go and get stuff whenever they need it, and the materials are stored all over the shop. If I walk around to keep track of them, then I'm not running the CNC."

"So why don't you have Steve Maturin run it?"

"He hates that machine. And he's my best guy at building tops.

He's way faster than anyone else. If I put him on the CNC, then we don't get as much done, and he's even unhappier than usual."

"So that's why you're working so much OT?" Will says yes, he's working long days and weekends to keep up with all his tasks, but he likes the money and he likes learning something new.

Both of us know that there's got to be a better way to organize the shop, but we don't have extra resources—cash or people—to throw at the problem. Our only solution is to try modest improvements while still producing work.

Getting back to the original question, scheduling, I tell Will that we should concentrate on the jobs we took without deposits. We want to finish those and ship them while we have cash. If we can get all of them done in November, we should be able to collect our balances before the end of the year. That might allow me to pay Christmas bonuses. And I don't say it, but I'm also hoping to take home a little money myself.

On Monday, November fifth, I report the last week's sales and our cash position. We booked $38,093, but only $924 of that landed in November. I'm starting what promises to be an expensive week with $154,463.95 on hand. Later I head to the shop. I know what every machine and tool does. I can identify every type of wood we use and every project. I have a good grasp of how the money works. Why isn't it enough? How can I have worked on this business for so long, learned so much, and still be so far from mastery? We do good work, but it's not always easy. Why not? How can we get control of our processes?

I think I see the problem. None of the different links in our production chain—sales, engineering, shop floor, finishing, shipping—talk to one another. They each get a job, do their thing, then pass it on. Steve Maturin, the Heroic Solitary Craftsman, was happy to operate that way. Will Krieger is heading down the same road. Even though he and I talk to each other, the shop floor is still running the old way. Will is putting in huge hours trying to monitor all the links in our production chain. But he's overloaded—caught in an operational role, running the CNC. Even though he's a much better foreman than Steve, he can't do it all himself. The shop is too big, the work is too complex, there are too many guys doing things too many ways. Useful information is not passed from person to person, but rather from each person through Will. That's presuming that guys are even sharing their ideas and complaints. They were all trained by Steve Maturin, who did not encourage innovation or communication. Nick has told me that when he was working on the bench, he came up with lots of ideas to do better work, but that when he took them to Steve, he never once got encouragement. Eventually he stopped trying to share. He simply did things the way he wanted to and didn't worry about how anyone else worked. He became a very fast, accurate builder, too. Meanwhile, his fellow workers, many of whom would have benefited from better skills and technique, struggled and often failed.

What can I do to encourage innovation and communication? Give an inspiring speech? Or stern orders? Can I succeed by describing my new understanding to Will Krieger and leaving it up to him? I don't think that will work. Maybe a regularly scheduled, all-hands meeting to discuss operational ideas, separate from the Monday meeting? That will eat up a lot of production hours. Does every single person need to attend a meeting in order to get the most benefit from it? Maybe I can work with a smaller group and get more bang for my buck.

My musings are interrupted by Emma with the mail. There's a big envelope from Independence Blue Cross. It's that time of year: time to decide whether to renew our health insurance. We're too small to have a dedicated human resources department, so I perform this task and all other HR work.

Doctors, hospitals, and health insurers treat small employers like me as convenient sources of cash, relying on the fact that it takes so much time for a boss to investigate the options, and to understand what is being offered, that most will surrender and buy the first choice presented to them. In 2005, insuring a single worker in an HMO cost me $206 per month. Insuring a family of four cost $606. Five years later, in 2010, those costs had more than doubled—the single premium stood at $425, the family premium was $1,247. Faced with those hikes, I forced my employees to contribute more and more of the cost each year. Now we pick up 66 percent of the cost, and the workers pay 34 percent.

Why do I offer insurance at all? (I'm not legally required to, though that may change.) Two reasons: first, I need to buy it for myself, and it's much cheaper for me to do that as part of a company group than by shopping on the open market. And second, because I want my company to be the kind of place where workers can stay for a long time. I try to offer compensation and benefits that allow them to raise families and have decent lives without having to search for better employment. Call me a softy, but I want them to succeed and prosper, and it makes me feel good to help that happen.

On the day I actually have to pick a plan, though, I'm not feeling so happy. I take another look at the stuff that Independence Blue Cross has sent and quickly discard it. It's useless. No description of all the choices available, and no pricing whatsoever. "Call your agent!" is repeated frequently.

My agent, as it turns out, e-mails me in the afternoon. They've sent me a spreadsheet with the pricing for this year and the steps I need to renew, plus descriptions of the forty-nine different plans being offered. Forty-nine plans! It's like looking into an abyss. One tab of the spreadsheet has a detailed description of my current plan, with thirty-seven separate copays and coinsurances. Every plan comes with a similar grid. If I want to shop the offerings of just this one company, I need to compare 1,813 different pieces of information, and that's just Independence Blue Cross. I don't have time for that.

I give up on finding a better choice and sign up for the same plan as last year. Having made that decision, the real work begins. IBX wants to know not only the name and address of each employee who might sign up, but also the full name, social security number, and birth date of every one of their dependents. They already have some of that information, but I need to double-check that everything is correct and talk to each employee to make sure that nothing has changed. It's a whole day of tedious clerical work. Then I'll have to explain my decision to the employees, and hand out sign-up sheets, at the next meeting.

On Thursday, a surprise: an order from Eurofurn, worth $10,810. Dan did all the preliminary work back in the spring and then forgot about it. We've heard nothing from them since Nigel and his henchmen came for lunch back in July, and we've received no business from them since the middle of June. Once sales started coming in from our normal clients, I moved them to the back of my mind and left them there.

Dan prepares an invoice for the deposit. Out of curiosity, I total up the value of the jobs we've received from Eurofurn this year. It's just $47,846. Then in my database, I look at how many hours we've spent building their jobs versus the number of hours we got paid for. We're more than a hundred hours behind our estimates. I've put a huge effort into these people. So far, it's been a big loss.

On Friday afternoon, I review the week's numbers. November is following the usual pattern, despite the changes to our sales process. We've sold just two jobs, totaling $18,717. Incoming cash has been even worse. We've picked up just $7,661, all pre-ship and final payments. As I predicted, we're bleeding cash: the payroll, rent, and vendor bills have cost me $66,581. I'm down $41,611 for the week and back in negative territory for the year.

On Friday, after Will and I go over the numbers, I ask, "How often do you gather all the guys together for a meeting?" He tells me that he gets the bench guys together now and then for an announcement or to demonstrate proper use of one of our machines.

"How about the whole shop? Bench guys, finishing, everyone?" He's never done that. "So how do you know the best solution to any problem? How do you know that what's good for the bench guys isn't screwing up the finishing room? Or shipping?" He responds with a statement in the form of a question: "I just think about it?"

I keep after him. "Are you sure that works? I've been thinking about stuff for twenty-six years but I'm discovering that my solutions come from fantasyland. I don't really know what's going on anymore. The shop is just too big; everyone's in a corner doing his own thing. I'm not experiencing things the way the rest of you do, and you aren't experiencing them the way I do. That's got to be true of everyone. What looks like a solution to you will be a problem to me."

He agrees, so I continue. "Our meetings, you and I, have been going really well. I'd like to do something similar with an expanded group and focus on identifying and fixing production problems. I want to make sure that someone from each department is attending, so that we can come up with solutions that work for everyone. Bonus, everyone will be hearing about the solution at the same time. So you won't have to run from one end of the shop to the other repeating your explanation of what you want to do. What do you think?"

He considers the idea, then asks, "Who will be on the committee?"

"I don't want to bring in the whole shop. It's too expensive to shut down production. But I do want someone from sales, engineering, build, finish, and ship to sit in. Nick, Andy, you, Dave, and Bob. I'll be in charge to keep things moving." Will thinks that it's worth a try, and we settle on eleven-thirty next Thursday morning. I decide to call it "Operations Committee."

On Monday, after devoting the meeting to the health insurance renewal, I get an unsettling e-mail from my contact at the big defense company. His boss, the CEO, has been fired after being caught in an affair with a subordinate. The news makes the front page of the *New York Times* business section.

I try to muster sympathy for this guy whose private life has made the national papers, but I'm mostly concerned with losing the order. Andy hasn't ordered the wood yet, and I tell him to hold off.

Later, my contact calls to confirm that the job will be canceled. We have one of those "wutcha gonna do?" conversations; then I point out that we have a valid purchase order, and that the job is in process. He hems and haws a bit. I offer to let them cancel if I can bill them for the time we've put into it. We agree that I can keep $3,915 of the $18,000 deposit; I'll have to refund the rest.

This cancellation comes at a bad time. I'm going to be short on cash until we get paid for the net-30 jobs, and I'll be paying my expenses for the rest of November out of what I have on hand plus whatever deposits we collect from new sales. The only bright spot is the credit card bill. We haven't charged much since I paid it off last month, and the upcoming total is just $5,857.86. If we don't make some sales, I'll bottom out at around $40,000 in cash at the end of the month. After that, the net-30 payments will start to arrive, but only if there are no shipping delays and no installation problems.

The next morning, I log in to the Defense Department's Web site and check the status of our invoices. The site is for any company doing business with the military, and it has some amusing drop-down lists describing the range of products that are being bought, from solid-fuel rocket motors to naval patrol vessels to potatoes. There's another drop-down for quantities delivered, ranging from grams to drums to railcars. Somewhere a junior officer is receiving a railcar full of potatoes and can use this system to affirm that it has arrived on time and in good condition. And thirty days later, the money is deposited in the seller's bank account.

I search for our jobs by product, NAICS code 337211: Wood Office Furniture. Two of our jobs have been received, but not formally accepted, so I'll have Emma prod them to complete the paperwork.

On Wednesday, Dan sells a job worth $19,630 to a gas company in Colorado. And on Thursday morning, Nick gets a nice one: $32,182, from a repeat customer. Both clients promise to send deposit checks. We should have that cash next week.

The last two military tables are assembled and ready for crating. One, a very large U-shaped table for an army base in Arizona, sports an especially flamboyant combination of maple and Bolivian rosewood, along with a huge inlaid logo in the center of the U. The other, for a Special Forces battalion in Florida, is made from more modest woods but has an even better logo panel. At the end of each arm of the U, we've inlaid a shield-shaped panel, about three feet long and two feet wide, with a huge black widow spider above an Apache spear. My guys like to do this kind of work. Military logos are usually cool looking, and it's a thrill to hear about our clients on the news. After Osama Bin Laden was killed, I pictured the returning special ops unit gathered around the table we'd made for them in 2010.

———

ON THURSDAY, we have our first Operations Committee: Nick, Andy, Will, Dave, and Bob, each representing a link in the production chain. They sit and stare at me, a little nervous. It's not Monday. We've never had meetings any other time.

I start by repeating what I told Will last week: that we've all been working in isolation for too many years. Each person has been a Heroic Solitary Craftsman, dealing with their problems by themselves. That approach leaves us with no way to collectively solve our many problems—no avenues for good ideas to be brought to the attention of management; no forum for discussing ideas to determine whether they work for all of us, or cause problems for someone else in the shop. And no way to make sure that good ideas are still being used a week, month, or year later. This committee is intended to solve all those problems.

I outline for them how I think it will work: anyone can bring up a problem, anyone can suggest a solution, and everyone should think about whether that solution raises a different problem. We will meet weekly, every Thursday at eleven-thirty. I don't want the meetings to be very long, and if the topic raised doesn't affect every part of the production chain, then the people who aren't concerned can leave and get back to work. I conclude with a question: "Who wants to start?"

Silence. All the guys are waiting for somebody else to go first. Then Will Krieger says that he's noticed an issue with the data-port lids we're making. There's a visible sense of relief from the others. This is the kind of problem they understand: technical, finite, and fixable. For the next forty-five minutes, they kick around ideas, and by the end of the meeting, we've found a solution that we all agree will work.

We don't have any whiteboards or chalkboards. So I screwed a large sheet of cardboard to the wall. At the end of the meeting, I take a Sharpie and write:

11/15 Data-port lids: *Concept Done Sustain*

I tell everyone that we'll list the problems we discuss each week on the cardboard. We'll start every meeting with a review of past problems. We'll be able to see exactly how each is progressing, whether they need more work or are now consistently being done. I've been mulling over how we can track what we've worked on, and this seemed like a simple idea to start with. The next day I ask Will how he thought it went. "It was good," he says. "I think we should keep doing it."

HENRY ARRIVES HOME on the Saturday before Thanksgiving. He'll stay for a week. Next Monday, he's sitting with the crew, eyes on the donuts, while I go through the numbers. Last week was good in all respects. We booked $52,150 in new orders and received deposits from a couple of them. It was a light spending week—just my AdWords credit card and some vendor bills. We ended the week with $6,561 more than we started it, and we now have $102,105 on hand. I have payroll and a bunch of other bills, and I have to give my defense customer their money back—more than $70,000 altogether. If I don't get some cash, I'll have less than a week of funds on hand.

I'm worried, but not as panic-stricken as I was in June and July. All the military jobs are shipped, and the first three have been installed without problems. I should be receiving the money in mid-December. Sales have been OK, and we still have lots of work from October in our queue. If I'm prudent, and we sell anything in December, I should be OK.

Thanksgiving and Christmas are the biggest upcoming problems. The guys often skip the day before or after a holiday, and this year Christmas falls on a Tuesday. We'll lose six of the next thirty working days. Even worse, shipping slows down as well. Truck drivers like to see their families, and so our shipments take longer than usual. I'll need to make sure that jobs are crated and ready to go well before Christmas.

Thanksgiving week, sales are usually slow. Not this year. We book three more orders, worth $38,953. Two are Dan's, totaling $31,048. Nick does the other. I spend a lot more time watching Henry than working, but I do stop in to pick up checks that have arrived. We receive $27,468 and spend $70,674. I finish the week with $58,899 on hand—my lowest balance since July. I'm down $78,256 from my position at the start of the year. If I can even get back to a $100,000 balance by year's end, I'll be satisfied.

The following Monday, I report to the crew. Five working days left in November. Sales so far: $110,744. What are the chances that we'll close $90,000 in new orders this week? History would say low, but we had weeks in October that were better than that. Should I follow my most optimistic estimate or the worst-case scenario? I prudently assume that nothing more will come in this week, but that we'll get some sales in December. It shouldn't be a bad cash week: no payroll, and the credit cards, health insurance, and rent have been paid. I can last a week with no new sales, but they'd better pick up after that.

I spend the rest of Monday and Tuesday doing all the things that I do every day, but not really concentrating much. On Wednesday, I fly to San Francisco to see Peter. I'll be staying with my sister, and Nancy is staying home with our youngest boy, Hugh. Henry is back at school.

On Thursday, I visit Peter's office, a couple of blocks from Union

Square. It's smaller than mine, and crowded. Peter and his coworkers sit shoulder-to-shoulder at a single long table. They're peering at oversize monitors. In the rest of the space are a couple of small conference rooms, a very well-stocked kitchen, and a hang-out area with comfy sofas. There are maybe fifteen people working this morning. I'm greeted with brief smiles and handshakes, but they all quickly return to their screens.

I ask Peter to show me what he does. His screen shows two columns of text—computer code. It looks like gibberish to me. The lines on the right match the lines on the left, with a few discrepancies—a letter or comma, or sometimes a couple of lines that are different from its counterpart. These are highlighted in a different color. The left side shows the existing code, the right shows whatever changes Peter is making. He spends long days parked in his chair, staring at this mess, and thinking.

I ask him: how do his bosses know who's doing a good job? He tells me that, first and foremost, good workers solve the problems they are given. The code that runs a Web site is an ever-evolving entity. The Web site is updated constantly as new functions are added, and it has to be rebuilt to handle more traffic as the user base grows. It's tricky. Updating the code without crashing the site is like trying to build a boat while sailing it across the ocean. You start with a rowboat, and if things go well, end up with an aircraft carrier.

That scenario guarantees problems. The engineers do their best to test the code before it goes live, but everyone is under incredible pressure to launch, whether it's perfect or not. So new blocks of code get shoved into the existing code base, often with little documentation. This can cause strange, unforeseen interactions with what's there already.

In our shop, once a table is shipped, it no longer interacts with our ongoing processes. If we lived in Peter's world, we might find that a change in how we build a table suddenly caused all the tables we'd ever built to collapse or burst into flames. On the other hand, software engineers can fix their whole code base from any place that has Internet. Our logistics challenges don't exist for them.

Peter's company measures productivity by the number of lines of code that have been tested and integrated into the new site. He's currently near the top of the whole team. He's working such long hours that sometimes he stays at the office for a couple of days in a row. "How does anyone know what to work on? How do the bosses know where everyone is?" Peter explains that the bosses hold regular meetings with each staffer and give regular updates to everyone about the overall state of the Web site and the company. His Web site, like many start-ups, generates no revenue. Cash comes from investors, who hope for a huge payout if the company is acquired by one of the monsters in the industry—Facebook, Google, Apple, or Amazon. There are also smaller investors looking for any company that can gain traction.

For Peter, the dream is still alive and well. His new company is getting repeated injections of cash, and their user base is growing. Peter and his coworkers have been told that they can expect substantial year-end bonuses, and if he stays for a year, he'll have stock in the company.

The site is functioning smoothly for the moment, so Peter and I spend a couple of days sightseeing. He seems to be very glad to have a break from the office. He tells me that he's given up exercise, and that his life consists of working and sleeping, nothing more.

As we walk around town, we keep seeing sleek white motor coaches: the famed tech buses, equipped with Wi-Fi and food, that shuttle employees back and forth between San Francisco and Silicon Valley. One has a Google logo painted on the side. Later, I look up how much they cost: about five hundred thousand dollars each. I've paid Google $627,416 since I started using AdWords. I've bought them a bus, and paid for food and a driver for a year.

This reminds me of something odd that happened last year. In my mail I found a smallish cardboard box. The return address: "Google, Mountain View, CA." It's a mug, with "Google" on the side. No note. Apparently this is their attempt to express gratitude to a steady customer. I had already spent more than seventy-five thousand dollars with Google that year, and I got a two-dollar mug. I haven't heard anything from them since. Granted, Google makes searching for anything on the Web cheap and easy, and connects me with buyers whom I would never otherwise meet. But how would a hotel, casino, or restaurant treat a customer who spent six hundred dollars a day, every day? Any of them would do something a little more impressive to keep me happy.

I fly back to Philly on Sunday. It's been a good visit. Peter seems to be doing well as a software engineer, at least professionally. His personal life is more of a struggle, since he doesn't have time to try to make friends, and San Francisco is not a good place for someone too young to go to a bar. But he insisted that he's doing well, and that he wants to stay until next fall.

DECEMBER

DATE: MONDAY, DECEMBER 3, 2012

BANK BALANCE: $66,033.55

CASH RELATIVE TO START OF YEAR ("NET CASH"): -$71,120.77

NEW-CONTRACT VALUE, YEAR-TO-DATE: $1,917,928

The temperature plummeted last night, and the office is freezing. The shop is warmed with gas-fired heaters, but the office, facing the wind, is always much colder. The chill is incentive to keep the Monday meeting short. I start with November sales—just $121,971. I'd rather concentrate on better news. The build total was good: $195,699 in a month that was two days shorter than normal. Our shipping total was better: $239,579. I dismiss the crew and think about what I didn't say. One decent month has not brought us to profitability. Year to date, we've built $1,834,731 and shipped $1,851,423. And spent $1,906,454. No matter how you measure it, either on a cash flow or accrual basis, I've lost money.

And individual performances? Dan won November, with $71,290 sold. Nick sold just $40,087, although he still has a commanding lead for the year. I'm even further behind, with just $9,670. Is that success or failure? I don't want to be selling and haven't made much effort recently. I'll call it success. I decide to ignore these low sales totals. It looks like the pattern of the previous three Novembers has repeated itself, despite our new methods.

On Tuesday, I have my sixth session with Bob Waks. We review how Dan and Nick have done since July: much, much better. Bob reminds me that I'm still far behind my targets and that I should probably replace Dan. I know that I'm not going to fire him before Christmas. That would be cruel. I promise a long, hard look after that.

ON SATURDAY, I lunch with a friend who is struggling with his own business. Mike Vogel first met me in the summer of 2011, shortly after he quit his last job. He described his vision: a mash-up of a gym, a school, and a woodworking studio. He would open a nicely equipped woodshop, then sell memberships to people who lacked their own space and tools, and offer woodworking classes as well. I asked him how far along he was. "I've rented the space. Now I have to renovate it. It's just an empty warehouse right now." The location was good, not far from wealthy neighborhoods full of potential customers.

I asked when he'd be opening his doors. He said that, with luck, it would take a year to fit out the shop. Uh-oh. "That's a long time. How much money have you got?" Mike had spent ten years working on Wall Street and he'd been frugal. He had two hundred thousand dollars in cash, and equity in his home worth about a hundred thousand. He had opened a seventy-thousand-dollar line of credit. He planned to use all of it for the build-out and to operate until he reached positive cash flow. He'd signed a five-year lease that, like most commercial leases, required him to personally guarantee the cost of the whole term. He was betting his cash and his house that the idea would succeed.

I met with Mike regularly, and every time I remembered my own business launch. For years I struggled with problems that can now be solved in a few seconds on Google, but in other ways I had it very easy. I didn't need a large amount of starting capital. A five-thousand-dollar inheritance covered a simple set of tools and my first six months of rent. Nancy had a full-time job, which covered our living expenses. I didn't need to hire people in order to get started—I worked by myself for two years. And I didn't need to present myself as anything other than what I was: a very small operator. Before the Internet, there was no requirement that I build a Web site or dominate social media. It was understood that beginners looked like beginners.

Mike had to solve a lot more problems before he could open his doors. Before he could expect a penny in income, he had to build a shop, stock it, and hire workers to interact with his members and teachers to teach his classes. He had to come up with courses. He had to establish pricing schemes for both membership and classes and build a marketing campaign, including Web site, Facebook page, and e-mailed newsletter.

Opening day, this last April, brought a new set of challenges. I thought that he would have difficulty finding customers. A membership woodshop? What's that? He'd have to educate an indifferent world about this new thing. Mike wasn't worried about that; he was more focused on his lack of woodworking skills. He wasn't sure he could teach his staff if he wasn't a master craftsman himself. I reassured him that basic woodworking isn't all that difficult and I was happy to help him with whatever technical issues came up.

Neither of us predicted his biggest headache, the issue that has dominated our conversations since opening day: staffing. Mike had no experience being a boss to a group of workers and wasn't sure how many people he'd need. Even worse, he needs skilled and competent people, but his business model doesn't allow for high wages. So he's stuck with young folks, just out of college, who haven't found steady work elsewhere. Mike has hired enthusiastic people, but they have no experience and can barely support themselves on the salaries he can afford: twelve dollars an hour to start. I told him that he won't get much for that and he certainly won't keep anyone worthwhile for very long. This has turned out to be true. The people he wants to keep have left for better pay, and the ones that have stayed are less competent. One key employee, Amelia, is extremely loyal and reliable, but she constantly makes idiotic mistakes. Which is a problem when she's in charge of maintaining the Web site and Facebook page, dealing with members, and collecting payments.

He's been complaining about her for as long as I've known him. I've challenged him to fire her. He won't. For better or worse, she's the only one who understands the systems that she's cobbled together. He can't imagine how he'll get through the period between her dismissal and the arrival of a new person, and he doesn't want to interview a potential hire while Amelia is around.

I wouldn't call Mike a mellow guy, and the stress of the situation is eating at him. At lunch, he's working through a long list of complaints. I point out that in a lot of ways he's done well. I didn't expect him to even open his doors, but he got to that happy day without going broke. It cost him $225,000 or so. He's been surprisingly successful at signing up members, and he's been cash positive since August. Really, he should be proud of himself. He took a huge risk and he hasn't failed yet. That's success for a very small business.

He counters with a litany of negatives: he's not paying himself, and he'll never get his $225,000 back, let alone make any return on the investment. And he's really tired of dealing with faulty employees. I tell him I know how he feels, although I've never had his staffing problems. Mike and I discuss my wage scale. I'm sure that I'm paying more than I need to, since nobody has ever quit, but I'm able to attract and keep competent people. I lay out my expectations for different amounts of money:

Minimum wage (in Pennsylvania, $7.25/hr): I don't hire at this wage. It might work for unskilled, youth, or temporary workers, but that's not what I want.

$10/hr: My starting wage. I expect a reliable worker who shows up on time and works at a steady pace, but not much in the way of skills. Should be able to perform simple tasks (taking out trash, unloading materials) correctly and understand enough English to follow simple directions.

$12/hr: If the $10/hr person can learn some technical tasks, and perform entry-level work without supervision, I can pay more. They also need a valid driver's license and should be willing to work extra hours when required. (They would be paid overtime per Pennsylvania law.) They should understand complex spoken English. This is also where I start workers who want to become skilled woodworkers but have had no training. These workers require significant attention from management and coworkers, so we can't pay them much. They must immediately demonstrate a good work ethic, curiosity, and willingness to take direction. And they must have "good hands": woodworking talent. This is not evenly distributed in the population and can't be taught.

$13.50/hr: A worker on the training path will get a raise to this level as a reward for reliability, hard work, and increasing skills.

$15/hr: Starting wage for someone fresh out of woodworking school. Most training programs emphasize skills that are, in my shop, obsolete. We rarely work with hand tools and our equipment is much more sophisticated than that found in schools. These green workers will still need very significant training, and we'll also need

to determine whether they have "good hands" and a good work ethic.

$18/hr: A worker who has had both schooling and some work experience, or whose skills and work ethic have been vouched for by their former boss. I still need to see whether this person can reach our required level of speed and accuracy, much higher than the industry average.

$20/hr: A worker who has been with me long enough to learn our procedures and can do most tasks without error. I will keep a worker in this wage range until he can do a very wide range of items without a problem. This might take a while—some pieces only get built now and then. Also, at this level, a worker shouldn't need constant attention from management.

$25/hr: This person should have mastered every aspect of his job. He should be able to manage a helper and contribute ideas that improve our operations. This is also where I would start a worker with previous experience doing work very similar to ours.

$30/hr: This is foreman pay, for complete mastery of both our particular skills and the wider demands of the trade. This worker should also be an energetic, innovative leader who can monitor all shop activity and provide direction to other workers. He/she will also drive innovation in our procedures and work closely with me and the office staff. In my experience, at this level, a person works a lot of overtime. I pay OT, instead of putting the foreman on salary, to reward that effort.

SO THAT'S MY WAGE SCALE. For the first ten dollars an hour, I get reliability; the second ten, a worker with skills adequate for our regular production; and the third ten, all the old-style hand skills.

We're custom makers, so we often need to do something that could be done by machine, but will require a large investment in programming and tooling. That's when the master-level workers shine. They can jump in and do something tricky, quickly, and keep moving.

Mike listens to all that and tells me that he might be able to bump three guys to thirteen dollars an hour after New Year's. He won't be paying a Christmas bonus. Maybe he'll take his people to dinner, but that's all he can afford.

After Mike leaves, I consider whether my guys deserve Christmas bonuses. Will Krieger and Dave Violi have been putting in huge hours, but they're getting overtime for that. As for the rest of the crew? Nobody else has come close to the hours that Dave and Will have put in, or put much effort into improving shop operations. Dan and Nick have not resisted the new sales methods, but they didn't think them up, either. I know who really deserves one: me. I'm the one who, in response to the crisis of falling sales, tried everything I could think of to save us. I swallowed my pride and asked for help, and then looked at how I've run the company for a quarter century and realized that it wasn't good enough. I made hard choices and lived with the consequences. And I'm the one who hasn't had a paycheck since April.

The next eleven working days, leading up to Christmas, are remarkable: nothing bad happens. Will Krieger keeps the shop running smoothly. There are no machine failures, no employee misbehavior, and we are beating our time estimates. Dan and Nick close six deals worth $98,388. We're amassing cash: the remaining military payments arrive, and we get money from new customers and completed projects. Two new buyers pay their entire bill up front to get the cash off their books before the year ends. From the beginning of the month to Christmas Eve, we take in $233,170 and spend $150,897. The net gain, $82,273, takes me past my starting balance at the beginning of the year. By Monday the twenty-fourth, I've got $147,111 in the bank.

Monday, Christmas Eve. Twelve of the fifteen employees have shown up to work. At the meeting, I tell them that our annual sales will be very close to last year's totals. We finished 2011 with $2,138,572 in new orders, and as of today, we stand at $2,066,064. I expect a few more jobs in the last days of the year, as bosses with extra cash rush to spend some of it and reduce their tax load.

Ron Dedrick raises his hand: "How about our bonus? We have money, and sales are back where they were last year. And you gave us a big bonus then. Are you going to do it again?"

It's the question I've been dreading. I swallow and deliver my answer: "Maybe. I'm not comfortable with our cash cushion. We're positive, but we've been negative most of the year. Bonuses are expensive. Do you remember what you got last year?" I had been very generous, giving the lowest-paid workers fifteen hundred dollars, and the higher-paid guys four thousand dollars each.

"You guys got a nice surprise. Well, that added up to forty-eight thousand dollars, not including payroll taxes. But we also had a lot more cash, so I could afford it. A year ago, I had $280,000 in the bank. Today I have half that." Stony looks from the crowd. "I'll tell you what. Next Monday, New Year's Eve, is the last payday of the year. I'll make a decision then, based on our cash position. But I'll tell you right now, it won't be anything like last year. I just don't have the money." Unhappy looks all around, which I find a little bit disgusting. All year, I've paid them on time and in full, even when it was a struggle. I resent the implication that they are entitled to a bonus after such a bad year. I'm tempted to point to the donuts and say, "There's your bonus, gentlemen," but I restrain myself. Instead, I end the meeting and walk back to my office.

I'm back in at nine a.m. on the day after Christmas. In 2013, I'd like a lot more data on our customers. I decide to start tracking both our inquiries and sales by client type. Not what kind of company they work for, but whether they are a big boss, the assistant to the boss, a corporate buyer, or one of the dozen other categories that I identify and add to FileMaker. I suspect that the types we call "low-level assistant" never lead to a sale. I can't prove it, but next year I'll know for sure.

On Thursday, we get a call. Surprise, surprise, it's the CEO of Brand Advantage, Mark Jones. They still owe me $7,448. Is he going to pay?

"Paul, I'd love to pay you. But I don't think it's gonna happen. We're shutting down after the New Year. I'm sorry it turned out this way. I just wanted to call you, not leave you hanging."

I give him half-hearted thanks for his consideration. He takes this as his cue to explain how Brand Advantage flamed out. He'd been in advertising for years and became a specialist in promoting brands at sporting events. Then he headed out on his own, figuring he'd be getting the big bucks. He opened his doors in April and persuaded some clients to sponsor a series of events in the fall. We walked into the middle of an unending disaster. None of his clients renewed their contracts, and some haven't paid him. He's going to shut down and go back to being an employee.

I make sympathetic noises, wish him luck, and hang up. Maybe he's lying to get out of paying me what he owes. Maybe he was never cut out to be a boss. Or maybe he's just unlucky. Like Mike Vogel, his business model required a lot of things to go right from the beginning.

ON FRIDAY, Will and I have our last meeting of the year. We share chuckles over incidents that weren't so funny at the time; then I ask if he has any New Year's resolutions. He does:

"I want to move us to something more like a production line. When we have everyone building their own tables, it's a mess. A bunch of guys always end up needing one of the machines at the same time, and everything is out of adjustment. And the guys are walking all over the shop all day. It's a huge waste. I want to get all that under control."

I think about this for a minute and then point out that the older guys aren't going to like it much. They've got Heroic Solitary Craftsman baked into them at this point. I don't know whether they'll tolerate that kind of change. We agree to give it a try and see how it works out. But not until next year.

MONDAY, DECEMBER 31. Everyone's here on New Year's Eve, I presume to hear my decision about bonuses. I give them the numbers. Dan sold two jobs last week worth $35,749. That brings our total for December to $184,333, and our total for the year to $2,102,261. We also picked up more cash last week—we've had positive cash flow for the entire month. My bank balance stands at $217,427. Because of that, everyone will each see an extra five hundred dollars in their paychecks. This news prompts some smiles, but everyone remembers the much larger bonus they got last year. Too bad. There won't be any bonus for me. I want plenty of cash on hand for 2013.

Before I go, I shake their hands, thanking them for their work during the year. I'm especially grateful for Dave Violi, who put in 360 hours of overtime, and Will Krieger, who rose to my challenge and did a superb job. I'm delighted to thank Andy Stahl, who kept pace with the shop, and to congratulate Dan and Nick for beating their 2011 sales totals. I thank Emma for all her help with my Middle East trip and for keeping the office running smoothly. I thank Bob Foote for keeping the work moving out the door and managing the helpers. I thank Ron Dedrick for his good craftsmanship and cheerful attitude; Sean Slovinski, Tyler Powell, and Kristian Scheld for working hard and doing a nice job. And I steel myself and walk over to the corner of the shop where Steve Maturin is smoking a cigarette. "Thanks, Steve. I appreciate your hard work." He shakes my hand, but, as usual, says nothing. Just a nod.

On the way home I think about the problems I've left unsolved. Steve Maturin is gloomy all the time now, even though his work is still impeccable. Dan is doing better as a result of Bob Waks's training, but he's still not consistently hitting my targets. He ended up with $647,056 this year. Nick sold $1,034,273. I ended up with $420,932. I'm not sure how I'll be able to retire from sales and get to $2,400,000 next year without a different salesman.

I haven't heard anything from Dubai since I sent the last proposal in September, but we shipped Eurofurn's November order and we've been paid. I think Will's vision for more specialization on the shop floor and a streamlined production process has much more potential than any adventures on foreign shores. If we can keep the shop busy with orders, anyway.

I'll start 2013 with $178,948 on hand. I'm up $41,794 from the beginning of 2012. When I come back to the office on Wednesday, I'll reset all the sales and production numbers to zero, start my twenty-seventh year, and see what happens.

Postscript

As I write these words, I'm starting my twenty-ninth year as a boss. They were all challenging and kept me very busy. And except for 2012, they lacked a narrative arc. So what do my very eventful year and the other years have in common? This: I never knew what the next day would bring. I still don't. That's what I was trying to get across in this book: the unpredictable nature of running a small company. The way that ordinary duties interact with randomly occurring events, and the way big decisions need to be made with incomplete information. More than anything else, I've had to be flexible and ready to respond to any challenge. And that's been fascinating. I suppose if my business had become successful and had grown to the point where I could hire people to do all the day-to-day stuff, I might grow bored. I'm not there yet. I still go into the office every day, say hello to Nick and Dan (who are doing very well), and walk around the shop floor to see what's happening. And that's a great gift. Despite vast economic forces arrayed against us, my little workshop is still alive, still putting out high-quality work for happy clients.

I swore in the Introduction that I wouldn't be giving you any lessons. Now you know why. I'm sure that many of you, more experienced in financial, managerial, or legal matters, were appalled at the errors I made. Fair enough. There's only one thing that I know will work for everyone. Get help. Find someone who knows you, knows your business, and who is willing to consult with you frequently. It's preferable to have more than one mentor, just in case your preferred source of advice is wrong. Running a business can be a very lonely experience. I assure you, nobody's troubles are unique. And fellow business owners are happy to share what they know.

In my years writing for *The New York Times*, I exchanged e-mails with hundreds of readers. It was fascinating, and I've missed that exchange of ideas. If you think my advice can be useful, please write to me at paul.c.downs@gmail.com. I'll do my best to help.

One last thing: thank you for reading my story.

Acknowledgments

In December 2009, I came to the conclusion that my business was about to fail. I turned to the Internet to see if I could prepare for the experience of closing my doors, and found no useful information. I wrote to Loren Feldman, then an editor at *The New York Times*, and offered to document my experience. His invitation to write for the *Times* started my second career as a writer. I'd like to thank him for his guidance, support, and friendship.

This book would not exist without encouragement from Paul Lucas, my agent. In September 2012, he asked me whether I had ever considered writing a book. Not really, I replied, but I would be happy to give it a shot. I don't think he was picturing the story you just read, but he patiently helped me complete my first draft, and has been my champion in the publishing world.

My business would never have survived its early years without the unflagging support of my father, Anthony Downs, and my brother, Tony Downs.

And I'd like to conclude with thanks to my wife, Nancy Bea Miller, and my children, Hugh, Henry, and Peter. Even when I exposed our private lives and finances to the world, they have stood with me.

About the Author

Paul Downs founded his business in 1986, fresh out of college. He's been at it ever since, and has no plans to shift gears.